Warnham
and the Great War

Church Street.

Warnham
and the Great War

THE WARNHAM SOCIETY

The Warnham Society
Warnham, West Sussex

Visit our website at www.warnhamsociety.org.uk

First published in United Kingdom by The Warnham Society in 2014

ISBN 978-0-9506966-2-1

Designed by Touchmedia
Set in Melior
Printed and Bound in the United Kingdom by Berforts Information Press

This book is dedicated to the people of Warnham,
for the immense sacrifices they made in the Great War of 1914-1918.

Contents

The Forge, Bell Road.

Preface

This book was conceived as part of the centenary commemorations in 2014, to be a tribute to the 25 men and one woman on the Warnham War Memorial who died in the Great War of 1914-18. Initially the intent was to compile a series of biographies to be displayed on the Warnham Society website. However, once research had started in earnest it was clear that not only were there additional names which should have been included on the memorial, but also there were many more men with Warnham connections who had served in the armed forces and had the good fortune to survive. Given that Warnham is the connecting thread between all these individuals, some acknowledgement has also been made to the contributions of those they left behind on the Home Front.

With the scope of the project much enlarged, the Warnham Society revised its plans and formed a project group to take on the work. It soon became obvious that to pay homage to the many people now identified, a book would be the most appropriate vehicle.

The members of the group are all residents of Warnham and have brought a variety of complementary skills to the work. The project group's aim throughout has been to honour every person identifiable from the various records available, and ensure that their stories are on record for all to see.

The project has attracted a lot of local attention and the Parish Council have willingly agreed to fund publication. As a direct result of the research undertaken to produce this book 17 new names will be added to the Warnham war memorial, thanks to funding from the Hodgson family bequest. Clearly Warnham is still very proud of its heritage and all those who fought, and the many who died to protect it.

Steven Lancaster
Warnham, Sussex
June 2014

Introduction

A common misunderstanding about village war memorials is that the names appearing on them were somehow dictated by central government or the War Office as being appropriate for that location. In fact memorials were entirely funded by local communities who decided on their own list and generally this was composed of names submitted by the families of the fallen. Inevitably this process produced anomalies. Sometimes families had moved away so there was no-one to make a submission. Some families might be associated with several locations and so a name could appear on more than one memorial. Names may have been omitted because for some reason someone objected to their inclusion. Casualties may not have had family in the village so would not have been included unless a friend or employer spoke up for them. Not surprisingly therefore the original list of names on the Warnham war memorial was found to be incomplete.

Of the 46 biographies in this book, 43 are for those connected with Warnham who died during the war (42 men and one woman). A further three biographies are included for notable locals who received gallantry awards. The complete list of Warnham names was constructed from several sources, but primarily includes anyone who was on the original war memorial; or was born in Warnham; or gave Warnham as their address whilst serving in the war; or was buried in Warnham.

Despite efforts to be inclusive, inevitably there will be omissions. Heavy reliance has been put upon service records to identify people, but many of those records were destroyed by enemy bombing during the Second World War. Even the records that survived are often incomplete and difficult to decipher. Nonetheless by using surviving service records together with the Parish Magazine, local newspapers, regimental war diaries and lists of war dead the vast majority have been found.

This book is an attempt to tell the story of Warnham's Great War. What the book is not is an account of the conflict itself. Some details of battles and troop movements are included where they help to tell an individual's story, but the reader must look elsewhere for the overall political and military history.

The Project Group:
Steven Lancaster (*Chairman*)
Elizabeth Bridges
George Elliott
Rachel Hamer
Susan Overton

Life in Warnham at the time of the Great War

The old Parish Magazines were published by the Diocese and covered the eleven parishes in the Rural Deanery of Storrington. Warnham was part of this group, and for the 40 years of the Rev Richard Bowcott's ministry, local affairs were well reported and the magazine was a useful monthly newsletter for the village, particularly during the Great War.

Rev Richard Bowcott, Vicar of Warnham 1882-1921.

Although generous in his writing on village affairs, the Rev Bowcott only wrote one 'Vicar's letter' each year. On 1 January he regularly urged his parishioners to be 'of very good cheer, to love one another and to come to church'. It took a world war to break him of this routine when in September 1914 he was moved to put pen to paper and address the village in an article entitled The War:

> *We find it well-nigh impossible to think of anything else. But a very short time back and there was peace. Work was undisturbed; homes and families felt secure, and the blessings of peace were ours. And then, like a man's hand, a little cloud was seen in the sky over Eastern Europe. There did not seem to be any reason why the quarrel between Austria and Servia should not be settled as between the parties engaged.*

His message continued in the same vein for a page or so defending 'our statesmen' and calling his fellow villagers to patriotism and self-sacrifice for King and Country.

The Defence of the Realm Act (DORA) was passed in the United Kingdom on 8 August 1914, during the early weeks of the Great War. It gave the government wide-ranging powers during the war period, including authority to requisition buildings or land needed for the war effort, or to make regulations creating criminal offences. As a result the leaders of the community in Warnham got together, formed yet another committee, and made far-reaching plans for action in case of invasion. This was an elaborate exercise and the details are shown elsewhere in this book.

Captain Corbett.

Even before the outbreak of war, some of the young men of Warnham were enlisting and for several months there had been mobilisation of troops from the Territorials. In April 1914 the Parish Magazine extolled the virtues of the Territorials, the Boy Scouts and the Church Lads' Brigade 'which foster qualities of the right sort and make for discipline and self-control'.

The CLB was a church youth club with a military flavour. Captain W H Corbett, who was in charge of the Horsham Company, was a Church Army Captain. Besides the religious and social sides of the organisation the boys practised shooting and drilling and formed a brass band. All this became more relevant at the beginning of the war and recruitment increased. The names of ex CLB members who joined up were regularly posted in the Parish Magazine. A company of the CLB was formed in Warnham and the November 1914 magazine reports:

With the winter months we shall restart the Company work. It has been a stirring time for the whole nation and the CLB has not been behindhand. Between 5,000 and 6,000 old members joined the Army at the outset of the war before any appeal for a separate battalion of CLB men had been made. The October report saw this battalion an accomplished fact, and it is attached to the King's Royal Rifles. The Brigade is intended for boys who have left school or are just leaving, and it is the only organisation which was formed for the express purpose of training lads between the ages of 13 and 19 in churchmanship, manliness and discipline.

In June 1915 there is further news of the CLB from which it is seen that playing at soldiers was quite a lot of fun:

The Company spent a most enjoyable day on Bank Holiday with their comrades from Horsham. Some 60 odd travelled to Pulborough. On arrival we marched out with the band to the Common. Two hours spent in skirmishing and attack gave all a good appetite for lunch. We then marched back to the village, and dismissed with two hours' liberty. Tea – and that a very good one – at the Railway Hotel followed at 5 pm. Afterwards the river attracted most of us, and the 'fall in' came all too soon. It was an ideal day, and we are very grateful to the officers and lads of the Horsham Company for the opportunity of spending such a healthy and helpful time.

But these young men's movements were peacetime organisations just brushing themselves up for war. What was now a novel sight for the people of Warnham was a large military encampment in the field between Warnham Court and the Mill Pond. This extensive collection of tents, horses, men and arms had grown rapidly and all were busy and active and training hard. In June 1914 the Vicar urged his parishioners to welcome these men and it seems that many of them attended services in the Parish Church. One of the officers, Lieutenant Tomlin, gave the following details:

The soldiers here are a collection of men from Cavalry Regiments and Engineers and form the personnel of the communication system of the Cavalry Division. There is a similar camp near Winchester for all the communication units of the Infantry Divisions. The methods of communication in the Cavalry consist of wireless telegraphy, cable telegraphy, visual flat signalling and heliograph, despatch riders on horses and bicycles, motor cars and motor bicyclists. These means of signalling etc are organised so as to correspond with the brigades into which our Cavalry is divided. Each Brigade sends an officer and so many men to the summer camp, and the 1st Signal Squadron Royal Engineers is a headquarters unit for keeping touch between the headquarters of the Cavalry Division and the different Brigades. The wireless sets are of two kinds (a) Big stations which can send about 100 miles, and (b) Some smaller stations which are only capable of sending about 20 to 25 miles. We are in daily communication with Aldershot and the big camp near Winchester. The camp is composed of men from the 9th Lancers, the Signal Squadron of the Royal Engineers, the 15th Hussars and the 19th Hussars.

St Margaret's church before the War Memorial was erected.

In January 1915 the Vicar addressed his parishioners with a lengthy and solemn letter:

> *The year which has just dawned upon us finds this country in a condition of war which is without a parallel in the memory of living man. Perhaps there has been nothing to equal it in the history of the world, if we consider the forces which are engaged on either side, the issues which are involved, and the appalling loss of life which the struggle entails . . . It is not so much that we are in doubt about the final result, for we are confident that victory will sooner or later be with us and our allies. But it is the question of the duration of the War that troubles us, and the toll which will have to be exacted before the end is reached threatens to be heavy and severe.*

He continued in this style assuring everyone that they were battling for principles, King and Country and the Church. All this was no doubt to stir up loyalty and to comfort those whose sons, brothers and husbands were being wounded and killed in France.

The January 1915 edition of the Parish Magazine published the first list of local men serving in the forces. More names were added in February making the total by then 101. This list was updated each year and 'a handsome card and a frame' containing all the names were donated by Miss Lee-Steere to be placed in the church porch. A facsimile of the only surviving copy of this handwritten document is on the inside of the back cover of this book.

By this time various groups in Warnham were beginning to work for the war effort. Mrs Bowcott recorded that with the money raised by a house-to-house collection, material had been bought and 103 garments had been made and sent to the Red Cross Depot in Horsham. In addition 20 small cushions stuffed with chipped flannel, suitable for resting damaged limbs had been sent to local hospitals.

The good citizens of Warnham had really got going on the many things which were now needed for the war effort. Throughout the following years there were constant reports of eggs being supplied to hospitals for the wounded. Many dozens of warm mufflers, gloves and socks were knitted and sent out to the troops, together with books and magazines and regular parcels of goodies. In February 1916 The War Office sent a requisition to voluntary organisations for 1,500 mufflers and 500 pairs of mittens. Warnham contributed 55 mufflers and 58 pairs of mittens knitted by 13 Warnham ladies.

In February 1915 a parcel of hospital comforts was sent from Warnham to the French Base Hospital No 12 at Le Havre and the letter of thanks particularly mentions pillows supplied by Warnham Stores. This was just part of a continuous effort by the village, and particularly the women and schoolchildren, to raise money, to knit and sew and send off parcels to the troops in France, to hospitals and convalescent homes and institutions for the disabled.

Warnham Stores in Church Street at the time of the Great War.

The staff in the hospitals for wounded soldiers frequently acknowledged parcels of fruit and vegetables and especially mentioned grapes. These were a considerable treat in those days and particularly during the war when imports were severely limited. Some of the big houses in Warnham had hothouses and were able to supply this luxury. At the same time the villagers of Warnham did not forget their old charities which they continued to support. The magazine published frequent letters of gratitude from the Waifs and Strays, Dr Barnardo's, Horsham Hospital, the Hospital for Women and many others including the Union Workhouse in Horsham, thanking the village for garments, eggs, fruit, vegetables, flowers and money.

The village also had concern for Belgian Refugees and in November 1914 the magazine reports:

We think it right to record that two cottages have been kindly placed at the disposal of those who arrange for the housing of Belgian Refugees – one by Mrs Gregson of Ends Place and the other by Mrs Lambert of Durfold. A committee was formed with Miss Muriel Lucas as Hon Secretary, to procure the necessary funds for maintenance. A sum sufficient for this purpose was promptly promised by some of our kind friends. But Sussex is now a prohibited area, and our plan has so far as this is concerned been frustrated. The offer of the houses still holds good, and perhaps later on some use may be made of them as convalescent homes for the wounded. Meanwhile much useful work is being done by people of all classes for the comfort of our soldiers and sailors.

In 1915 there is a report of socks being knitted for the Belgian Soldiers' Fund. In June of that year:

Miss Frances Bowcott and Miss Muriel Lucas have been collecting money to provide a soup kitchen for Belgian soldiers. A sum of from £50 to £60 was required for the purpose. They are now able to announce that, thanks to liberal friends, the amount has been raised, and the kitchen will be known as the 'Warnham Soup Kitchen'.

In December 1916 a special collection was made on Christmas Day to raise money for the Relief Fund to assist in helping Belgian children who were said to be in a distressing state.

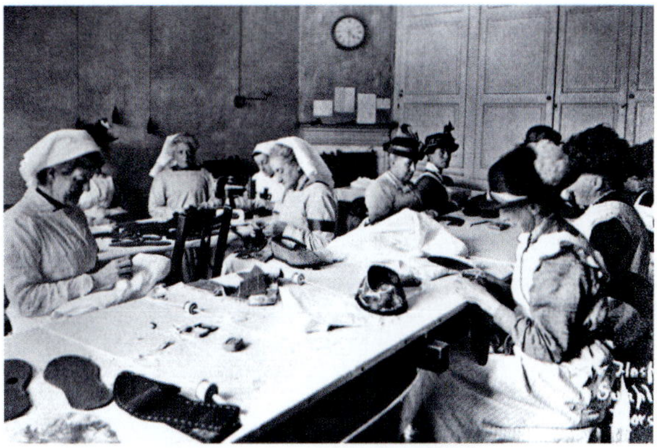

Volunteers working at 8 Causeway in Horsham preparing slippers and other comforts for the wounded.

Belgian refugees leaving Antwerp in October 1914.

Each year of the war the village made an effort to send Christmas parcels to Warnham men:

CHRISTMAS PARCELS TO WARNHAM MEN IN THE FIGHTING AREAS
A very fine response has been made to the appeal of Mrs Bowcott for the above object. At the time of writing about £35 has been received, also £1. 9s. 4d. from the Whist Drive. The following will be included in the parcels:

Tin Horlicks malted milk tablets	*Tin cocoa and milk*	*Tin shortbreads*
Tablet boracic and cold cream soap	*Writing pad and pencil*	*Tin cigarettes*
Tin peppermint bulls eyes	*1 pair socks*	*Tin Oxo cubes*
Holly and mistletoe	*Crackers*	

Other items suggested: shortbread, peppermints, diary, laces, matches, salmon paste.

A large number of Christmas Parcels were sent each year to 'Warnham Boys' and these generated a spate of heartfelt and warm replies from hospitals and bases in Ireland, England and France. The letters were similar in their content: they were all well written, courteous and grateful with a little bit of news. Many of them were from ex manual workers all of whom had left school at 14 and they do credit to these young men. This example makes a brief reference to the Christmas Truce in 1914 which was widely talked about and severely disapproved of by the high command.

Malo-les-Bains, Dunkirk

I must thank you all for your kindness in sending the parcel, which I received nearly minus paper, but all the contents intact. Well, I daresay you would like to know how I spent the Day of Days – one which I think will for ever live in my memory. I received yours on the 24th and we all thoroughly enjoyed the biscuits. The weather was ideal – a lovely starry night, hard and crisp, with a clear half moon shining. During one period of the evening I was working by the church, which although badly battered, still has its tower standing amid the ruin and desolation around; a village larger than Warnham entirely deserted. My thoughts were with you all at Warnham and that you were spared this Christmas such pain and tragedy, in fact the impression on my memory I shall never be able to describe. Peace and Goodwill was sung here in the trenches – our enemy scarcely 100 yards distant. Many carols were sung as I have heard in the dear old village. Greetings were exchanged between our trenches, and in several cases friend and foe met mid-way and exchanged cigarettes and returned to their own trenches to have 'Peace and Goodwill' for a short time. The day passed away cheerfully, being provided with lots of good things. I hope you will be able to understand the scribble, as there must be many degrees of frost and I can hardly feel the pencil and we are not lucky enough to have tables and chairs. With hearty wishes to you all for a happier New Year.

Yours faithfully H A Yea

Hubert Yea, who was in the 59th Company, Royal Engineers, was the third son of Alfred Yea, caretaker of the Warnham village hall for many years. This letter from Malo-les-Bains must have been written by Hubert when his unit was resting in reserve. Soldiers in the front line were never allowed to indicate their location.

Another letter of thanks comes from Esmé F Chinnery. Sadly in the same edition of the magazine there is a report of the memorial service held after his death in a flying accident in Paris on 18 January 1915.

The Vicar also records in the magazine that a significant day for the recruits from Warnham was 17 July 1915 when the 4th Battalion Royal Sussex sailed for Gallipoli on *HMS Ulysses*. They travelled via Alexandria and Port Said, arriving in Suvla Bay on 8 August.

German and British soldiers during the Christmas truce in 1914.

At Christmas 1915 79 parcels were sent to Warnham men in various places: France 40, Egypt and Malta 11, India 1, Italy 1, Germany (prisoner of war) 1, Sailors 9, England (in hospital or convalescent) 16. Here are a few extracts from some of the many unnamed letters published in the Parish Magazine, which give little snippets of life in the army:

'I have just returned from the trenches where the mud and water was up to my hips. The parcel from friends at the Village came as a great surprise.'

'I am writing to thank you and all concerned for the parcel which was so kindly sent to me. We are stationed up in the mountains so you can guess it is very cold, but we have plenty of work, so do not think about this. The snow is now over two feet deep, and we find it very difficult getting the wounded away from the trenches, as some of the roads through the mountains are only just wide enough for a car, with several hundreds of feet drop on either side, so one has to be very careful.'

'The cocoa and malted milk was much appreciated during the long night watches on the bridge; we have been lying here since we left the Dardanelles, where it was quite exciting enough to be safe, especially on the night when we landed the Australians at Gaba Tepe, the place which is now known as Anzac Cove. We were lucky, however, as we lost only four men killed and six wounded.'

'I have just received an excellent parcel from Friends at Warnham and wish to thank them all for their great kindness. Our Battalion, having left Gallipoli, is now quartered in the desert near Cairo. It is a little better than the fighting line . . . We had what they termed a "short route march" over the desert. My word, it was some march, as the Yankees would say. Sand, sand all the way. It helps one however, to realise the difficulties of an army fighting in these parts.'

In September 1915 Mrs Beatrice Hodgson made an appeal for jam – it being the time of year for blackberries, apples and plums. Every household was asked to contribute two pots of jam or honey which would be sent to the Committee of the Brighton War Hospitals as 'an extra in the way of jam at tea-time, which will be greatly appreciated by the men.' In October an effusive letter of thanks was published 'for the splendid consignment of jam from Warnham.' This effort went on throughout the war, the schoolchildren being especially thanked each year for the large quantities of blackberries they had picked. The school is mentioned very regularly as having helped with the war effort. The children collected pennies, made items for sale, collected newspapers, knitted socks and gloves and were always ready to lend a hand. Appeals were made for salvage of all kinds, particularly metal and also for bones which would be turned into glue.

The same magazine contains an unusual note: *'SANDBAGS FOR THE FRONT. The following also helped to make sandbags: Gladys Cocks, Eva Ayling.'* It seems the girls were doing their bit and had turned their hands from fine sewing and knitting, to stitching up sacking.

Eggs were sent out in great numbers to various hospitals. Between May and June 1915, 752 were despatched, and the villagers of Warnham sent an average of 800 a month for most of the year when the hens were laying. The eggs were regularly collected by various people and despatched every Wednesday. Most villagers kept hens and many thousands of eggs were given. And of course in those days they were all free range and organic and so tasty and nutritious. As well as sandbags, eggs, food parcels and the many other demands being made on the population, by 1915 recycling was very much the order of the day. Once more the magazine took the lead:

OLD NEWSPAPER COLLECTION
Throughout the country considerable sums have been raised by this means for charitable objects. We hope to do this here through the CLB and to send parcels with the proceeds to old CLB boys at the Front. All can help by sending single newspapers or small bundles to the school by the children. Heavier quantities will be called for. Books and letters are not useful.

April 1916 gives even more details of mufflers, bed socks, day socks, shirts, limb pillows, slippers and many other comforts made and provided by the women of Warnham. But it also tells us of other ways in which women were helping the war effort:

WOMEN'S WORK ON THE LAND
The Secretary for the Horsham Rural District for 'Women's Work on the Land' has asked Miss Lee-Steere to keep the register of women in Warnham parish who are willing to assist farmers (preferably in their own parish) during the scarcity of male labour, owing to the war. Will any who are willing to help in this way, either by the week, day, or part of a day, send their name and address to Miss Lee-Steere, Haisthorpe, Warnham.

Women's Forestry Corps felling trees in Sussex.

At the turn of the century there were still a large number of small mixed farms in the Parish, none of them very profitable. The only mechanisation was the steam-driven threshing machine and even that required a large team of men to feed it with fuel and water and to handle the sheaves. It was not until the end of the war that the first American-built tractor arrived and this would have been beyond the budget of most small farmers. Although efforts were made to plough up more land on which to grow food, there was nothing like the 'Dig for Victory' campaign in the Second World War. Agricultural labouring employed large numbers of working class boys and when they went off to war the farms were left very short of labour. This was where their mothers and sisters came to the rescue. Much of the produce collected by the village for despatch to the troops came from cottage gardens, smallholdings and the big estates.

Despite the importance of the work done by the Women's Land Army, the government still felt that it was appropriate to remind women of the standards expected of them. *'You are doing a man's work and so you are dressed rather like a man; but remember that because you wear a smock and trousers you should take care to behave like an English girl who expects chivalry and respect from everyone she meets.'*

While acknowledging the contribution of women to the war effort and the undoubted necessity of their labour particularly on the home front, there was a slight feeling of unease from the government and others in authority (almost exclusively men) that this might be the thin end of the wedge and their womenfolk, having experienced some financial independence, might acquire a taste for it.

An interesting comment entitled 'Women's Position' appeared in the Church Monthly in 1917.

> *As an increasing number of women are taking the place of men in numerous occupations and their position in the country's service develops, there are many influences operating upon their position in this country. In some cases they are showing themselves to be quite capable of the work assigned to them. Oftentimes they have to labour against much prejudice, but in typing and secretarial work they had obtained an assured position before the war, and other occupations seem likely now to retain their services permanently.*
>
> *What the effect will be upon men's work remains to be seen, but two strong arguments will operate probably against dismissing them. Sentiment will be strongly in their favour and probably also economy, since women necessarily require smaller remuneration. As their work becomes better appreciated there may result a changed attitude of mind which will have its effect upon lower grades of labour so that sweated industries will cease to take their appalling toll of*

women's energies under conditions hardly removed from slavery. In many cases, alas, the women will become the chief support of the family when he, who bore the responsibility, has been maimed for life.

All these things will tend to change the relationships between the sexes. The Church can contribute to ensure that the change is one for the better. If the women gain strength of character, endurance and initiative, the lives of their husbands and brothers will not have been given in vain, but there will be need for care that in the process they do not lose the womanly graces and by a greater share in the battle and bustle of life be deprived of the gentle charm which characterises the true woman.

Two cheerful members of the Woman's Army Auxiliary Corps.

In April 1917 the following appeared:

NATIONAL WAR SERVICE
Meetings have been held by the School Managers with a view to organising a class for boys for instruction in digging and planting, and by the Parish Council for the canvassing and visiting men of serviceable age. The matter is pressing and it is certain that an adequate response will be made.

This half sentence about canvassing men presumably means putting pressure on those who had not yet joined up. After the failure of the Derby scheme, which had been devised to appeal to the consciences of those not already enlisted, the government passed the Military Services Act of January 1916 bringing in conscription for single men and childless widowers aged 18-41. But it seems that many still found ways round this legislation and it was reported that although 43,000 had joined up, 93,000 had failed to appear, 748,587 had claimed exemption and 1,433,827 were said to be in reserved occupations essential to the war effort. By this time the heavy death toll and huge numbers of wounded in hostilities which relied more on men than machinery, had created severe shortages of troops and the matter was critical.

By this stage of the war besides the crisis of manpower, German U-boats in the North Atlantic had sunk many merchant ships bringing food, particularly grain, from abroad. The shortages of food and fuel were causing hardship and in May 1917, King George V was moved to issue a Royal Proclamation to be read out in churches on four successive Sundays. This rather pompous and stiff document, all in one sentence, exhorted his subjects to practise the greatest economy and frugality in their use of grain both for themselves and for their horses. The Royal Proclamation is reproduced elsewhere in this book.

The women of Warnham were constantly being urged to be thrifty and to this end 'Patriotic Economy and Thrift Exhibitions' were regularly held in Horsham to which they were invited. Some Warnham women attended one in June 1917 where:

> *Mrs Yea won first prize for a 'converted' garment – a most serviceable jersey and pair of knickers made out of old stockings. The second prize went to Annie Wood for a bedspread which soon found a purchaser, and Lily Nightingale gained a third prize for a hearthrug made from oddments.*

In the same month:

> *COOKING AND WAR ECONOMY*
> *Miss Anderson came to speak to us on these subjects on Monday, the 18th, in the afternoon at 3 and in the evening at 8. Her demonstrations on how to cook were most practical and to the point, and her address on our duty during the war was excellent and worth hearing. We have been fortunate in securing her services for a week early in September, when she will give cooking classes at the Village Hall.*

All very worthy though one cannot help feeling that these country women, who had been bringing up large families on very small incomes, could probably have taught Miss Anderson a thing or two about thrift and economical cooking. A few weeks later the writer laments the fact that these classes were very poorly attended.

In August 1917 the magazine records the erection of a shrine in memory of those from the village who had given their lives in the war so far. Twelve names were already on it and it was the gift of Colonel Sir Arthur Davidson and his two sisters. Presumably this was removed when the war memorial was erected in 1920.

Poster from 1919.

Money was being collected regularly throughout the war, by frequent sales of work, whist drives and other fund raising events, house-to-house and street collections, and direct appeals for donations. These funds were mostly used to buy items to go in parcels for the troops, or to buy materials for sewing and knitting garments. Some money was sent to the Red Cross and in January 1918 £156 was collected for the YMCA Hut Appeal. At the very beginning of the war the YMCA provided 250 huts all over the country from which to serve hot drinks and food to soldiers. These were sited mostly near railway stations and ports. Soon they extended their role into France and Belgium and established hundreds of huts and small roadside canteens, some of these only small stalls, wherever troops were stationed or fighting. This exercise was soon supported financially by donations and fund raising schemes in every corner of the country, including Warnham.

A War Savings Scheme was also started towards the end of the war and this flourished with regular reports of investments made. Around this time the Parish Magazine had to be reduced in size owing to the shortage of paper. Another clue to hardships being experienced was an appeal in October 1918 for people to save coal.

The Coal Controller has asked us to draw attention to the very serious shortage of coal for our country this winter. Every bit of coal saved will help us and our Allies to win the war. The most careful economy should be exercised and in all houses, large and small, as few fires as possible should be burning. This matter should be taken very seriously and even though it may involve some inconvenience or even hardship, it is a nothing to the life of our soldiers in the trenches, and of our sailors tossing in all weathers on the seas. 'Be hard' is the message issued to the German people and we, with our infinitely better food supplies, should be able to show them that we too are able, for patriotic reasons, to bear a little hardship.

The country people of Warnham no doubt kept their cottages warm with supplies of wood which were plentiful around the village, but most of them cooked on kitchen ranges for which coal was needed.

There were many food shortages, made worse by the lack of imports. In rural Warnham these problems would have been less serious as people always had the means of providing for themselves. They all had gardens and were serious vegetable and fruit growers. They kept hens and rabbits and bees and some had pigs and goats and even a cow. There were many small mixed farms and the countryside provided wild rabbits, mushrooms and blackberries. There may have been little tea and sugar, and few oranges and bananas but country people would not be seriously hungry. Those in towns fared less well, the black market was rife and malnutrition was seen in poor communities. Sugar rationing was introduced in December 1917 and this was followed by rationing of butter, margarine, lard, meat, bacon and ham, jam and tea. As in the Second World War imported goods were the most difficult to obtain and everyone was urged to 'Dig for Victory'. Women in particular were targeted with pleas to grow more vegetables and keep the families fed while their men were at the front. Butter was scarce and supplies of margarine very low. In Warnham the allotments, which were already an important amenity, were extended over several acres on the land which is now Freeman and Lucas Roads and Gardeners' Close.

HORSHAM
FOOD CONTROL COMMITTEE
NOTICE.
BUTTER & MARGARINE.

Consumers are required to register at once for supplies of Butter and Margarine.

The original Household Sugar Card should be taken to the Retailer for stamping for this purpose, and Consumers will be restricted to one Retailer.

On NO account may the individual Sugar Cards be used for this purpose.

Retailers of Farm or Dairy Butter are required to Register, by letter, with the Food Office, Town Hall, forthwith.

22. JAN 1918.

Queuing for margarine in Horsham.

Three very unappetising recipes appeared in the Church Monthly, attached to the Parish Magazine, in 1917.

HOMELY COOKERY
ECONOMICAL WAR TIME RECIPES

CORNFLOUR SHAPE

Three good tablespoonfuls of cornflour, mix smoothly in a little water, add 1 pint of quite boiling water (add one teaspoonful of sugar if wished). Boil briskly eight minutes, stirring briskly. Pour into a shape and turn out when cold. To be eaten with jam.

PLAIN SUET PUDDING

Chop very finely 3 oz suet, mix in a basin with ½ lb of flour, half a teaspoonful of salt. Mix quarter teaspoonful of carbonate of soda in a ¼ pint of water. Stir into the flour well, add a little more water if required. Put into a basin and boil three hours. This can be eaten with meat or with syrup or jam.

INVALID BEEF PUDDING

Have ready ½ pint beef tea. Take 1 tablespoonful of fine breadcrumbs; beat up 1 egg with half the beef tea, the breadcrumbs and a little pepper or salt; butter a cup, pour in the mixture and place in a saucepan in boiling water and steam 10 minutes. Put on a plate and pour the remainder of the beef tea nice and hot over it.

After the breaking of the Hindenburg line at the end of September 1918, although hostilities were continuing along the Western Front, the German Chancellor, sensing defeat and influenced by the public opinion of his half-starved population, spent most of October exchanging notes with the Allies on terms for peace. After a good deal of wrangling most conditions were agreed and these were presented to the Germans on 8 November. The Armistice was signed in a railway carriage in Compiègne Forest at 5 am on 11 November and hostilities on the Western Front officially ceased at 11 am. For the past 90 years the coincidence of this date has been a gift to commentators who relish in the evocative words 'the 11th hour of the 11th day of the 11th month'.

Warnham Post Office and Stores.

The celebrations throughout this country were huge, not least in Warnham where two big church services were held on 12 and 16 November and much rejoicing was recorded by the Rev Bowcott in the Parish Magazine of December 1918. But after the initial and quite understandable euphoria and sense of relief, the horrors of the previous four years became dramatically real to the villagers when they realised how many of their young men had perished and how many of the returning soldiers were plagued by nightmares and had lifetime afflictions from wounds or gas.

Although hostilities had ended, hardships continued for many years to come. Fearing mass unemployment, government plans for demobilisation only released a limited number of men each month, beginning with those who could prove that they had jobs to go back to. The Spanish flu was taking its toll and is mentioned in the magazine several times and there are still regular reports of the continuing need of parcels for the troops and eggs for the wounded. All the thanks letters were put on display in the post office, and extracts from some of them were published in the magazine.

Early in 1919 an interesting thanks letter was received from a former Warnham bell ringer:

> *Dear Vicar*
>
> *Just a line to thank you for the nice parcel that you have sent me. I cannot thank you and the dear old friends of Warnham too much for it. I was very pleased with it all – the soap, the Oxo tablets and the writing paper I find very useful, and the chocolate and biscuits were very nice too. I have travelled through France and Belgium, and the people were very pleased to see us in the large towns through which we passed. They cheer and wave flags as we go along.*
>
> *I have been with the 2nd Dragoon Guards. I was with them when I first crossed the frontier into Germany on Dec 1st. That day I shall never forget. After we crossed, we passed through a forest of fir trees about two miles long, and then we came to some large towns with factories and very open country with good soil where they grow sugar beet, and we saw women working in the fields. I must tell you I had the honour of crossing the Rhine. We then came back to Cologne. This is a very pretty town and a very fine bridge that we crossed over. The people in Germany are very nice to us; they treat us all right. I am now sleeping in a civilian billet and have a nice little room, like being at home. I had a very nice Christmas. And now I am wishing you and your family and all the dear Warnham friends a happy New Year. May we have a better one than the last four have been.*
>
> *Yours faithfully, JOHN COOK*

In 1919 the village, and the country, were reeling from the horrors and tragedies of war and torn between celebrating, mourning and trying to cope with the problems brought on by Spanish flu and the massive unemployment among the returning troops, particularly those who had been badly wounded or were suffering from shell shock. The Parish Magazine reflects all of this and various efforts were made to jolly everyone along as on Empire Day at the School:

> *We were glad to see so many of the parents and friends. The children sang patriotic songs, and they gave intelligent answers to Mr Stroud* [the headmaster] *on the subject of the Flag and the Empire. Mr Martin Lucas most happily addressed the children. He reminded them of the pride of the old Roman who rejoiced in the fact that he was a Roman citizen, and he told us that ours is a greater trust, whose glory it is that we are British citizens. He told us that when he made his*

tour round the world, the thing that impressed him not least of all was the fact that the British flag was almost everywhere, telling him of the freedom and the security of Britons all over the world. The ceremony in the school being over, we went out to salute the Flag, which was hoisted by two of the senior children, and with the singing of the National Anthem the company dispersed.

On Saturday 19 July 1919 'Peace Celebrations' took place in the village. A short service was held on the Cricket Field at 2 pm and the rest of the day was devoted to festivities which included sports followed by dancing in the evening. Everyone was entertained to tea and the field was taken up with coconut shies and other side shows. Warnham certainly knew how to put on a good show when it came to sports and entertainment for the whole village. Since 1906 the 'Flower Show and Athletic Sports' had been laid on with considerable aplomb. These annual events, mostly held at Warnham Court, were hugely successful and attracted hundreds of people including many from outside the village. In the days before annual paid holidays, the Flower Show and Sports was the main leisure activity for most people. In 1914 this event was suspended but it was re-instated in 1920 though sadly with some of the former athletes no longer there or no longer fit enough to compete. Other village events slowly came back. November 1919 saw the return of the annual cricket club dance which had been suspended during the war and celebrated the renewal of play, the first practice being held on 3 May 1919.

The County Times also reports a peace celebration taking place near Warnham Station. The community in that area were close knit and slightly separate from the village. Most of the residents of Station Road worked together at the brickworks and there are several instances, particularly connected with the Flower Show, when they 'did their own thing', though they most likely also attended the big event in the village.

The first Armistice Day Service was held in the Church at 7 pm on 11 November 1919 and the two minutes' silence was observed throughout the country at 11 am on that day. These ceremonies are still held annually 95 years later.

In October 1919 the magazine reported the formation of the Comrades Club.

An inaugural smoking concert was held at the Sussex Oak on October 11th at which General Sir John Nixon GCMG KCB took the chair. An admirable and lucid speech from the Hon secretary of the Horsham Branch, Mr Trotter, resulted in the prompt enrolment of about 60 members, and with speech and song – and some songs that were mostly speech – the evening went merrily and everybody felt that a good start had been made.

This feeling was fully justified by the next smoking concert on the 25th when the following officers and committee were elected: Major C R Stone, DSO MC, captain and Hon treasurer; Mr T Burrage, Hon secretary; committee General Sir John Nixon GCMG KCB, Capt C E Lucas, Capt K S Stubbs and Messrs Cannon, Greenslade, Gregson, E Nightingale, Packham, Secrett and Vincent. Membership has reached 80 and a discussion about the Warnham War Memorial brought into prominence the spirit of comradeship and responsibility which animates the Warnham Post, and which will prove to be a stimulating and united influence in the future history of the village. All ex-soldiers, sailors and airmen are urged to lose no time in joining the Warnham Post. The subscription at present is only 1s a year; and civilians willing to promote a continuance of the spirit of comradeship and pledged to act as true friends to all ex-service men may become associates on payment of a subscription of not less than 10s 6d a year. In view of the alluring programme of concerts, smoking concerts, lectures etc which the committee is preparing for every fortnight during the winter, it is hoped that the decision to admit associates may appeal to those of us who would not wish to be left out of so excellent a movement.

The smoking concert, by modern standards a very unhealthy and disagreeable event, was a very popular entertainment in Victorian times and continued to be held until well after the Great War. The concerts were strictly confined to an audience of men who were encouraged to smoke while listening to live music. Ironically these events were particularly popular with cricket and football clubs.

When reporting the Peace Celebrations held in July, the writer lamented that many of the servicemen had not yet been demobilised and promised to lay on something for them later in the year. This was done in December.

WELCOME TO THE RETURNED SERVICE MEN
'The best evening we have ever had in Warnham' this was said by one of the men as he left the Village Hall after the dinner and entertainment on Saturday, Nov 22nd 1919, and it may be taken as expressing the opinion of everyone who was present. We had looked forward to this day during the long years of the War – the day when we should welcome our men and lads back to the old village. The invitation included not only those who had gone from Warnham but also those service men who were now living amongst us. About 180 had accepted the invitation, but illness and other causes kept some away and about 156 sat down to dinner.

The dinner was following by a smoking concert. In January 1920 the Vicar reported the successful launch of the Comrades Club led by Major Christopher Stone and numbering 128 members.

All over the country villages and towns were erecting memorials and in Warnham in the summer of 1919 an appeal was launched. Mr Lucas opened the appeal with a gift of £50 which was soon matched by the same amount from Mrs Wharrie, and contributions came pouring in. In its usual style, Warnham formed a committee, 'The War Memorial Committee'. The chair was sometimes taken by Mr Lucas and sometimes by the Rev Bowcott. The members were a group of local people from all walks of life, including several ex-servicemen. The Vicar collected and accounted for the contributions and Mr Lucas took on the job of organising the building of the memorial through his London based architect, Arthur Blomfield.

Initially it was intended to erect a memorial inside the church and the £200 required for this was quickly raised and work set in motion. While this was in progress it began to dawn on the committee that many villages were erecting outside memorials and they too decided that this would be an appropriate thing for Warnham. The design of a handsome cross was approved and estimates were sought. All this was the subject of a busy hand-written correspondence between Mr Lucas and Mr Blomfield who were on first name terms. J W Whitehead & Sons, Stonemasons of Kennington were given the work of providing both memorials.

There was some discussion as to a suitable location for the cross and at one point Mr Lucas said that he was thinking of giving a piece of land opposite the school to be used as a village green and he thought that area might be a suitable site for the memorial. However no more was recorded about this proposal and it was decided to erect the cross just outside the church. Some years later, on 5 May 1933, his son Captain Eric Lucas did in fact make a gift of the land to the Parish Council for recreational purposes and it remains to this day the village green.

Additional works were needed to accommodate the outside cross and this was dealt with by Mr A S Hodgson who sought estimates from local firms. The cheapest estimate for installing the cross (£59) came from A E Ayling and this was accepted though he later required another £6.10.0d. for repositioning the middle section of the wall. Charman's, a local blacksmith, undertook to lay paving and provide posts, post caps and a metal chain.

A further appeal was launched which resulted in a final total of £551.13. 7d. from just over 400 subscribers. As the total expenditure, including £187.15.0d. for the inside tablet, amounted to £540.13.0d. they broke even. The Vicar kept a record of all contributions in a little notebook carefully recording the name of each donor and the amounts given, even the tiny gifts from children and all this information was later painstakingly transferred into a ledger. The amounts given ranged from twenty or more of 1d, mostly from children, to the highest which was £60 from Mrs Coole, whose son is buried in the churchyard. Most of the gifts were below £10, about half of these less than £1 and reflect the status of the givers. The better-off gave around £20, the tradesmen £5-£10 and most others less than £1. Some of the donors were relatives of those on the memorial.

A public meeting was held on 30 October 1919 to finalise the names to be included on the memorials and a list was approved. At this meeting Miss Emily Steere suggested that the seats round the outside memorial should be omitted owing to the temptation to the children to play there. This was discussed and no decision given – but the seats are still there.

The war memorial was dedicated on Sunday 3 October 1920 and the following account appeared in the Parish Magazine of November 1920:

> *DEDICATION OF WAR MEMORIAL*
>
> *The bell-ringers rang a peal at 3 o'clock on Sunday afternoon, Oct 3rd, while a crowd of about one thousand people was assembling in the roadway outside the Church to take part in the dedication of the Memorial Cross, to the glory of God and in memory of the gallant men of Warnham who lost their lives in the War. Deeply moving as such an occasion was bound to be, the impression of it was much enhanced by the playing of the Dead March from Saul by the band of the 4th Batt Royal Sussex Regt; by the words spoken by Mr C J Lucas, JP who unveiled the cross, and by the Vicar, who dedicated it; by the prayers and the singing of 'For all the Saints' and the National Anthem; by the beautiful rendering of the Last Post and the Reveillé by two buglers from the Horsham Church Lads' Brigade; and by the numerous wreaths which were laid at the foot of the cross.*
>
> *We all felt that we were present at an historical scene in the life of the village which, as the Vicar reminded us, those whom the cross commemorated must so often have remembered with loving and passionate thoughts during the campaigns from which they never returned; and that the Girl Guides and the Boy Scouts in their uniforms, and the other children present – and their children after them – would henceforward look upon the Warnham Cross as a precious trust, and as a fine symbol of the spirit which animated the village in the days when it was threatened with invasion by the enemy.*
>
> *We felt too, how much sincere gratitude we owe to the architect, Mr Arthur Blomfield, who made this striking example of his art as a gift to Warnham; to the Memorial Committee who translated our aspirations into action; and especially to Capt C E Lucas for his admirable organisation of the unveiling ceremony; to Major Eric Godman who brought over the band and a detachment of the 4th Batt Royal Sussex Regt to help us; and to the large contingents of Comrades of the Great War, whom Mr W H B Trotter and Major E F St John brought over*

A latter-day remembrance parade on a wet November day in the 1990s.

> *from Horsham and Slinfold respectively, to honour, with our own branch of the Comrades, the memory of our fallen. So representative a gathering has seldom been seen in Warnham, and as the Union Jack fell to the ground and revealed the cross upstanding in its magnificent simplicity, surely none present can have failed to feel with humility and pride and thankfulness that the dead and the living alike were honoured by the symbol of the Eternal Sacrifice.*

Further names were added on two additional tablets after the Second World War. Although these days we do not have a gathering of one thousand people on Remembrance Sunday, it is a matter of considerable pride that each year the church is always packed for this solemn and dignified service of commemoration.

Warnham War Memorial.

WARNHAM WAR MEMORIAL.

The Memorial erected outside the Church will be unveiled and dedicated on Sunday, October 3rd, 1920, at 3.30 p.m.

ORDER OF PROCEEDINGS.

People to assemble outside the Church at 3 o'clock.

3.30. Mr. Lucas will unveil the Memorial.

Dedication by the Vicar.

Prayers and Address by the Vicar.

Hymn—"For all the Saints who from their labours rest"

For all the Saints who from their labours rest,
Who Thee by faith before the world confess'd,
Thy Name, O Jesu, be for ever blest. Alleluia!

Thou wast their Rock, their Fortress, and their Might;
Thou, Lord, their Captain in the well-fought fight;
Thou in the darkness drear their one true Light. Alleluia!

O may Thy soldiers, faithful, true, and bold,
Fight as the Saints who nobly fought of old,
And win, with them, the victor's crown of gold. Alleluia!

O blest communion! fellowship Divine!
We feebly struggle, they in glory shine;
Yet all are one in Thee, for all are Thine. Alleluia!

And when the strife is fierce, the warfare long,
Steals on the ear the distant triumph-song,
And hearts are brave again, and arms are strong. Alleluia!

The golden evening brightens in the west;
Soon, soon to faithful warriors comes their rest;
Sweet is the calm of Paradise the blest. Alleluia!

But lo! there breaks a yet more glorious day;
The Saints triumphant rise in bright array;
The King of glory passes on His way. Alleluia!

From earth's wide bounds, from ocean's farthest coast,
Through gates of pearl streams in the countless host,
Singing to Father, Son, and Holy Ghost, Alleluia! Amen.

First verse of the National Anthem.

The Last Post and Reveillé.

People are requested to come in good time so that due arrangements may be made.

All those who may like to bring Flowers are requested to place them at the foot of the Memorial after the Ceremony is over.

Warnham and the 1911 Census

Just three years prior to the outbreak of the Great War, the UK underwent its most detailed census to date. The results of that census have now been released to the general public and so we have been able to compile a comprehensive understanding of the population of Warnham at that time.

The census enumerated each person's whereabouts on the night of Sunday 2 April 1911. Inevitably there were people normally resident in Warnham who were away for some reason and so have been excluded, and there were visitors from elsewhere who have been included. Fortunately the number of these people relative to the village population is very small and so does not distort any analysis.

The census recorded the following for each person:

Whereabouts on census night
Full name
Relationship to the head of household
Age
Sex
Marital status
For married women, how many years married, how many children born alive and how many still living
Occupation and industry/service sector
Whether an employer, employee or self-employed
If working from home
Birthplace
Nationality
Whether deaf, dumb, blind or mentally disabled
Number of rooms in their dwelling

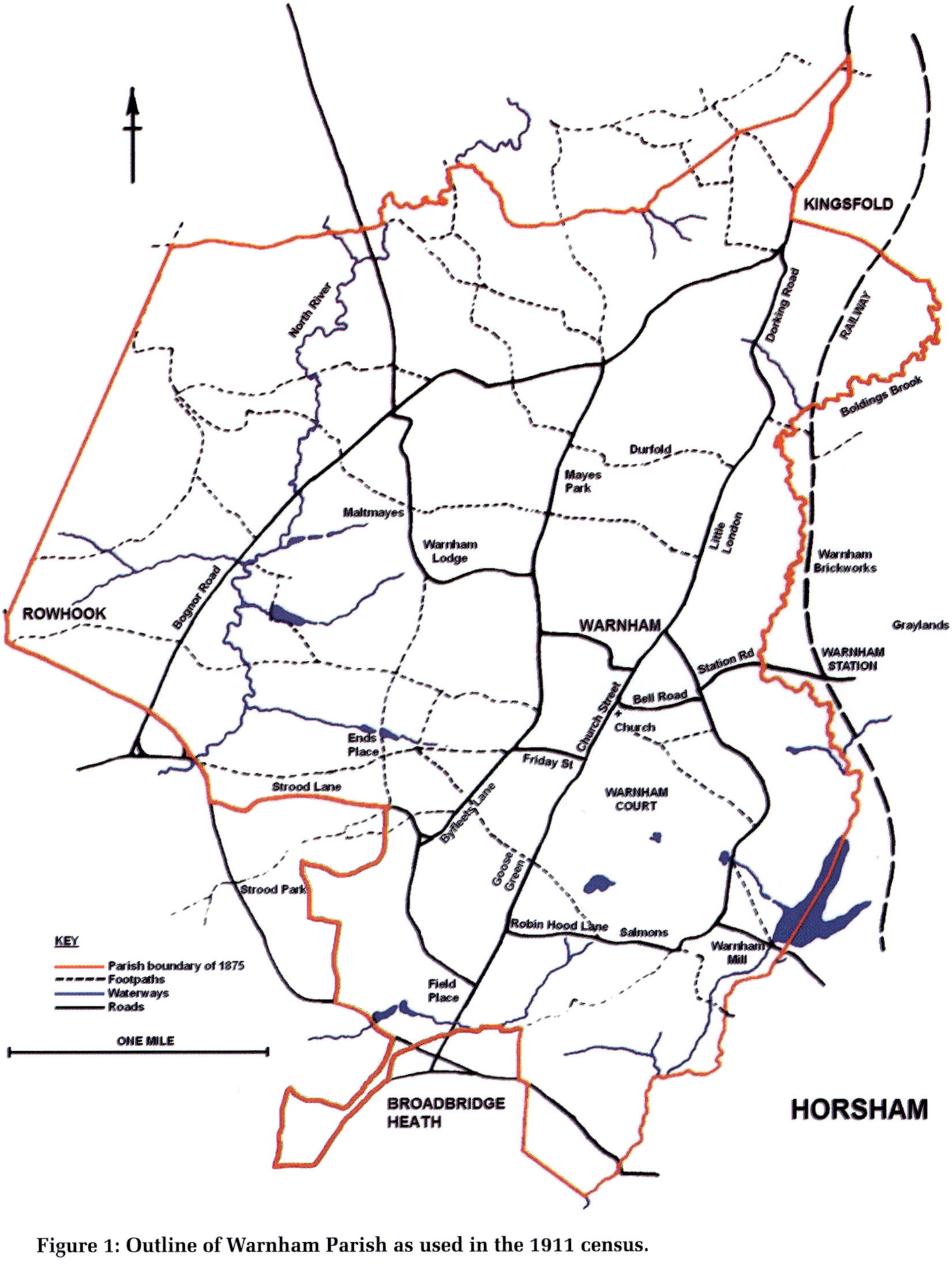

Figure 1: Outline of Warnham Parish as used in the 1911 census.

Age Profiles

It is worth noting that as well as providing more information than previous censuses, particularly with regard to the numbers of children born, this is the only census we have where the original forms completed by the head of the house still exist. Only transcriptions by local enumerators exist for earlier censuses. This means the information provided in 1911 should be more reliable.

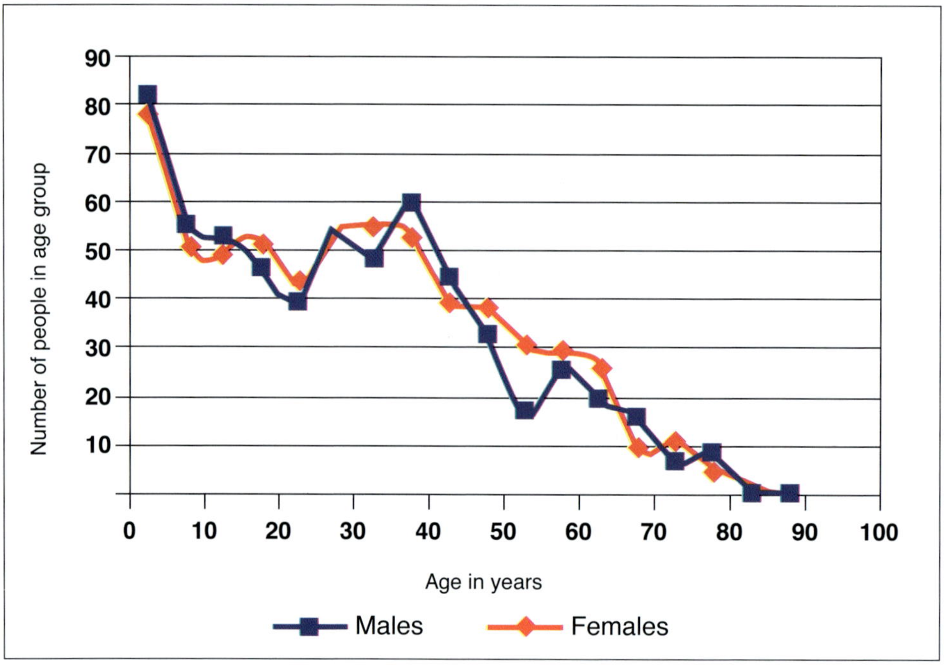

Figure 2: Age profiles of population in 1911.

286 properties were enumerated, and the population of Warnham totalled 1,190 men, women and children. Looking at the age profiles of the population in Figure 2 we see that they are broadly similar for both sexes. Perhaps the most notable difference though is around the age of 52, where it seems there are twice as many women as men. This may well indicate that men were more likely to die in their fifties than women, perhaps a symptom of the tough physical demands of an agricultural existence. The oldest inhabitant was Sir Henry Harben aged 86, who owned the Warnham Lodge Estate.

Overall 49.28% of the village population was male and 50.72% female, which is in close agreement with the national average at the time of 48.4% male to 51.6% female, as given by the official General Report of the 1911 Census by Bernard Mallet.

Birthplaces

People's birthplaces are also of particular interest, as they show just how mobile people were. From the census information it appears that only 31% were actually born in Warnham. Those born in Sussex accounted for 63% and the rest were from further afield, with a handful from outside the UK. It seems the population was a lot more mobile than we might imagine, in some instances travelling from one end of the country to the other to find work.

Figure 3 plots these birthplaces for all those Warnham residents born in the UK. We have had to be mindful of the fact that a clear majority of two-thirds did not come from Warnham when deciding whom to include on our revised Roll of Honour from the Great War. The village could not have functioned with its strongly agricultural economy and its great houses without the influx of these people. We cannot just restrict the Roll to those born in the village, but must also include anyone who gave their residence as being in Warnham.

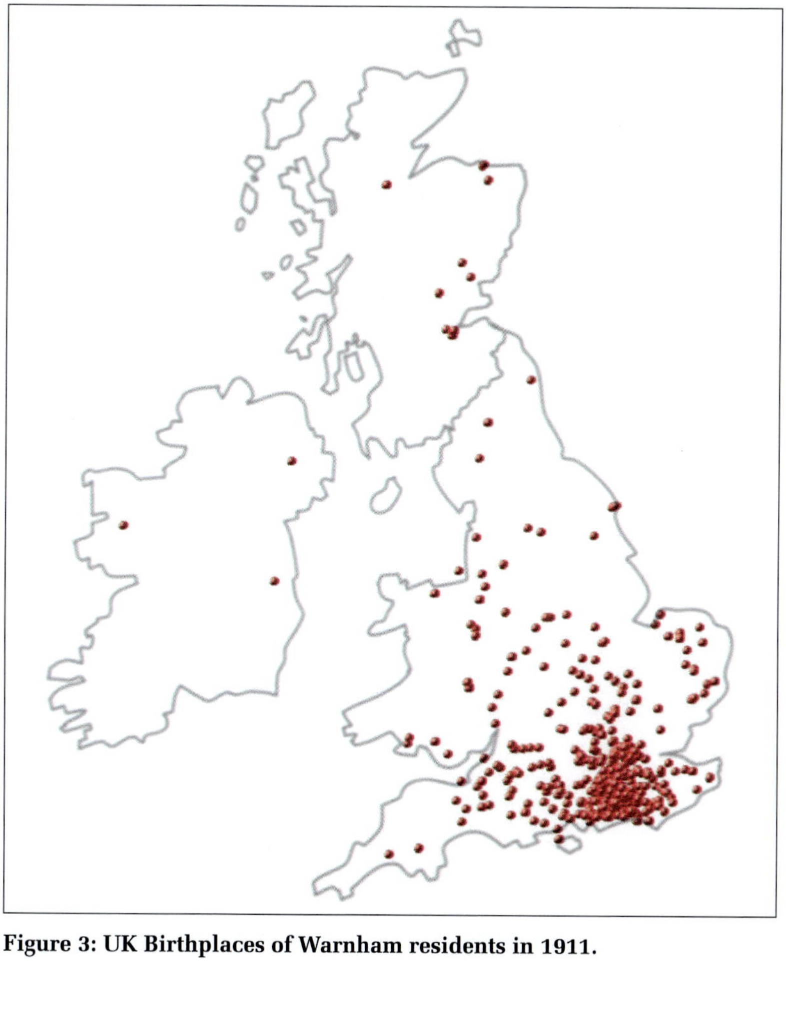

Figure 3: UK Birthplaces of Warnham residents in 1911.

Occupations

The census also provided valuable information about people's occupations. 602 were specified as bringing in an income, although this tended to be just the men. Presumably women and children also earned money with low-paid jobs, but these were not normally specified on the census unless they were the main bread-winner. Of those specified 602 earners, the majority of 505 were classified as workers, plus 27 employers and a further 70 living off 'own means'.

What is perhaps surprising is that the largest employment sector was service and domestic, which accounted for a third of all jobs and included not only household servants but gardeners, grooms and other estate workers. Despite being a rural community, agriculture accounted for just less than a quarter of jobs.

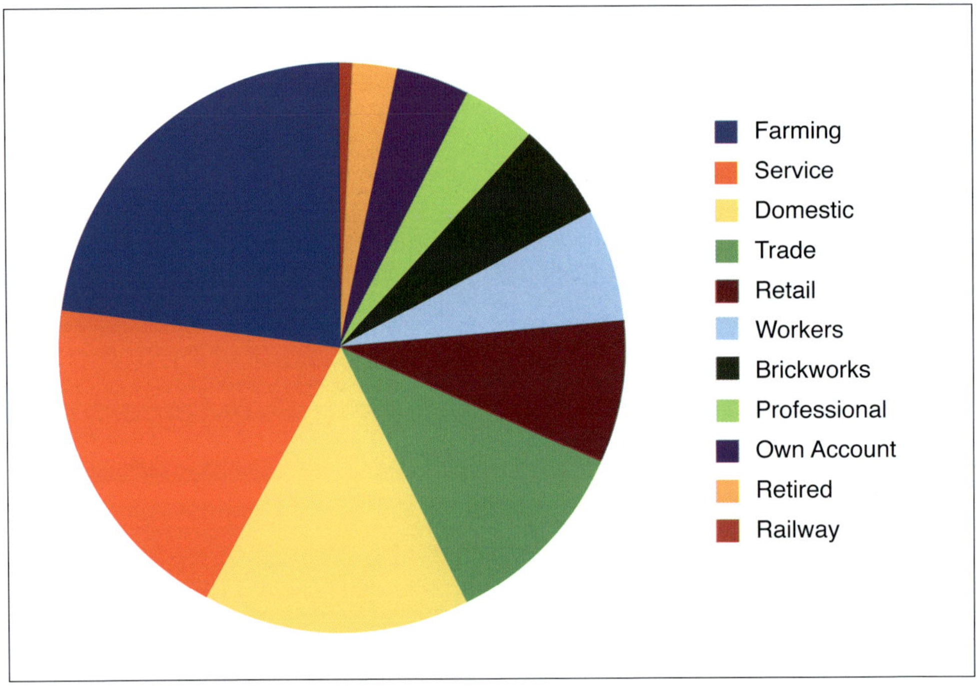

Figure 4: Breakdown of occupations given in the Warnham 1911 census.

Warnham School in the Great War

Warnham School c 1900.

Although there had been a school building in Warnham since 1851, the school above was built in 1873 following the Elementary School Act of 1870. After local discussion it was agreed that a single mixed school to accommodate 160 children, with separate junior and infant schoolrooms, a parochial reading room and a schoolmaster's house be built on a new site. The first headmaster was William Morris who opened the school in 1873 and gradually built up the numbers. His only child, also called William, was born in the School House in 1890 and sadly was killed in 1916 in the Great War. William Morris remained in Warnham until just before the turn of the century when he retired and was succeeded as headmaster by Thomas Stroud. At the outbreak of war there were 180-190 pupils attending, the total somewhat increased by a number of children from

London. Children attended school from the ages of 5 to 12, although later in 1918 the leaving age was raised to 14 years. Mr Stroud, the headmaster, was in charge throughout the war period and he finally retired in 1923.

In many ways the impact of the war was limited. The school's log book reveals that the main preoccupations were the weather and sickness. All the children walked to school, some well over a mile, and this significantly affected attendance. For example on 8 March 1918 because of the snow, only 50 pupils arrived. School was abandoned and many wet feet had to be dried! Illness was a grave concern, especially chicken pox and measles, and many cases of ringworm involved difficult journeys to Worthing Hospital for X-Ray treatment. Regular school inspections continued both from the Diocese of Chichester to monitor religious education and from local government inspectors to maintain the standard of the curriculum.

However there were important ways in which the pupils at Warnham were made aware of the war. The Parish Magazine reported in November 1914: *At the hour of 12 every day the School bell is rung, and the children are asked to join in a short Prayer for our Soldiers and Sailors, and for our Allies.* There were several causes for which they collected money. In July 1915 their collection for the Children's Huts being erected for soldiers was acknowledged by Lord Kinnaird in a special scroll from the Secretary of the War Emergency Fund. A receipt for £1 5s 3d sent by the children at the school to the Secretary of the Overseas Club for Christmas gifts to the soldiers was received in 1916 and 11s 10¾d was contributed to the YMCA Hut Week in January 1918. Towards the end of the war each Monday between 12 noon and 1 pm some pupils went to the village hall to put their money into the War Savings Association. In addition the children were very busy sewing and knitting many things for the war effort. Letters such as these were sent to thank them:

> 7th March 1916 . . . *Lady Jellicoe acknowledges, with grateful thanks, 7 helmets, 3 pairs of mittens and 4 scarves from Mrs Stroud, Warnham School, for the sailors.*
>
> 17th July 1918 . . . *Lady Smith-Dorrien would be grateful to Mrs Bowcott if she would please thank the children of Warnham School very much for the 19 most excellent hospital bags received. They are most acceptable and Lady Smith-Dorrien thinks it very kind of them to have taken so much trouble. They are in great demand.*

The school was also the depository for collected newspapers. On 23 November 1917 Messrs Barnes sent sacks from Horsham to collect the horse chestnuts gathered by the children for the government. They took 5 sacks (10cwt) and said they would bring sacks for the remaining 4 cwt the following week. The Ministry of Supply put out this request:

Thomas Stroud with some of the pupils in 1909.

Collecting groups are being organised in your district. Groups of scholars & boy scouts are being organised to collect conkers. Receiving depots are being opened in most districts. All schools, W.V.S. centres, W.I.s, are involved. Boy Scout leaders will advise you of the nearest depot where 7s 6d per cwt is being paid for immediate delivery of the chestnuts (without the outer green husks). This collection is invaluable war work and is very urgent. Please encourage it.

The purpose was a closely guarded secret so the enemy would not learn of the process. The conkers were used in a newly-discovered method for producing acetone for cordite in shells in a secret process carried out in factories in Poole, Dorset and King's Lynn in Norfolk. Just as much fun was the task of picking blackberries by Standard III upwards on a series of five afternoons from 9 to 21 September 1917. These were taken to Mrs Hoare at Warnham Court.

An episode that highlights an unusual aspect of the war is recorded in the Log Book by Mr Stroud on 26 March 1918:

46 children absent this afternoon. They followed an aeroplane which hovered about the village during the dinner hour and then came down in the neighbourhood. I sent two teachers to fetch them back but the aeroplane had gone up and the children had followed on still further away and were quite gone.

It must have been an amazing sight.

The staff was also affected in various ways. The Management minute book records that on 14 October Mr Pratt, the assistant master, resigned and they resolved to appoint Mr Edwin Cooper of Horsham who had applied for the post. He was appointed on 17 December 1914. However on 27 February 1915 he requested leave to go to Horsham to pass for the army, and on 22 March he reported to Horsham recruiting centre as a volunteer. He enlisted as 3123 Private E Cooper in 'D' Company of the 4th Battalion Royal Sussex Regiment in which other soldiers from Warnham were already serving. He wrote this letter to his pupils from Bedford where 'D' Company were training for the ill-fated Gallipoli Campaign. It was printed in the Parish Magazine in August 1915.

> *This letter from Mr Edwin Cooper, who gave up his post at our school to serve his country, will be read with much interest by the children and their parents. It strikes the right note, and we shall all like to read it.*
>
> Bedford, Monday, July 12th 1915
>
> *To all the scholars of Warnham CE School. Dear Children, Since the time that I left Warnham School to enlist in the army of His Majesty King George V, I have been waiting to go to the fighting line to help those brave men who have been battling for us against the cruel Germans ever since last August. Sometimes I thought that our battalion would never go abroad, but the other day the call came. We have been ordered to go to fight at the Dardanelles. I think we shall set sail probably from Avonmouth at the end of this week or at the beginning of next. Whether I shall be spared to come back alive to you or not I cannot tell, but I hope I may. I am trusting in Him of whom you read in your Bible. Well, dear children, I must say goodbye. Think of me as I do of you. From your loving teacher and friend, EDWIN COOPER.*

Edwin did in fact survive the Gallipoli campaign and moved with the battalion to Palestine. He was killed there on 26 March 1917 on the first day of the first Battle of Gaza.

The women on the staff were also clearly affected. On 5 June 1917 Mrs Packham requested an afternoon's leave as her husband was returning from Salonika. She later asked for 4 days' leave to be with him later in June and again on 20 November for an afternoon when he returned to military duty. Mrs Greenop also requested time off when her husband came home on leave in March of that year.

All through the war much was made of Empire Day. In 1915 this fell on Whit Monday, and so it was not celebrated until 22 June. The headmaster wrote:

> *The Vicar, Mr Wharrie of Warnham Lodge, people from the village and parents of the children assembled at the school at 11 o'clock. Speeches were made by the Vicar and Mr Wharrie. Patriotic songs were sung by the children. The master questioned the children about Empire Day – its meaning, responsibilities and duties. After this the children assembled outside the school to sing 'God save the King' and salute the flag. Mr Wharrie very kindly gave each child sixpence on the occasion. There was a half-holiday in the afternoon.*

As the war progressed, the day was marked with more ceremony. For example on 24 May 1917, Empire Day itself, Mr Stroud reported:

> *Empire Day was observed in the following manner – Lessons were given to all classes on Patriotism, the Empire and the Flag during the morning attendance. Soon after 11 o'clock the Vicar, Mr Lucas, Commander Lucas and the Rev J N Tanner, also several ladies and parents came to the school. Patriotic songs were sung and the Vicar, Mr Lucas and Commander Lucas addressed the children. The last gentleman offered to give prizes to each of the upper standards for the best essay in each standard on . . .* [there is a gap left here]. *The essays to be sent within a fortnight from the date. At 12 o'clock the children lined up in front of the School when the Flag was hoisted and saluted. Hearty cheers were given and then the children dispersed for a ½ holiday.*

The schoolroom in the 1920s, showing little had changed since the Great War.

The end of the war was not marked by the school at the time. From 22 October the headmaster reported that a large number of sick children were absent from school. By the 28 October there were only 112 pupils attending and he wrote to report the serious situation to the medical officer that evening. The following day, by order of the Education Committee, the school was closed until 15 November along with all the schools in West Sussex. By the time they returned the war was over. It is certainly possible that this was linked to the generally poorer health of the population by this time and to the influenza epidemic that began in the spring of 1918 and swept the country that winter.

However, on 11 November 1919 Armistice Day was given due prominence. All the upper children were given a lesson on the importance and meaning of the signing of the Armistice and the coming of peace. The pupils stood silent for two minutes at 11 am and the boys saluted. Mrs Bowcott distributed the mugs which were presented to the children in commemoration of the 'Peace'. The proceedings closed with the singing of the National Anthem. The children collected 17s 3d towards the cost of the war memorial and no doubt attended the dedication with their parents on Sunday, 3 October 1920.

Your King & Country Need You.

A CALL to ARMS

An addition of **100,000** men to His Majesty's Regular Army is immediately necessary in the present grave National Emergency.

Lord Kitchener is confident that this appeal will be at once responded to by all those who have the safety of our Empire at heart.

Terms of Service.

General Service for a period of 3 years or until the war is concluded.
Age of Enlistment between 19 and 30.

RATES OF PAY:

1s. 3d. to 10s. 6d. a day, according to Branch of Service and qualifications.

How to Join.

Full information can be obtained at

or any Post Office in the Kingdom or at any Military Depot.

GOD SAVE THE KING.

W. P. DICKINSON, PRINTER, HIGH STREET, MAIDSTONE.

Kitchener's Call to Arms which was widely published on 7 August 1914. His target of 100,000 was reached well before the end of the month.

Map of the Western Front

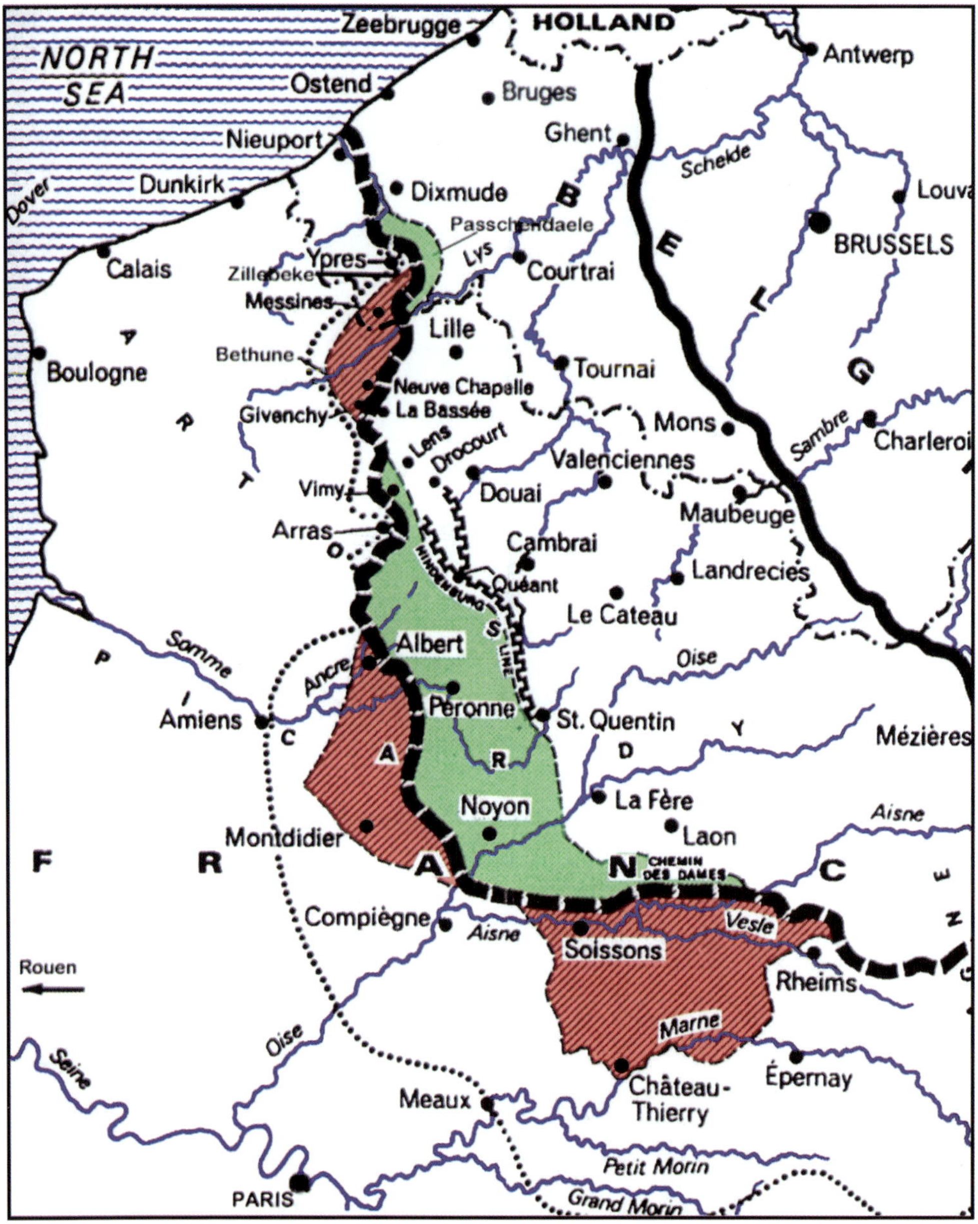

Key

- Limit of German advance in September 1914.
- General front from end of 1914 to 30 June 1916 (prior to Somme battles).
- Allied gains in 1916 and 1917.
- German gains during 1918 offensives.
- Armistice line on 11 November 1918.
- Frontiers in 1914.
- Capital cities.
- Other cities and towns.

Park Street, Horsham 4 August 1914. Troops of the 1/4th Battalion (TF) Royal Sussex Regiment leaving to take up guard duties at Newhaven.

Biographies of Warnham's casualties in the Great War

The biographies that follow form the main part of this book. Three of them are for notable survivors, but those that died as a result of their service are listed below chronologically, set against the key events of the war. For convenience of reference the biographies follow in alphabetical order.

Key Events	Warnham Casualty	Date of Death
1914		
United Kingdon declares war on Germany	Rush, Arthur	24 Aug 1914
4 August	Worsfold, Albert	14 Sep 1914
Battle of Mons	Blackwell, Alfred*	7 Nov 1914
First Battle of the Marne	Bennett, Albert Henry	18 Dec 1914
First Battle of Ypres		
Britain declares war on Turkey		
1915		
Battle of Neuve Chappelle	Chinnery, Esmé Fairfax*	18 Jan 1915
Second Battle of Ypres	Hayler, Frederick Charles*	28 Jan 1915
Invasion of Gallipoli	Reed, Thomas Peter*	11 Apr 1915
Sinking of the Lusitania	Bates, William George Henry*	26 Apr 1915
Battle of Loos	Dalrymple, Ian Douglas	5 May 1915
British and French land in Salonika	Wallis, Duncan Boyd*	23 Jul 1915
Evacuation from Gallipoli	Kemp, William Valentine	13 Aug 1915
	Charman, John Edward*	21 Aug 1915
1916		
Start of conscription	Ottley, Cadwaladr James*	21 Jan 1916
Battle of Verdun	Munday, Charles*	18 May 1916
Battle of Jutland	Richards, Albert Wilfred*	25 Jun 1916
Russian offensive	Burchell, Thomas William	21 Jul 1916
Battle of the Somme	Grant, Clifton Brown	27 Jul 1916
David Lloyd George becomes	Edwards, Harry*	7 Oct 1916
Prime Minister	Hards, Arthur Eldred	10 Oct 1916
	Miller, George Henry*	14 Nov 1916
	Morris, William Charles F	20 Dec 1916

Key Events	Warnham Casualty	Date of Death
1917		
German forces re-group at the Hindenburg line	Bowles, William Ernest	7 Apr 1917
	Miles, Frank Alfred*	16 Apr 1917
America declares war on Germany	Muggeridge, John Edward C	22 Apr 1917
Battle of Arras	Burchett, Cecil*	14 Jun 1917
Battle of Messines	Simmonds, Frank*	20 Sep 1917
Third Battle of Ypres (Passchendaele)	Wood, William Charles*	20 Sep 1917
Third Battle of Gaza	Picton, Frederick*	24 Oct 1917
Russian revolution	Charman, Albert	29 Oct 1917
Battle of Cambrai	Comper, Alfred Charles*	6 Nov 1917
British take Jerusalem	Miles, James William*	6 Nov 1917
Russia signs armistice	Nightingale, Albert John	30 Nov 1917
	Edwards, Fred	27 Dec 1917
1918		
German spring offensive	Dinnage, Ernest James	21 Mar 1918
Battle of the Lys	Eames, Jonas*	30 Mar 1918
Second Battle of the Marne	Spink, William Alfred*	16 Apr 1918
Battle of Amiens	Worsfold, George	24 Apr 1918
Battle of St Quentin canal	Salmon, Dorothy Lottie*	8 May 1918
Turkey signs armistice	Higgins, Thomas James*	2 Aug 1918
Germany signs armistice 11 November	Woodman, Percy*	5 Sep 1918
	Winchester, Charlie*	14 Oct 1918
	Grant, Reginald Walter	26 Nov 1918
1919		
	Coole, Arthur Evans*	14 May 1919

* On original Warnham War Memorial.

William George Henry Bates

Captain

1st Battalion (Prince of Wales's)
Leinster Regiment (Royal Canadians)
82nd Brigade 27th Division
Formerly Lancashire Fusiliers

Killed in action Second Battle of Ypres
26 April 1915, aged 36

William Bates was the son of the Reverend William Wheatley Bates MA of Toronto. His mother, Emily, was the daughter of Manasseh and Emma Leeson, extensive landowners in Canada. He was born in Thornhill, Toronto on 12 October 1878. He received a private education and then from 1894-1896 attended the prestigious Trinity College in Toronto, a college founded as a College of Divinity.

The original Gothic Revival Trinity College, c 1852 by the architect Kivas Tully.

It is not known why he decided on a military career but in 1901 William Bates enlisted in the Lancashire Fusiliers hoping to take part in the Boer War in South Africa. However the regiment was ordered to Crete and remained there until the conclusion of the campaign. He served in the ranks for over two years, but on 7 November 1903 he was commissioned into the Leinster Regiment and promoted Lieutenant on 15 December 1906 and Captain on 12 September 1912. He had a distinguished and varied career in the army before the Great War serving in many parts of the Empire: Crete, Malta, Gibraltar, South Africa, Mauritius and India. While he was in South Africa he became an Instructor in the School of Musketry where he invented automatic elevating and traversing machine gun gear. After his death this was to be tested at the Hythe School of Musketry from 1916.

Captain Bates was married at St Margaret's Church, Warnham on 10 August 1912 to Mabel, the youngest daughter of Mr and Mrs Hastings Castor Draper of Little Daux, Warnham. They went out to India together and there a son, Lionel William Leeson, was born on 25 May 1913, and soon after a daughter, Pamela Dorcas, was born on 2 June 1914.

Captain William Bates.

When war broke out in August 1914, Captain William Bates was with the regiment in Fyzabad in India. They returned to England landing in Plymouth on 16 November 1914. The battalion moved to Winchester and came under the orders of the 82nd Brigade in the 27th Division. They embarked for France on 20 December and landed at Le Havre the next day.

The British Expeditionary Force had managed to defend Ypres, the last sizeable town in Flanders in Allied hands standing in the way of the German Army sweeping onward to the sea. The campaign drew to a close towards the end of November 1914 just before Captain Bates and his battalion reached France. To probe Allied defences, cover the movement of troops to the Eastern Front and test their new weapon, chlorine gas, the Germans prepared for a limited offensive in spring 1915 against the Ypres Salient, a bulge in the Allied lines. As Ypres provided a defensive position from which to protect French ports on the English Channel, it had to be held. The 1st Battalion Leinster Regiment played a key part in this action known as the Second Battle of Ypres which was fought from 22 April to 25 May.

Captain William Bates was shot through the head on Monday 26 April 1915. His commanding officer wrote to his wife:

> *Your husband was one of the bravest and most gallant men I know, and his death leaves a gap which cannot be filled. I can only add that he died like the gallant man he was.*

A fellow officer also wrote:

> *The regiment can say of him that he never asked a man to do a thing that he would not do himself. He simply did not know fear, and would always tell us that dying was part of the game. It isn't only we officers who admired him, but every man who knew him would have followed him anywhere – everywhere he led.*

Members of 'D' Company, 1st Battalion, The Prince of Wales's Leinster Regiment in the front line 1915.

The West Sussex County Times when reporting his death also extended sympathy to his widow and two children under two. And in the Warnham Parish Magazine the Reverend Bowcott added:

Captain Bates was well known to us having married the daughter of Mr and Mrs Draper of Little Daux. He was killed on 26th April while on duty in the trenches in Belgium.

He also quoted the letter from his commanding officer.

Captain William George Henry Bates has no known grave and his memorial is on Panel 44 of the Menin Gate at Ypres. He was awarded three medals, the 1914-15 Star, the Victory Medal and the British War Medal in commemoration of his war service.

The Menin Gate at Ypres.

Albert Henry Bennett

L/10378 Private

2nd Battalion
Queen's (Royal West Surrey Regiment)
22nd Brigade 7th Division

Killed in action at La Boutillerie
18 December 1914, aged 19

The Bennett family were resident in and around Horsham for many generations. Albert's grandparents, Henry and Elizabeth, had both been born in Warnham and all their children, including Albert's father William, were also born there. The family moved for a few years to Newfoundout in Southwater but in the 1870s returned to the village where they lived at Station Cottages, Warnham. At the age of 13 William was a general labourer, marrying when he was 20 and moving with his wife, Ada, (another Warnham girl) to 64 Trafalgar Road, Horsham. After a year or two he got a job at the brickworks, probably at Capel, and by 1901 was a foreman brick maker. The family by then had moved to Chapel Cottage, Capel.

Albert, born in Warnham on 11 November 1895, perhaps at the home of his grandparents, was the middle one of Ada and William's three surviving sons, the first, Arthur, having died at the age of two. There is no trace of Albert on the 1911 Census and his family were by then living in Leatherhead. All the military records for Private Bennett were damaged in the bombing in the Second World War and there are only fragments of partially burned papers still existing. Albert was working as a milkman when he had a medical examination in September 1912 as he signed up with the Army Reserve at Guildford. He was attached to the Queen's (Royal West Surrey Regiment) known colloquially as 'The Queen's'. A few months later, in April 1913, he was discharged from the Reserve when he enlisted in the 2nd Battalion Queen's at Guildford. The 1st and 2nd battalions were the only Regular battalions in the regiment.

Before the war, the 2nd Battalion, together with other Regular Army units had been comfortably stationed at Roberts Heights in Pretoria. These battalions were mobilised for war on 10 August 1914. The *SS Kenilworth Castle*, a Union Castle Liner, was hastily requisitioned as a troopship and sailed from Table Bay with a large number of troops on 27 August, stopping briefly on St Helena and arriving in Southampton on 19 September. The 2nd Battalion Queen's, together with the 2nd Warwickshires, 1st Royal Welsh Fusiliers and 1st South Staffs made up the

22nd Brigade, part of the 7th Division. On arrival in England, the 22nd Brigade was stationed at Lyndhurst in a temporary camp on a piece of land which is now the golf course. During the following week they were given 24 hour passes for a brief visit home. For the remainder of the month, together with the 21st Brigade, whose battalions had also been recalled from relatively easy peacetime postings (Guernsey, Gibraltar and South Africa) they were subjected to a harsh regime – route marches, weapon training and military exercises in preparation for the Division's move to France. We can assume that Albert was with the Battalion throughout all this.

On 4 October the Division, including the 2nd Queen's (30 officers and 988 other ranks), having marched the nine miles from Lyndhurst, embarked at Southampton, crossed the Channel and landed at Zeebrugge. They then moved south to join elements of the British Expeditionary Force coming from the River Aisne after the retreat from Mons, including the 1st Battalion Queen's, before moving west to take up positions to the east of Ypres. During October and November the 1st and 2nd Battalions were heavily involved in the First Battle of Ypres. Fighting near the village of Zonnebeke they suffered severe defeats and horrendous losses. The British armies in France now consisted of shattered units of the Regular Army, most of which had been all but destroyed at Ypres. They were now in the process of being rebuilt by receiving new drafts from the Territorials and Service battalions of the New Army.

Once the fighting of the First Battle of Ypres had died down, the British units were relieved by the French and the BEF moved south, now holding a sector of the Western Front from south of St Eloi to Givenchy. The 2nd Queen's dug in near La Boutillerie, a small village half way between Armentières and Neuve Chapelle. During the next few weeks there were various attempts to gain some ground. On 18 December 1914, the 2nd Battalion, together with the 2nd Royal Warwicks, launched an attack on the Well Farm position at La Boutillerie. The 2nd Battalion War Diary [WO 95/1664] records many difficulties and possibly a lack of planning. The writer is critical and refers to:

> *. . . the short time given to prepare for an attack against a strongly entrenched position and at night. The details of the scheme were not circulated to each individual man as they should have been. Owing to the difficulties of getting men through communication trenches they were not actually in their places until 4.45 pm. The Artillery opened a terrific fire on the enemy's trenches from 4.15 – 4.45 pm to cover the advance of the Warwicks. This Artillery fire apparently did no damage to the enemy but wounded a few of our own men and let the enemy know that we were going to attack them.*

The writer (probably the CO or his adjutant) continues with a very detailed account of a muddled exercise with considerable lack of communication. Heavy losses were sustained by the Brigade and some confusion ensued:

Owing to the arrival in the trenches of 2 more Coys Welsh Fusiliers as well as wounded and also Queen's and Warwick's returning, the trenches were very congested and great difficulty was experienced in reorganising the firing line and evacuating wounded. This was accomplished by 2 am. Search parties were out all night collecting wounded. The fire was terrific – machine guns to our front and one enfilading attack. The fire dropped a bit towards midnight and altogether about 6 am.

The Brigade suffered very heavy losses that night amounting to 22 officers and 958 other ranks, including Albert Bennett. The War Diary also records an interesting interlude the following day:

At daybreak Germans were seen beckoning to our men to come out and collect wounded and bury dead. Several of our officers including the MO and 30 men went out. About 80 Germans and 10 German officers also came out and there was a local armistice. A sniper on our right killed one officer of S. Staffords and one of our men but there was no firing from our front. The Germans buried a lot of our dead and we collected wounded, some of whom were taken into the German trenches and others into ours. As our dead and wounded were mostly near the German wire the enemy took possession of their rifles etc. Our officers conversed with the German officers and unfortunately two of our officers 2nd Lt Rought and 2nd Lt Walmesley were enticed into the German trenches and taken prisoner, so also were 7 stretcher bearers. These officers and men were not missed until after the armistice. The armistice was brought to a sudden close owing to one of our guns shelling the enemy's trenches.

These encounters were to lead to the 1914 Christmas Truce in which men of the 2nd Battalion Queen's were involved.

Albert Bennett, one of the few survivors of the 2nd Battalion after the First Battle of Ypres, was 19 when he was killed in the battle at La Boutillerie. His body was never found or perhaps never identified, but he is remembered on the nearby Ploegsteert Memorial, Panel 1 & 2. He is also remembered on the

Ploegsteert Memorial.

Leatherhead Town War Memorial and on the Church Lads' Brigade Triptych in All Saints Church, Leatherhead. He was awarded the 1914 Star, the Victory Medal and the British War Medal.

The writer of the War Diary goes on to give a very good first-hand account of the Christmas Truce in this area:

24th In the trenches – Enemy quiet and not much sniping. In the morning enemy were evidently keeping Xmas – many flares going in rear of their lines. Weather fine and frosty.

25th Xmas Day – At 11 am an armistice began – It started opposite the left of the Wiltshire Regt – the Regt on our right. Many German officers and men came out of their trenches to midway between the two lines – parties were sent out to collect and bury the dead who had been killed on the 18th – graves were dug in the centre between the lines. 71 bodies were collected chiefly Warwicks. The body of Lt Ramsay previously reported missing was found near the German trenches and taken back to the dressing station to be buried in the churchyard.

The Germans were nearly all belonging to the 55th Regt – several Staff officers also came over – these were quite a different class to the infantry officers, who were of a very low class. All professed themselves as confident as to their being able to end the war in their favour. They had no opinion of the Russians who they considered already beaten. All gave the appearance however of being fed up with the war. Armistice concluded at 4 pm with agreement to resume it at 9 am the following morning as dead were not all buried.

26th. Armistice recommenced as arranged at 9 am. A large number of staff officers appeared during the day – all were immaculately dressed without a speck of mud on them, mostly in fur lined coats. They furnished us with a list of officers lately taken prisoner and asked that their relatives might be informed. They also promised to try and obtain the release of 2nd Lts Rought and Walmesley, who had been taken prisoner during the armistice on 19th inst.

German soldiers wearing sheepskin coats.

Owing to frost the ground was very hard and the graves were not completed till 1 pm when the chaplain read the burial service in the presence of the digging party, some officers of the Queen's and 8 or 10 German officers. The body of 2nd Lt Barnard, Royal Warwicks was found and buried. Armistice concluded at 3.30 pm.

Alfred Blackwell

1214 Trooper

6TH DRAGOON GUARDS (CARABINIERS)
4TH CAVALRY BRIGADE 2ND CAVALRY DIVISION
FORMERLY 7TH BATTALION KING'S ROYAL RIFLE CORPS

Killed in Flanders 7 November 1914, aged 31

Alfred Blackwell is one of our more interesting characters, as despite there being no evidence he ever lived in Warnham he appears on the memorial.

Alfred's father, Henry Blackwell, a groom, and Sarah Marson had married in Paddington in January 1879. They had five children of whom Alfred, born in Marylebone in 1883, was the fourth. The family all lived in two rooms in a tenement house with four other families at 71 Hall Place, Paddington. Early in 1894 Henry died at the age of 43 and the following year Sarah remarried. Her husband was Jabez Warren of Hanwell. By the turn of the century Sarah and Jabez were living in Ealing with a collection of children from their previous marriages and their daughter, Florence. Sarah was soon widowed for the second time when Jabez died in 1903.

From the 1901 Census we know that Alfred had a spell in the army as a regular at the beginning of the century serving in the 7th Battalion King's Royal Rifle Corps. There is no trace of him in 1911 but he most likely remained in the Reserve. He enlisted in Stratford and no doubt his previous service was the reason why at the beginning of the war he was mobilised into a unit which was sent to the front line very early on, unlike the Service Battalions of new infantry recruits who spent the first six months of the war training in England. In the minutes of the Warnham War memorial committee held on 30 October 1919 there appears the following:

> *The question whether the name of Mr Blackwell who was killed in 1914 and whose widow has since lived in Warnham should be included, was raised by the Vicar. 9 votes were recorded on each side and the chairman put it to the vote again and the decision was 13 to 10 votes in favour of inclusion.*

If Albert had been resident in the village it remains a question as to why there should have been any doubt as to his eligibility. Mrs Blackwell later contributed 1/- to the War Memorial fund.

The 6th Dragoon Guards were a very old regiment dating back to the 17th century and their nickname 'The Carabiniers' originally meant a soldier on horseback armed with a short musket. The Carabiniers, having served in the Crimea, in India and in the Boer War also had the honour of parading in 1906 at the Bangalore Durbar. By 1914 they had returned to England and their War Diary [WO 95/1137/1] records on 9 August that the 6th Dragoon Guards was stationed at Canterbury, had completed mobilisation and was awaiting orders. During this period they occupied themselves with regimental parades and training exercises. At 3.40 am on 15 August they left by train, crossed the Channel and arrived in Le Havre at 2.30 pm the next day. They travelled by train to Rouen and on to Hautmont from where they moved on to Verberie having marched every day for a week. The Carabiniers were still a mounted regiment and there are frequent references to 'saddling up'. Obviously the troops had horses with them and maybe some of the reported marching was in fact on horseback. The War Diary also records on many occasions 'grooming and exercising the horses'.

After reorganisation in October, the 6th Dragoon Guards became part of the 4th Cavalry Brigade in the 2nd Cavalry Division occupying part of the Ypres Salient near the Messines Ridge. The Division remained in France and Flanders for the whole four years of the war.

Despite rapid advances in motor transport, the invention of tanks and development of aeroplanes, horses were still widely used in the Great War. Over eight million horses died on all sides during the war. Thanks to the sterling work of the Army Veterinary Corps, nearly three million horses were treated for battle wounds and two million of these were returned to duty. At the beginning of the war the older generals planned for cavalry charges, but the charge near Mons in 1914 was practically the last seen in the war. Machine guns, trench complexes and barbed wire made such charges impossible. However horses were still invaluable in transporting food and ammunition, hauling guns, ambulances and other equipment over rough, waterlogged ground peppered with craters and strewn with dead trees and other debris. At that time mechanised vehicles were unreliable and frequently broke down or got stuck in the mud.

As told in Michael Morpurgo's touching story of *War Horse*, fit animals were requisitioned from farms and transport businesses for use in battle. This caused many a heartbreak. A number of Remount Depots were set up all over the country to accommodate and mobilise newly acquired horses and from these stables fresh animals were sent out to the front as replacements for those dead or injured. As the war proceeded the supply of horses for the Allies began to run out but owing to a sea blockade this shortage became even more acute for the Germans who were unable to import any fresh animals or any food to feed those they already had. Providing fodder was a constant problem and many animals were lost through starvation and disease, particularly sores and skin problems. Apart from the obvious dangers of war – gun and shellfire and gas, these creatures suffered badly from living in the open in the extreme cold and wet of winter and, in Palestine, from the heat and the lack of water. Many highly bred sensitive animals suffered from shell shock and would refuse to move or go berserk. The big bus companies in London and other cities were beginning to move over to motorised vehicles and were pleased to sell their strong horses to the military and these creatures had the reputation of being the least sensitive to the sounds and smells of battle.

There are conflicting reports about the beginnings of the battles of Ypres but early in October huge numbers of German soldiers had swept into the town, demanding money, food and fodder for their horses. Some accounts say they left after a couple of days and the vacuum was soon filled by the British. Others tell of the British army driving them out. Whatever the correct account, the result was that by the third week of October the British were in possession of Ypres and stayed in possession for the duration of the war. The Germans made many attempts to capture Ypres and bitter fighting took place on this stretch of the Western front. The French and British forces had denied the German commanders a route across Belgium to the French coastal ports of Calais and Dunkirk. Ypres was a crucial location in the 'Race to the Sea', when the Allied Armies and the German Armies were engaged in an attempt to outflank one another in a desire to reach and secure the ports on the northern French coast. The efforts of the Allies in preventing the Germans from gaining access to the coast led to the development of the Ypres Salient and the stalemate and sporadic fighting which occupied the spaces between the three main battles of Ypres. In the constant effort to defend Ypres in the difficult line of the Salient the city was shelled incessantly and reduced to rubble.

The 6th Dragoon Guards fought with distinction in the First Battle of Ypres which took place from 19 October until 22 November 1914. Before the activities of 7 November, Alfred and his colleagues had been involved in desperate fighting near Wytschaete particularly on 1 November when, heavily outnumbered by the enemy, they had found themselves surrounded but had managed to fight their way back. Bitter and costly battles went on all along the Salient for some days and it was on 7 November, a misty and wintery day, that Alfred Blackwell was killed in action between Messines and Wyschaete, about 5 miles south of Ypres. In recognition of his active service so early in the war, Alfred was awarded the 1914 Star, together with the Victory Medal and the British War Medal. He is buried in the Nieuwkerke (Neuve-Eglise) Churchyard (Plot C2) a mile or two from where he fell.

William Ernest Bowles

26163 Private

Royal Defence Corps
Formerly 20401 Private
2nd Battalion Royal Sussex Regiment
5th (Royal Irish) Lancers
4th (Volunteer) Battalion
Royal Sussex Regiment

Committed suicide at Warnham
7 April 1917, aged 43

William Ernest Bowles was the son of Jane and William Bowles of Lewes, where he was born early in 1874. His father died in 1881 leaving Jane a widow with three daughters, the youngest just a baby, and her only son William aged 7. In 1892 Jane married George Green from Bromley and settled in Newhaven. By 1911 Jane was a widow again and living at 9 East View Terrace, Newhaven with her 38 year old son, William, who by then was an army pensioner.

William Bowles worked as a labourer before enlisting in the 5th Lancers at Chichester on 24 March 1890 giving his age as 18 years and 2 months when in fact he was just 16 years and 2 months. Before this he had served with the 4th (Volunteer) Battalion Royal Sussex Regiment, a kind of territorial unit whose main job was home defence. In 1893, while serving in India with the Lancers, William transferred to the Royal Sussex Regiment with which he served in South Africa from 1900 to 1902 during the Second Boer War. He was awarded both the King's and Queen's South Africa medals with Clasps, recording his presence in named actions. During another spell in India in 1906 William was awarded his fourth Good Conduct Badge and in 1909, the Long Service and Good Conduct Medal.

In 1910 when serving with the 2nd Battalion Royal Sussex, he applied for discharge from the Army which was granted at The Curragh in Ireland on 10 February 1910, enabling him to draw his pension after almost 20 years' service. His discharge papers describe his conduct as 'Very Good'. With his excellent service record it is surprising that William was never promoted and that he had remained a Private soldier throughout his pre-war career. There is no indication that William ever married and he gave as his next of kin his mother, Jane Green, living at Newhaven. By 1915 or possibly earlier William was back in the army with the Royal Sussex and later, in 1916, he transferred to the Royal Defence Corps.

The RDC was authorised by Royal Warrant in March 1916 published in Army Order 115 of 1 April 1916. The Corps was composed of soldiers either too old or medically unfit for overseas service. Their job was to guard railways, ports etc. in the UK, so securing the infrastructure for enabling the movement of men, equipment and materials to the Channel ports. They also performed guard duties at prisoner-of-war camps. Sometimes they were seen as being overzealous, resulting in questions being asked in Parliament. The RDC released many fit men for active service, so making up for the heavy losses sustained in battle. We are not sure why there was an RDC unit in Warnham; quite possibly it was to guard two important areas, the railway line and the ammunition now being stored in the brickworks which were under-used at this time owing to lack of demand for bricks.

The West Sussex County Times of 14 April 1917, under the heading *Determined Suicide At Warnham*, reported on the inquest on 7 April 1917 conducted by Mr F W Butler at the Sussex Oak Inn into the death of Private Bowles of the Royal Defence Corps, who had died that very day. Mr Eldred (Neddy) Hammond, landlord of the inn, was chosen as foreman of the jury.

The jury heard that Private Bowles was quartered with nine others of the Warnham Company at a house in the village and that he had not appeared at the 9 am parade. Lance Corporal Salmon who was sent to his billet to hurry him up found the deceased in his underwear, lying across the bed on his back with his head almost touching the floor, with blood on his chin. He concluded he was dead, noticed no gun and went back and reported to his sergeant.

Lieutenant William Powell Breach, in charge of the Warnham Company, corroborated this account saying that he had concluded that Bowles had been shot through the head and that he was quite dead. He had put a sentry in charge and informed Captain Shand of the Royal Army Medical Corps. Lieutenant Breach stated that Bowles had been under his charge for 16 months, that he was a very capable soldier and he had made him acting corporal. Bowles was formerly in the regular army and had seen a good deal of service in India but at times had been subject to attacks of ague [probably malaria]. Lieutenant Breach stated that he had cautioned him about 14 months ago about drink, but had not punished him and had had no trouble since. Private Bowles had returned from 48 hours' leave two days before and had taken his pay the previous day at 10.15 am. The witness stated that he appeared normal and there were no claims upon him.

Captain Shand who was in charge of the Military Hospital at Horsham, said he saw the body of the deceased at ten o'clock that morning at his billet and in his opinion the man had not been dead more than an hour or two. He gave a graphic description of the body, its wounds and the position of the rifle from which he concluded that

Private Bowles could have killed himself and that death must have been practically instantaneous. Ague, he noted, had a depressing effect on those who suffered from it.

Private John Mills quartered with Private Bowles said the deceased had been alone in the house that morning after his comrades had left. He had cleaned the deceased's room the previous day and thought he had been drinking. He had seen him the worse for drink before, but had never heard him threaten to commit suicide.

The jury returned a verdict that Private Bowles had committed suicide by shooting himself with a rifle whilst temporarily insane.

He was buried in Warnham churchyard on 10 April 1917. His grave, near the Old Forge, close to the wall, is marked by a Commonwealth War Graves Commission headstone giving his date of death, wrongly, as 17 April 1917. His name is listed on the Newhaven War Memorial as A E Bowles where he is recorded as having died at home. His death is also recorded on a memorial in Newhaven's St Michael's Church. He received no medals for his Great War service.

It is worth noting that the whole process from discovering William's body, convening the jury and receiving witness testimonies, until the time the jury gave their verdict took place within one day.

Grave of Private Bowles.

Thomas William Burchell

L/10653 Private

1st Battalion
Queen's (Royal West Surrey Regiment)
100th Brigade 33rd Division
(Before 15 December 1915 –
5th Brigade 2nd Division)

Killed in action near Amiens
21 July 1916, aged 24

At first glance, Tom Burchell may have a rather slender claim to being a son of Warnham, but on further investigation it is clear that he comes from a long line of Warnham people on his mother's side – her maiden name was Harriett Redford. He was born in Warnham and lived here for the first few years of his life.

This branch of the Redford family had been living in Warnham since the beginning of the 19th century and most likely earlier. Harriett's grandfather, William, was born in Warnham in 1796 and was an agricultural labourer living for many years with his wife Kitty and their children in Warnham Street (now Church Street). Their son Henry was born in 1839 and in 1861 was lodging with John and Mary Petter and working for them at Mays Farm, Kingsfold. After his marriage, Henry and his wife Mary lived first in a cottage on the A24 between Geerings and Chickens. After several years they moved with their children, including Harriett, to Warnham Place where later Thomas Burchell became their lodger.

The Burchell family (in the 1881 Census registered as Burchall) favoured the name of Thomas for their sons. Private Burchell's grandfather, Thomas was born in West Chiltington in 1844 and worked as an agricultural labourer. His father, also Thomas, was born in Billingshurst in 1870 and started as an agricultural labourer. By 1891 when he was 21 he was lodging with Henry and Mary Redford at Warnham Place where most likely he and Henry both worked on the farm. While here he met and married Henry's eldest daughter, Harriett Redford. Harriett and Thomas Burchell had seven children, the eldest of whom was Thomas William, born in Warnham in 1893.

By 1901 Thomas William's father had moved on from his work as a labourer to the job of miller's loader and obviously proved himself to be a useful employee as by

1911 he had been promoted to the job of Corn Merchant's Manager. As he sought better jobs, the family had moved around to Clayton and Haywards Heath and were now living in Balcombe. By this time there were still five children living at home including Charles Henry, two years younger than Thomas, who was working with his father as a corn merchant's assistant. Both Charles and his father describe themselves as 'working at home' so it is assumed that they were living in property attached to the milling business. By this time Thomas William had moved out of the family home and was lodging at Morley Cottages, Triangle Road, Haywards Heath with Amos and Mildred Newnham and working as a baker at the Co-op in Haywards Heath.

The army records for Thomas William are missing, presumably lost in the Second World War bombing, but we know he enlisted in Guildford in 1914 and was posted to the 1st Battalion Queen's (Royal West Surrey Regiment) which was a Regular Battalion and part of the 2nd Division. The 1st Battalion had been sent to France in August 1914 where the scale of casualties was horrific – by the end of the first week of November 1914 there were only 32 survivors out of a total of 998 men. Their ranks were filled by Territorials and men from Kitchener's New Army. On enlisting Private Burchell would have spent some months training in England while the 1st Battalion were fighting at Mons, on the Marne and the Aisne and at the First Battle of Ypres. He was awarded the 1914-15 Star so it can be assumed that he joined the battalion some time in 1915 probably at Aubers Ridge or Loos. When the 1st Battalion came out of the line in November 1916, only 17 men were left out of all ranks that had gone to France in 1914.

British soldiers playing cricket in 1915.

By the time Thomas joined the battalion, probably early in 1915, by far the majority of officers and other ranks were New Army men. The battalion had been in the Béthune area since December 1914 and by May 1916 had transferred to the 100th Brigade of the 33rd Division, in a sector of the line on the western outskirts of Béthune, moving in and out of the line and into reserve in the usual regular pattern of 4 days in and 4 days in reserve. They were near the villages of Beuvry and Guinchy and the War Diary tells of regular action with the enemy, followed by recuperation while in reserve when baths were provided, church parades held and even a few cricket matches with tea took place. The War Diary [WO 95/2430] records all this in great detail.

By this time the slaughter on the Somme had greatly reduced the manpower in that area and with a few hours' notice on 6 July 1916, the battalion was given orders to move that night. They left at 1 am and marched nine miles west through Béthune to Busnettes where, after resting, they marched on to Lillers. Here they entrained in what were described as 'very dirty trucks for the troops' and travelled south to Saleux, south-west of Amiens, arriving in the early hours. They marched off at 5 am, via Dreull to Saint Sauveur arriving at 9 am and rested in billets until the middle of the day. They then received sudden orders to move at 2.30 pm and marched via Amiens to Daours arriving at 8 pm. Looking at the map this would appear to be very much the long way round, but presumably a more direct and shorter journey was not viable. Some men collapsed which was not surprising – they were wearing steel helmets, heavy uniforms and carrying full packs and it was a very hot day. They marched 8½ miles in the morning and 12½ miles in the afternoon.

The next day, the 10th, they rested in billets and all bathed in the streams and in the canal. On the 11th they marched on to Morlancourt 12 miles away where they were in billets for one night and, on the 12th, another 4½ miles to Bécordel where they bivouacked just north east of the village. From here they had a good view of Mametz Wood and the two Bazentins, then in the hands of the Germans. On the 14th the battalion was ordered to move off at 3.25 am and to dig in near Mametz Wood and there followed several days of mixed success in their efforts to gain ground near the two villages of Bazentin. By the end of the 15th there were five officers killed, 11 wounded, 28 other ranks killed and 62 missing. The casualties were said to be particularly heavy amongst the NCOs. On the 16th the exhausted battalion was relieved by the 5th Scottish Rifles and moved into support for a much needed rest. This was broken by shelling at 2.30 am, including gas shells which killed one officer and continued for several days. The battle continued with neither side making noticeable gains and climaxed in a stiff battle for High Wood with gas shells still causing considerable distress. These few days resulted in 6 officers and 35 other ranks killed, and over 300 wounded or missing. One of these was Thomas William Burchell who was killed in action near Mametz Wood on 21 July and is buried in Caterpillar Valley Cemetery, Longueval (Plot XV1.K.13). He was posthumously awarded the 1914-15 Star together with the Victory Medal and the British War Medal.

German observation post destroyed by shellfire in Mametz Wood.

Thomas's younger brother, Charles Henry, who had enlisted at Brighton early in the war, joined the 13th Battalion (3rd South Down) Royal Sussex Regiment, part of the 39th Division. He went to France with the battalion in March 1916 and was killed in action on the Rue de Bois near Neuve Chapelle to the east of Béthune on 30 June 1916. For some weeks during the early summer of 1916 the two brothers were stationed quite close to each other and it is possible they may have met up at some time. This battle turned out to be a rather pointless action with devastating results of which there are many graphic reports. The regimental diary [WO 95/2430] laments that:

> *The Sussex attack is not mentioned in the British Official History of the war, no doubt being more concerned with the very much greater events taking place on the Somme on 1 July 1916. The South Down units lost 360 killed and more than 1,100 wounded in this fruitless action, the intention of which was to distract the enemy from the Somme, pin down his reserves and improve the local tactical situation.*

The War Memorial in the parish church at Balcombe.

The losses in the Sussex battalions represented 60% of their troops. Charles, who was 21, has no known grave and is commemorated on the Loos Memorial. His parents were still reeling from this blow, when they were told of the death of their eldest son, Thomas, three weeks later.

Both soldiers are commemorated on the war memorial in the Parish Church at Balcombe, Sussex.

Cecil Burchett

GS/62137 Private

12TH (SERVICE) BATTALION ROYAL FUSILIERS
(CITY OF LONDON REGIMENT)
73RD BRIGADE 24TH DIVISION
FORMERLY 8TH (SERVICE) BATTALION ROYAL FUSILIERS
36TH BRIGADE 12TH DIVISION
3/1ST CITY OF LONDON YEOMANRY (ROUGH RIDERS)

Killed at Messines 14 June 1917, aged 20

Cuthbert Burchett married Sarah Jane Wallis at Ticehurst, East Sussex in 1884 and by 1891 they were living with their two children at Westmeston near Ditchling where Cuthbert worked as an agricultural labourer. Over the next few years the family grew to seven children and Cuthbert improved his status to that of farm bailiff. By 1901 the family were living in Clemsfold Cottages near Slinfold. Cecil, who was their sixth child, was born in Slinfold in 1897. By 1911 Cuthbert, who was still a farm bailiff, together with his wife and three of their four sons had moved to Old Barn Cottages, Kingsfold where Cecil and his older brother Cuthbert worked as farm labourers. The three girls were away from home as was the oldest lad. The 1911 Census makes cheerful reading in recording that seven children had been born alive to the marriage and that they were all still living – not always the case in those days.

In 1915 Cecil joined a Territorial Force unit, the 3/1st City of London Yeomanry then moved to the 8th Battalion Royal Fusiliers which landed in France on 10 December 1916. He was quickly posted to the 12th Battalion Royal Fusiliers with whom he served in and around the Loos and Lens trenches. In April the battalion was present at the opening of the Battle of Arras from where Cecil would have had a grandstand view of the successful storming of Vimy Ridge by the Canadians. By May 1917 the battalion had moved near to Ypres to prepare for the coming Battle of Messines, which lasted from 7 to 14 June.

The aim of the Second Battle of Messines was to remove enemy forces from a ridge where they dominated the positions of the British and Commonwealth troops. The battle is memorable for being a great success and the manner of its achievement. General Plumer who commanded the Second Army had begun planning and preparing the attack from 1915 onwards. A key element of his battle plan was to create and detonate a number of mines under the German front line. This hazardous work was carried out by British and Commonwealth tunnellers, many of them former miners. A second element was to apply the lessons learned from previous battles by effective co-ordination in the use of mines, artillery, gas canisters, air power and, of course, infantry. Plumer, by then aged 60, was regarded as a plodder and had the moustache and receding chin to reinforce this misjudgement. The evening before the battle he remarked to his staff: *'Gentlemen we may not make history tomorrow but we shall certainly change the geography'*. He did both.

Zero hour was fixed for 3.10 am on 7 June 1917. The allied guns fell briefly silent. It was all quiet on the Western Front – at Messines at least, so much so that birdsong was heard. At 3.10 am the silence was shattered when 19 mines were detonated under the German front line; two others failed to explode. The noise was deafening; it was heard in London. The effect was devastating. Then the artillery opened up allowing the infantry to capture Messines Ridge. There was fierce fighting with heavy casualties on both sides. The enemy counter-attacked, but to no avail and by 14 June the whole ridge was in Allied hands. Victory had been achieved at a cost of about 25,000 casualties on each side, one of whom was Cecil on the last day of the battle. The battalion lost its Commanding Officer (the second CO to be killed – another was soon to follow), the Adjutant and the Medical Officer.

An edited transcript of the 12th Battalion's War Diary provided by Barry Fleming whose father fought in the battle and survived the war, reveals what the battalion did on 14 June and provides the backdrop to Cecil's death, without saying just how he met his end. Prior to the attack the battalion's adjutant had issued an Operational Order to each company defining the objectives and how they were to be achieved. Here is a summary of the battle:

> *The weather was fine. The battalion attacked at 7.30 pm on 14 June in conjunction with the 8th Buffs. All objectives were gained and the attack was highly successful. 28 prisoners were captured together with a machine gun after very stiff fighting. A line of outposts was established and consolidated.*

Details of the fighting reveal the strong resistance that was met and the efforts needed to clear the German dugouts. Efforts meant hand to hand fighting and a successful charge with the bayonet. The reinforcements summoned by the Fusiliers who had suffered heavy casualties, arrived under heavy shell fire. Good leadership and dash allowed the final objective to be taken. A line of outposts was established under persistent artillery and machine gun fire. The diary emphasises the importance of good communications achieved by runners and telephone lines. In order to guide stretcher bearers from the relay post to Battalion HQ and thence to the dressing station, a tape was laid along the route. But success came at a price – of the officers, two were killed and five wounded, eight other ranks were killed and 84 wounded. After the action the battalion was visited by the Divisional Commander who congratulated them on their good work.

The battle was over, what happened next? The answer is provided by a historian of the battle who wrote *'Despite the completeness and swiftness of the victory, the opportunity was missed to exploit the capture of the ridge by gaining a speedy foothold on the Gheluvelt Plateau'.* General Plumer was replaced by General Gough, immediately after Messines, to lead the dash to the coast. It never happened. Momentum was lost which was to have unhappy and costly results. On 31 July 1917 the Third Battle of Ypres began, in which Albert Chapman, another Warnham lad also with the 12th Royal Fusiliers, fought and fell.

The 19 exploded mines which erupted with nearly one million pounds of high explosives left craters, the largest being 80 metres wide and 12 metres deep. Many of these craters are now attractive ponds in farmland. Of the two mines which had not detonated in 1917, one exploded in 1955 killing a cow. All records have now been lost and the last unexploded mine has never been found.

The July issue of the Warnham Parish Magazine reported the receipt of a letter to the Vicar from Cecil's mother bringing 'the sorrowful tidings' of Cecil's death. By then Cecil's parents were living at 8 Hollands Road, Henfield. Cecil's three brothers served in the War – Harold with the 1st County of London Yeomanry, Cuthbert with the Royal Field Artillery and Victor in the Royal Marines and all three survived.

Cecil's body was never traced and his name is on Panel 6 and 8 of the Menin Gate in Ypres, the British Memorial to the Missing which bears the names of the 54,896 who died between 1914 and 15 August 1917 and who have no known grave. Cecil was awarded the Victory and British War Medals.

The panels on the Menin Gate showing the names of the Royal Fusiliers, including Cecil Burchett.

Albert Charman

228577 Private

12TH (SERVICE) BATTALION ROYAL FUSILIERS
(CITY OF LONDON REGIMENT)
17TH BRIGADE 24TH DIVISION
FORMERLY 1ST (CITY OF LONDON) BATTALION
LONDON REGIMENT (ROYAL FUSILIERS)
167TH BRIGADE 56TH (1ST LONDON) DIVISION
5TH (RESERVE) BATTALION EAST SURREY REGIMENT
HOME COUNTIES RESERVE BRIGADE (TF)

Killed in action near St Quentin
29 October 1917, aged 25

In the summer of 1888 James Charman, a farm labourer, married Ellen Chennell, both were born in Warnham. Three years later the 1891 Census shows Ellen Charman living at Kingsfold as a married daughter with her widowed father, other family and her two year old son, James. The same Census shows James Charman resident at Denn Farm, Ends Place, Warnham as a married son with his widowed mother and other family. No explanation is available as to why James and Ellen were in different houses for the 1891 Census. However in 1901 James and Ellen were both living at Berry House Cottage, Rudgwick with their sons James, Albert and Harry. All three had been born in Warnham. The middle one, Albert, was baptised on 27 September 1891. In 1911 the three brothers were living at Walthurst Farm, Loxwood, Billingshurst with their parents and working with their father on that farm.

Albert's service records were destroyed by enemy bombing in the Second World War but we know he was called up for military service in January 1917 as a Private in the 5th East Surreys. He arrived in France on 6 July 1917, where he served with the 9th East Surreys for a few weeks, probably for training. He and others then joined the 1st Battalion London Regiment from whom he received a new service number. On 21 July Albert and 24 other East Surreys were posted to the 12th Battalion Royal Fusiliers, who had been in France since September 1915 and had distinguished themselves at the recent Battle of Messines in which Cecil Burchett, another Warnham lad in the same battalion, had died.

The end of July saw the opening of the Third Battle of Ypres, also known as Passchendaele, after the village of that name. The 12th Royal Fusiliers were soon in action, suffering the heavy losses so typical of this terrible battle. Temporary relief was at hand when the battalion was transferred from Ypres to a position to the north west of St Quentin then in German hands. The German front line was west of the village of Bellenglise following the line of the Hélène Ridge looking down over Ascension Valley (no man's land) to our front line to the west.

Recent photograph showing the Bank on the right which gave great cover to the German assault group making their way to Somerville Wood for the raid that led to the death of Albert Charman.

On 29 October Albert and others were manning forward positions in Somerville Wood. Unbeknown to them a group of about 40 men from a Prussian unit led by an officer had made its way using natural cover and darkness to reach Somerville Wood undetected. They had come through the barbed wire and began an attack at 5.30 am. Though outnumbered the Fusiliers fought back with rifles and bombs and the German officer was soon killed. The enemy fled and apparently discouraged by the loss of their officer had not stopped to remove his identification. Albert Charman was killed and four others were wounded one of whom, Robert Parnham, died the next day. The CO, seeming to acknowledge their vulnerability, ordered the posts to be withdrawn which action was safely accomplished.

Albert Charman's grave – in the centre of the photograph with poppy cross.

Albert is buried with Robert Parnham at Vadencourt British Cemetery at Maissemy, Grave Reference I B 10. Albert was awarded the Victory Medal and the British War Medal and he is commemorated on the war memorial in the St John the Baptist Church at Loxwood.

John Edward Charman

TF/1738

1/4th Battalion (TF)
Royal Sussex Regiment
160th Brigade 53rd (Welsh) Division

Killed in action at Gallipoli
21 August 1915, aged 25

In the census of 1841 the Charman family are recorded as living in Warnham. Michael, the grandfather of John Edward (known as Jack), was born in Itchingfield and Jack's grandmother, Teresa, came from Southwick. All through the nineteenth century both grandfather and father, William, worked as blacksmiths living first in Warnham Street, now known as Church Street and then in Friday Street at Bell Cottages. The forge they worked in was where the present numbers 53, 57 and 63 are in Friday Street. By the outbreak of the Great War the family were living at 2 Cherry Tree Cottages in Friday Street.

Friday Street, Warnham.

Jack was born in 1890 to William and Ellen Charman. He was their youngest child. His elder brother, Albert, was an apprentice blacksmith to his father and he had two elder sisters, Nellie who was 14 years old and Minnie aged nine who attended Warnham School where later Jack was also a pupil. By 1911 he was working as a stationary engineer. He might well have been responsible for engines such as threshing machines. The West Sussex County Times states that he was employed at Warnham Lodge by Mr Thomas Wharrie JP and he is described as being an electrical engineer.

Jack had joined the Territorial Army some time before war broke out and enlisted into the 4th Battalion Royal Sussex at the Horsham recruiting office at 6 Park Street where he joined 'E' company with all the other Horsham based recruits. The 4th Battalion was mobilised on 5 August as part of the Home Counties Division. After a period of training in various parts of the country, the battalion was attached to the Mediterranean Expeditionary Force. On 24 April 1915 they were posted to the

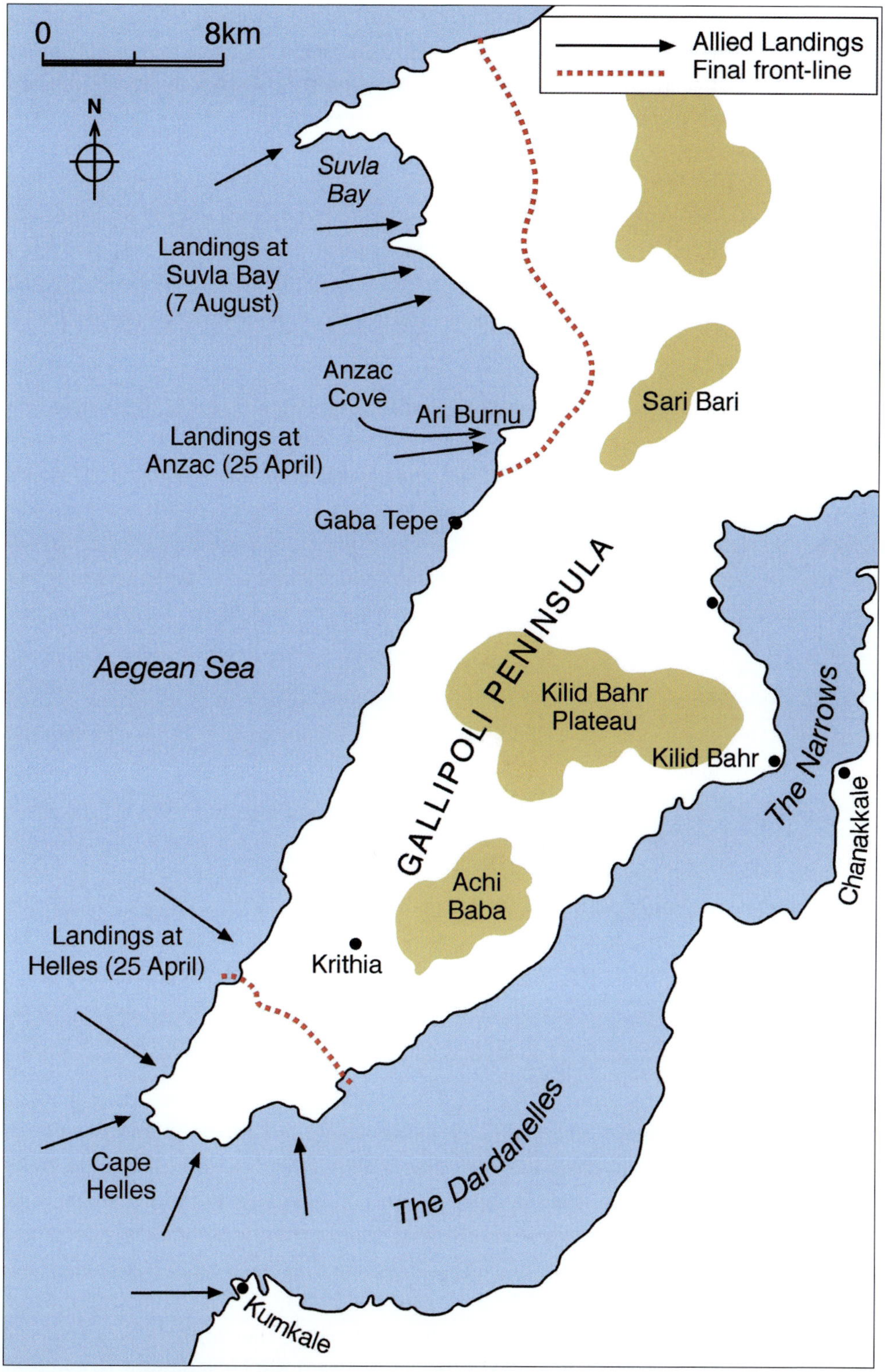

Map of the Gallipoli Peninsula.

160th Brigade 53rd (Welsh) Division at Cambridge in preparation for the journey to the Eastern Mediterranean and Gallipoli and at the same time the eight companies were amalgamated into four. 'E' Company merged with 'C' Company and from then on was known as 'C' Company and the battalion was renamed 1/4th.

The Gallipoli Campaign

By the end of 1914 as the First Battle of Ypres came to an end, a new phase of the war was beginning. In the West both sides were dug into trenches that stretched from the North Sea to Switzerland, and in the East the Russians had been driven back from Prussia. The war had become stationary. How could the deadlock be broken?

It was Winston Churchill who brought forward the proposal to the War Council – a naval attack on the Dardanelles. At first this was shelved but then the Russians requested a diversion against the Turks who had entered the war on the German side and advanced into the Caucasus. In January Churchill pressured the War Council to agree to a naval attack on the Gallipoli peninsula with Constantinople as the objective. It offered a way to break the stalemate in France, it promised to break the virtual blockade of Russia and it might persuade the Balkan countries to join the war on the Allied side.

No real analysis however was undertaken of the available resources, either of men or ships. Also there was apprehension in the naval command as to whether the plan was even possible. Indeed, Churchill, the newly appointed First Lord of the Admiralty, had himself said in 1911 'nobody would expose a modern fleet to such peril'. Moreover there was disagreement at the top between Churchill and Admiral Sir John Fisher, First Sea Lord, about how to proceed. On the other hand German bombardments of Belgian forts had been seen to be successful, so might not British bombardments of Turkish positions be equally successful? And, in any case, the Turks were not highly rated militarily. So the project continued. At this stage Churchill had no plans to use land troops for attack, but intended to deploy them later as a garrison for Constantinople. The British, Australian and New Zealand divisions in Egypt were put on alert.

Admiral Carden, commanding naval forces, opened his attack on 19 February 1915 and the marines landed successfully at Cape Helles. They failed, however, to make progress as the terrain was challenging and Turkish resistance became stronger. Bad weather meant that the fleet of old ships, with the exception of the new battleship, *Queen Elizabeth*, could make little headway through the heavily mined Dardanelles. Momentum was lost. On the eve of a renewed attack Admiral Carden collapsed and was replaced by Rear Admiral Roebuck. It was decided that military support was necessary, so on 12 March Sir Ian Hamilton was appointed Commander in Chief of what was now called the Mediterranean Expeditionary Force. He arrived just as the naval attack suffered a momentous reverse on 18 March – three battleships were sunk and three were crippled out of the total of nine. No progress was made. A joint operation was now agreed.

Over the next month there was little evidence of systematic planning or co-ordinated organisation. General Sir John Maxwell was in command in Egypt, Roebuck commanded the navy and Hamilton the troops. Each focused on their own needs and competed for scarce resources and there was scant regard for security. The Turks also had their problems with a lack of supplies and, in spite of the serious situation, little sense of urgency. At the end of March a new German commander arrived, General Liman von Sanders, supported by effective subordinates – notably Colonel Mustafa Kemal who inspired the rather ragged Turkish army to great heights of courage. The Turkish troops were now well dug in but continued to benefit from being underestimated by the Allies.

The crowded beach at Anzac Cove.

Hamilton's plan was bold. There were to be attacks at Cape Helles and further north by the Australian and New Zealand troops (ANZACS) at what became known as Anzac Cove. Feint landings were to take place at Bulair and also at Kum Kale by the French. From these points they planned to launch an assault on the heights of the Sari Bair Ridge. The British and Anzac troops set off from Mudros on the Island of Lemnos on 25 April, full of hope. The first landings at Cape Helles were successful but they made little progress inland. The other beaches at Helles proved to be death traps. As the troops landed they were met with deadly fire from above. The Anzac divisions landed largely unopposed but because of the difficulty of the ground, their heavy kit and the increasingly fierce counter attacks led by Kemal, they were unable to take the heights. This initial setback really meant the failure of the whole campaign. The Turks brought up reinforcements and together with the natural advantages of their position were able to fend off all further pushes. The toll in lives and casualties was tragically great on both sides. The troops had nowhere to go for respite from the constant bombardment, heat, flies disease and lack of water.

Hamilton launched a final assault in August 1915 – the largest attack in terms of numbers of the campaign. The aim was to land troops in Anzac Bay and attempt once more to capture the Sari Bair Ridge. A simultaneous landing began further north at Suvla Bay by the IX Corps which included the 1/4th Battalion Royal Sussex Regiment. This was commanded by General Sir Frederick Stopford, a man over 60 years of age who had no experience of battle.

On the night of 6 August the landings began and the troops found that at this stage Turkish resistance was slight. The next day the troops were not encouraged to press on and exploit this early advantage. By the time Hamilton arrived the day after, the opportunity was lost. Stopford had remained on board his ship with an injury. The troops did manage to link up with the Anzacs and under very heavy fire advanced to the point shown on the map. But they failed to secure the high ground. The Turks rushed reinforcements from Bulair and were spurred on by Mustafa Kemal. Casualties were up to 90% and in the end the troops once again were forced to protect themselves in trenches. Soon they began to suffer from bitter weather as the campaign became stationary. In mid-October Hamilton was recalled and was replaced by Sir Charles Monroe a much more decisive commander who recommended evacuation. Under the direction of Sir William Birdwood this was brilliantly executed on the nights of 18 and 19 December – the Turks were unaware of what was happening and there was not a single casualty. Helles was similarly evacuated in early January.

The entire operation sadly justified what Lloyd George had written before the campaign 'Expeditions which are decided upon and organised with insufficient care generally end disastrously'. However, considerable responsibility for the failure must fall on Hamilton and Stopford who failed to act decisively at crucial moments and showed an inability to grasp the whole picture. There were other factors too: the fact that the Turks always commanded the heights and that the Allies had only inaccurate, insufficiently detailed maps. Communication was often difficult between land and sea forces and always there was a lack of effective

The landing at Suvla Bay, Gallipoli, 1915, painted by Lieutenant R C Lewis during the action using the dye from cigarette packets.

artillery. All troops suffered from the lack of sanitation and hygiene so sickness, especially dysentery, was rife. The approximate number of Allied casualties was 250,000 including 50,000 deaths. The suffering of the wounded was terrible and the facilities for dealing with them hopelessly inadequate. The failure led to Churchill's resignation and the Cabinet formally resolved that the main theatre of war would now be focused on the Western Front.

The Royal Sussex Regiment

Jack Charman and the 1/4th Battalion began their journey to Gallipoli on 16 July in two trains from Bedford to Devonport where they departed next day on *HMT Ulysses*. They reached Alexandria in Egypt on 28 July and, after disembarking some soldiers at Port Said, arrived at Mudros the Allied base on Lemnos on 4 August. From there, three days later, they left for Suvla Bay landing in darkness.

On 9 August the Battalion moved inward from the beach to construct a trench and then moved on to Lala Baba. Skirting south of the Salt Lake they came under heavy fire as they advanced to take Hill 70. It was crucial to advance and occupy the high ground before more Turkish reinforcements could reach the scene. But poor communication and indecisive orders meant the opportunity was lost. Losses were heavy and the Battalion were relieved on 12 August and returned to the beach where they continued to work on the trenches. Another battle took place on 21 August the day that Jack's death is recorded.

Private John Edward Charman's name is on panel 125 of the Helles Memorial. He was awarded three medals, the 1914-15 Star, the Victory Medal and the British War Medal in commemoration of his war service.

From the Dardanelles Jack's Chaplain wrote this letter to his mother, Ellen Charman:

> *As Chaplain to the Sussex Regiment, I venture to sympathise with you in the loss of your son. I think it may help you to know that we buried him under a fig tree, in a lovely spot, and put a cross over his grave, which is all in good order.*
>
> *It will be some help to you to know that many of his friends were there. I have a parcel of his things which I hope to send back to you.*
>
> *I believe he was engaged to be married. I can only offer you all very heartfelt sympathy and assure you that he always did his duty and is now with Christ.*
>
> *Yours truly, Fred H Campion, Chaplain*

In the October edition of the Warnham Parish Magazine the Rev Bowcott tried to express the feelings of fellow villagers as follows:

MEMORIAL SERVICE – On Wednesday evening, the 15th, a service was held in our church in memory of one of our lads who was killed last month fighting for his country in the Dardanelles. We thought of the bright young lad who had lived amongst us from a child, and we sorrowed for our loss when we felt that we should have him no more amongst us. Jack Charman, as a boy, sang in our choir. He was also one of our bell ringers and thus he was closely connected with the old Parish Church. He has given his life for his country and his name is on the roll of England's gallant sons. The whole country mourns the loss of these lads and we offer our loving sympathy to those upon whom the sorrow falls most heavily – his parents, his brother and his sisters. May God bless and comfort them.

The Helles Memorial.

Esmé Fairfax Chinnery

WS/32276 Captain

Coldstream Guards
Attached No 4 Squadron
Royal Flying Corps

Died in an aeroplane crash in Paris
18 January 1915, aged 28

Esmé Fairfax Chinnery, born at Hatchford Park, Cobham, Surrey on 28 March 1886, was the sixth child of Walter Moresby Chinnery and the second child of his father's second marriage. In 1871, Walter and his first wife, Jane, were living in Black Horse Yard, Aldersgate, London. Walter worked at the Stock Exchange and soon began to rise in his profession. During the 1870s the family moved out of London into a substantial house at Rose Hill, Hampton, Middlesex. In 1880, Jane who was only 33, died. Walter continued to live at Rose Hill and the 1881 census shows him there as a widower with his children plus two nieces, described as 'Wards in Chancery', all attended by six servants including a governess. Walter was 37 and now a Member of the London Stock Exchange.

In 1883 Walter married Alice Emily Wilson who was 21, and 18 years his junior. Over the following years Alice brought up her stepchildren and produced four more of her own, including Esmé. Walter continued to rise in the world and by 1891 has acquired 23 Park Lane as his London address, where he employed ten servants including a butler, two footmen and a lady's maid. Sometime after this he bought a new country house and by 1901 the family were resident at Hatchford House, Cobham, Surrey, a grand residence kept going by thirteen servants including a housekeeper, two footmen and a lady's maid.

Esmé was educated at Eton College, playing cricket for the 1st XI in 1905, including the matches against Harrow and Winchester. He had one first class match for Surrey, making 47 not out in his one innings, but did not bowl in the match. Early in that same year, 1905, his father died at the age of 61. Esmé went on to Brasenose College, Oxford and while there became a freemason. In August 1910 Esmé was commissioned into the Coldstream Guards and that same year he became a member of the MCC. Walter had been a very wealthy man and it was likely that besides providing for his widow, he had left money to his children. Esmé, who was probably better off than most of his fellow officers, had the reputation of being generous and used to lend money to his mechanics and often paid off their debts for subsistence.

In 1909, four years after Walter's death, Alice married Christopher Stone, at that time an author with considerable private means 20 years her junior. In 1911 they were living at The Hill, Witley, Surrey in a large house with eight servants, including a butler and a footman, and as a sign of the times, a chauffeur. Alice by now was 46 and her much younger husband was almost the same age as his stepson Esmé. By this time Esmé had become an Ensign in the Coldstream Guards and presumably was home on leave at the time of the census. Two younger children of Walter Chinnery were also still living with their mother. Shortly after this Alice moved with Christopher and her family to Field Place, Warnham which became Esmé's home.

In April 1913, Esmé qualified as a pilot and joined the recently formed Royal Flying Corps, on attachment, receiving the temporary rank of Captain on 4 September 1914. The RFC was the air arm of the Army; its primary tasks were artillery co-operation and photographic reconnaissance. Later planes were armed with machine guns to fight aerial battles to gain control of the skies and then with bombs to attack enemy positions and industrial targets. On 1 April 1918 the much expanded RFC merged with the Royal Naval Air Service to form the Royal Air Force.

Captain E F Chinnery, Royal Flying Corps.

Esmé was a member of No 4 Squadron and was one of the first six RFC men to go to France in August 1914 to support the British Expeditionary Force. The BEF was soon in action with its French and Belgian allies in stemming the German army's advance towards Paris. This was accomplished at the first Battle of the Marne from where the enemy retreated to the high ground beyond the River Aisne. Esmé received a Mention in Despatches for his reconnaissance work in what would have been one of the earliest uses of aircraft in war. We presume that Esmé continued to provide aerial support to the Army whilst enjoying the occasional spot of leave in Paris.

The February 1915 edition of the Parish Magazine printed a letter from Esmé:

> *I am writing to you to ask you to be so kind as to thank the various friends at Warnham who were so very kind as to send me those charming and useful Christmas gifts. I was most pleased to get them and have put every one of them to great use. It is the feeling that one has been thought of when there is so much to occupy everyone's mind that touches me. The generosity of everyone at home and the frequency of such gifts are remarkable, and it is pleasant to think that every soldier in the trenches gets similar best wishes for 1915, and again many thanks.*
>
> *Yours very sincerely, Esmé F Chinnery*

Sadly in the same edition the Vicar reports his death:

> *Esmé Fairfax Chinnery of the Coldstream Guards, and of the Royal Army Flying Corps, killed in Paris on 18th Jan 1915. Such is the sad announcement. A gallant young officer, whose loss will be felt by the Army and by his country. Steadfast of purpose, with a high, clear sense of duty, he offered his life to the service of his King and Country, and he has paid the final sacrifice. All who knew him, knew also the sterling worth of this young life. We sorrow that he has been taken from us. We sorrow for those – for his mother and family – upon whom the blow has fallen, and we pray that God of His Mercy will comfort and sustain them. A short Memorial Service for him was held in the Parish Church on the morning of Thursday, Jan 21st.*

On 18 January 1915 Esmé was flying over Paris as a passenger in a French Voisin plane with a French civilian test pilot, M Delaporte. A witness reported that the plane was flying low and suddenly burst into flames before it crashed. Esmé was killed and the French pilot who was rescued died later that day. A memorial service was held for Esmé at the British Embassy's church in Paris. Unusually, his remains were exhumed and returned to England, a practice that was ended later in the war. Captain Chinnery was laid to rest at Hatchford churchyard, Cobham on 6 February 1915, his place of birth.

As well as his Mention in Despatches, Esmé was awarded the Victory and British War Medals and he seemed eligible for the 1914 Star with Clasp but this does not seem to have been awarded. He is commemorated on the Horsham War Memorial and on the MCC Great War Memorial at Lord's cricket ground, as is his half-brother Harry Brodrick Chinnery, a rather useful county cricketer. Esmé's will was proved on 2 March 1915, his executors being Christopher Stone and his half-brother Harry, later killed in action in 1916. Esmé, a single man, left an estate of about £16,000, a large fortune in those days.

Alfred Charles Comper Yates

200249 Corporal
1/4th Battalion (TF)
Royal Sussex Regiment
160th Brigade 53rd (Welsh) Division

Killed in action in Palestine
6 November 1917, aged 28

Thomas Yates DSM

M/3996 Leading Cook's Mate
Royal Navy HMS Victory
I RN Barracks

On the two war memorials in Warnham, inside and outside the church, Alfred is listed as 'Alfred Comper Yates' but in the official documents and on the CWGC database he is named as Alfred Charles Comper which was his correct name.

Alfred's maternal grandmother, Elizabeth, was the eldest child of Emily Tullett, widow of Joshua Tullett who in 1861 was living with her six children at Dismal Castle. This address was an appropriate one for the two-roomed hovel made of black stone set back a few feet from the corner of Green Lane and Northlands Road, just south of Curtis Farm three miles or so north of Horsham. Elizabeth was 14 and was working as a shoemaker. Ten years later Elizabeth married and lived in Trafalgar Road, Horsham with her husband, Thomas Comper, a railway porter, and their three small children. Her second child was Charlotte, born in 1869. Thomas and Elizabeth had several more children and later moved to 12 Spencers Road, Horsham.

Alfred was born in the Horsham Workhouse on 28 November 1888, when his mother, Charlotte Comper, gave her address as 24 Springfield Road, Horsham. At this time Charlotte, who does not give the name of Alfred's father, was probably in service at Springfield Road. In 1891 at the age of 22 and described as a 'General Domestic Servant' she was living with her parents, Thomas and Elizabeth, at 12 Spencers Road, Horsham. Also in this household were two little boys, Alfred aged two and his elder brother Arthur aged four, both described as 'grandsons' to the head of the household and most likely they were both children of Charlotte.

In 1892 Charlotte Comper, now aged 23, married Thomas Yates and they set up home in Friday Street, Warnham. Charlotte took Alfred with her and he was treated as the eldest son of this family, assuming for all everyday purposes the surname 'Yates'. The other boy, Arthur Comper, appears to have stayed with his grandparents. Maybe Thomas Yates decided that he could not take on more than one extra mouth to feed. By 1901 Thomas and Charlotte had four more children of their own and four more were born in the next few years. Their daughter, Hartie, died from diphtheria at the age of six during an outbreak of the disease in the village in 1903.

By 1881, a year or two before he married Charlotte, Thomas had been living with his parents, Thomas and Mary Yates, and one brother and sister in Friday Street. All three men at this time were agricultural labourers; the family had moved to Warnham from Buckinghamshire at the end of the 1850s. Thomas junior and his older brother, John, remained in Warnham for the rest of their days. Also in the household as a lodger was Felix Edwards, father of Harry and Alex whose biographies are also included in this book.

John Yates, who was an engine driver, lived with his wife Harriett at 14 or 16 Church Street. They married in 1889 and by 1901 had five children, two daughters and then three sons. They also had living with them George Cox who was described as 'step-son'. It seems likely that his mother had been widowed before she married John Yates. George was working at this time as a gardener at Warnham Lodge, but he was making his name as a professional first class cricketer playing for Sussex and on one occasion for the MCC. The three sons of this branch of the Yates family all joined up. Jack, a 21 year old motor mechanic, enlisted in the King's Royal Rifle Corps in 1914 and went to France in 1915 where he was wounded. Charlie, a farm labourer, was 18 in 1914, and had enlisted in the Reserve in 1913. He was soon mobilised into the 4th Battalion Royal Sussex Regiment and went with them to Gallipoli and on to Egypt and France. In 1914 he was promoted and later became a Sergeant. The youngest, Percy, who before the war was a bricklayer's labourer, enlisted in June 1916 when he was 18. He worked as a Pioneer in the Royal Engineers and was in France from 1917. All three brothers survived the war.

Thomas Yates and his wife Charlotte stayed in Friday Street with their large family until about 1910 when they moved into 3 School Hill (now 4/6 'Shatherum') where their daughter Florence was born. A year or two later they all moved up the road into what is now No 26. Mr Branch who ran the bakery at 18 School Hill (Kingshead Cottage) built these two brick houses, one for himself and the other which he let to the Yates family. It was here that the baby of the family, May, was born in 1911.

By 1911 Alfred was still living at home in School Hill with his mother, step-father and the five younger members of his eight half-siblings, and working as a carter on a farm. On the census return he is shown as a 'boarder' and given the surname 'Comper'. It seems he had not been officially adopted by Thomas. At the outbreak of war, together with some of his friends from Warnham, he enlisted in the 4th Battalion Royal Sussex.

After several months training in the Cambridge and Bedford areas, the 4th Battalion, now renamed 1/4th with the addition of many new recruits, sailed for Gallipoli in July 1915, arriving there on 8 August. With Alfred was his cousin Charlie and a number of his village friends including Jack Charman and William and Frank Miles. Alfred, Jack and William had all been bell ringers at Warnham and Alfred had played the double bass in the Warnham String Band. Fairly early on in his military career he was promoted to Lance Corporal and later to Corporal. This may be partly due to the fact that he was a few years older than his colleagues from Warnham but it could also be due to the good home he had had with the Yates family. He was fortunate not to have been left in the workhouse.

Entitled 'A Warnham Contingent' this is a group of the 4th Battalion Royal Sussex, in England during preliminary training, not destined for Berlin as they suppose, but about to be sent to Gallipoli. Lance Corporal Alfred Comper Yates is third from the left. Most of these men will be the subject of our biographies but sadly we do not know who they are.

The battles and hardships experienced by the 1/4th during the middle part of August 1915 are told in detail in the biography of Jack Charman. William Miles and Alfred Comper were both wounded during that battle, taken to hospital in Lemnos and later repatriated to England.

In December 1915 the 1/4th were evacuated from the peninsula and sent to Egypt where they became part of the Egyptian Frontier Force and indeed stayed in the Middle East until 1918 during which time most of the men were given no home leave. Alfred Comper Yates, having recovered from his wounds, joined his battalion in Egypt early in 1916 and for most of that year they had a relatively quiet time. Their main assignment was to keep the Turks from invading from the East and to guard the vital artery of the Suez Canal. In December 1916 the battalion took part in a campaign to drive the Turks from the Sinai desert.

This was the beginning of more activity for the Sussex men and during 1917 they were involved in all three big battles of Gaza to drive the Turks out of Palestine and to secure vital water supplies, essential for men and beasts in that parched land. The 1/4th was involved in the First Battle of Gaza at the end of March 1917. After initial success, some poor decisions made at staff level and from a distance, turned the promised victory into failure. The battalion lost a large number of men including their much admired CO, Colonel Ashworth, who had led his men from the front over open ground and paid the price. Edwin Cooper, a young teacher from Horsham who had been a school master at Warnham School, also died in this battle.

Alfred Comper Yates in Egypt.

A month later, under pressure from London, another attempt was made to take Gaza. The Officer commanding in Egypt, General Sir Archibald Murray, ordered a fresh attack from his HQ miles away in Cairo, and once again this was a failure. The Turks under their German commander, had strengthened their defences and dug themselves well in and become a formidable enemy. The British suffered enormous losses and very little gain.

In June, Sir Archibald Murray was replaced by Sir Edmund Allenby who had been given instructions to advance and capture Jerusalem. The Expeditionary Force was reinforced and Allenby, with revised tactics, ordered a new surprise attack which was successful. The vital water supplies and wells of Gaza were secured and the town fell on 1 November. On that same day the 53rd Division, including 1/4th Sussex, as part of 160th Brigade, was facing the Turks on a piece of high ground slightly north east of Beersheba where the sand of the desert had given way to rough stone and scrub. There followed five days of continual fighting along this line, the right flank of which was held by 53rd Division at Khuweilfe, resulting in neither side making any significant gains. Unlike the position in Flanders where there was too much water most of the time, here in Palestine supplying water for both men and horses was as serious a problem as the provision of food and ammunition. Many of the water courses had dried and the few wells in the area were very deep. Water supply was a constant and worrying logistical problem. The anxiety of thirst is brought home by the Official History:

> *The day was hot, and the troops, labouring over the rough and broken ground, suffered greatly from thirst. Major-General Mott ordered the 160th Bde to push on its advance guards and if possible occupy the hills in front, but it was quickly found that the enemy was in strength and prepared to fight hard for the position. No further progress was made that evening, though after sunset a patrol of the 4/Sussex, with an interpreter as guide, succeeded in working its way right round the Turkish position and approaching the wells behind it. The patrol, though fired on by a few Turks at the wells, was able to return to the British lines. But the longed-for water remained in the hands of the enemy and the exhausted troops who had finished the contents of the two water bottles which each man carried, were issued with only about a quarter of a pint apiece.*

In the darkness and mist of the early morning of 6 November a fresh attack was launched and after many hours of bitter fighting the Allies moved over the almost dried up watercourse, Wadi esh Sheria, the Turks drew back a few miles and the Allies held their line. This became known as the Battle of Beersheba. It was an important achievement and the springboard for the Allied troops who fought on to capture Jerusalem at the beginning of December. The news of this victory reaching England after many months of depressing reports from the Western Front, went some way to cheering up the population at home. It was the 'El Alamein' of the Great War. [War Diaries Ref WO95/4631]

But these victories took their toll. Warnham lost two of its sons – William Miles and Alfred Comper Yates, old bell ringing friends, both killed at Beersheba on 6 November 1917.

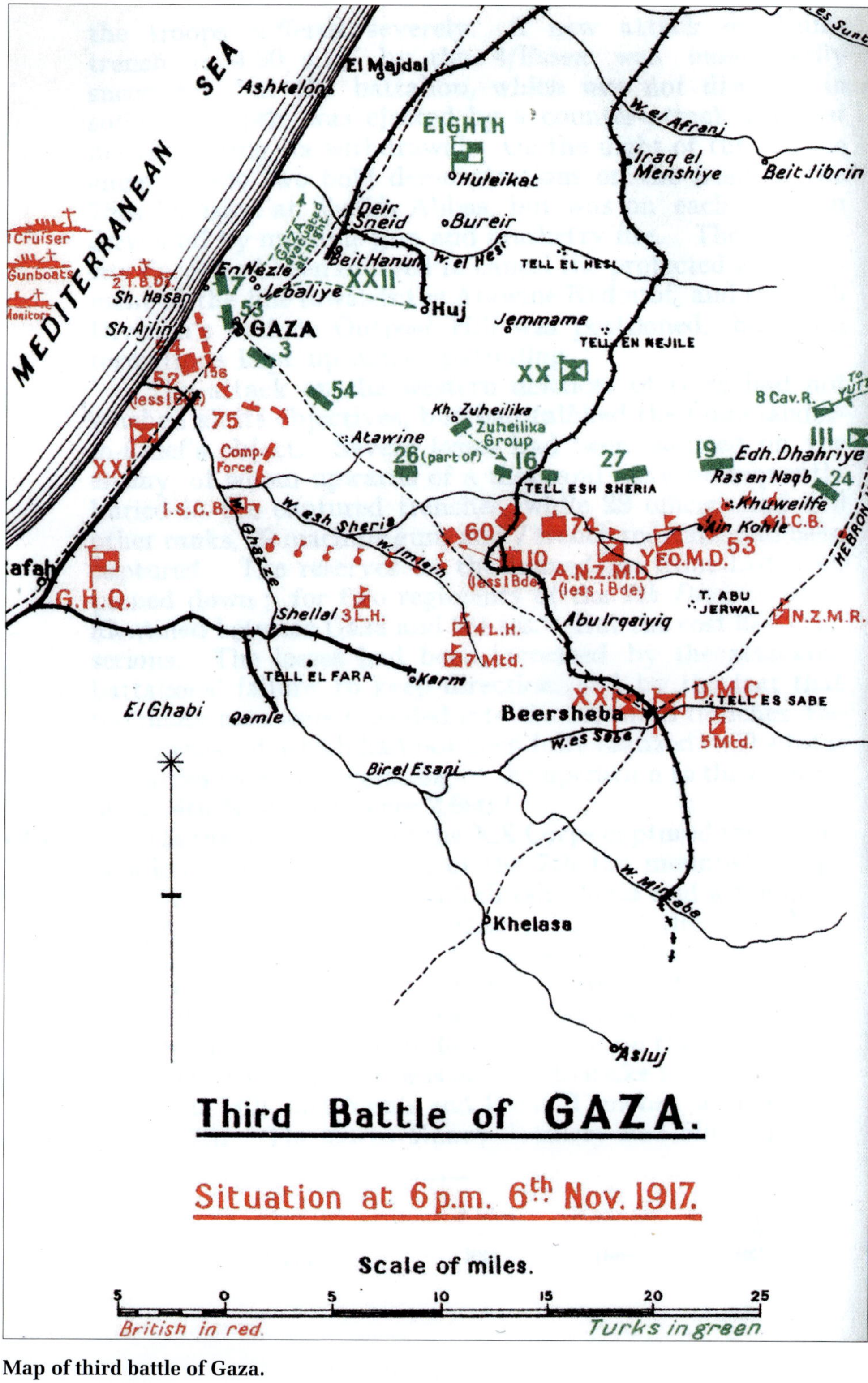

Map of third battle of Gaza.

In April 1918 Charlotte, Alfred's grieving mother, received a letter from the War Office together with a statement of income and expenditure. The expenditure was for items incurred by Alfred 'while in the field' and the income was the extra pay he had accumulated as Lance Corporal and later as Corporal together with £4 gratuity. The net balance due was £15.16.2d which the Paymaster was intending to send direct to Miss Rose Young as part of her legacy. Rose was Alfred's girlfriend and was in service at Warnham Lodge. In his military will, drawn up on enlistment, he had left her £20, with the balance to go to his mother. Rose later married and lived in Broadbridge Heath. She continued to keep in touch with the Yates family all her life.

Alfred was posthumously awarded the 1914-15 Star, together with the Victory Medal and the British War Medal and he is buried in the Beersheba War Cemetery, Plot G.50.

Tom outside his home in School Hill with his younger brother and sister.

Thomas and Charlotte's eldest child was yet another Thomas. He was born on 7 June 1892 and brought up in Friday Street, Warnham. When Tom left school he trained as a gardener at Warnham Court Gardens and by 1911 was working in Paddockhurst Gardens, Worth. Here he lived with six other young men, all gardeners, in a bothy on the estate. At this time Paddockhurst was a fine Victorian mansion which is now the main building of Worth Abbey School. The house and estate was owned by the first Viscount Cowdray who spent enormous sums on the gardens, winter garden and tropical fruit houses.

In January 1912, when he was 19, Tom Yates joined the Royal Navy as a ship's cook. He was attached to *HMS Victory* at Portsmouth Barracks which was (and still is) a shore establishment of the Navy. He was drafted to France on 9 October 1914 as cook for a Royal Navy Hospital and was promoted to the rank of Leading Cook's Mate. In recognition of his services abroad for the duration of the war, he was awarded the 1914 Star together with the Victory Medal and the British War Medal. It has not been possible to obtain any details of his experiences, apart from his work in the hospital in France.

But we do know that in 1917 Tom distinguished himself by winning a DSM for bravery in a fire at a hospital near Dunkirk in France. This was presented to him by the Vice-Admiral of the Dover Patrol, in Portsmouth on 27 October. The Parish Magazine of July 1917 reports:

> *'Somewhere in France' a hospital was set on fire and the whole building was being rapidly demolished. In the upper rooms three wounded men were in danger. There was no time to be lost. A stone attached to a rope-ladder was thrown into the window and Tom Yates at once went up to the rescue. One man was able to come down by himself. Tom brought down the second and went back for the third. The position was now critical, and a further crash unnerved the patient so that the rescue was a matter of extreme danger and difficulty; but it was accomplished, and we hear that Tom Yates has been awarded the DSM. It is a simple story of a brave deed. We are very proud of the men who have gone from amongst us and congratulate Tom and his friends upon the honour that he has won for himself and his village.*

Tom and Amelia on their wedding day.

We also know that soon after this event Tom Yates came on leave to marry his girlfriend Amelia Eugenie Stanford, the youngest daughter of John and Mary Stanford formerly of Warnham. Tom and Amelia were married at St George's Church, Bayswater on 11 September 1917.

As well as the DSM, in recognition of his actions that day, Tom was presented with a fine marble clock from his colleagues. The hospital, which may have been a naval establishment, was in Malo-les-Bains near Dunkirk, probably in a requisitioned

Tom's marble clock, which he passed on to his daughter, Malo, and is now in the possession of his granddaughter, Myra.

hotel. While he was there his first child, a little girl was born, and he asked that she be called 'Malo'. She was two years old before he saw her.

After the war Tom worked for the Gregsons at Ends Place and the family lived in Newman's Cottage at the bottom of Friday Street. He was a very keen and expert gardener and a strong supporter of the Flower Show. In 1933 he became caretaker of the Village Hall and moved into the accommodation there with his wife and three children, Malo, Edgar and Amy. The youngest Amy Andrews still lives in the village.

Arthur Evans Coole

Second Lieutenant

32ND SIKH PIONEERS

Died in hospital at Chatham 14 May 1919, aged 19

A formidable, non-military monument has been erected in Warnham churchyard over the grave of Second Lieutenant Arthur Evans Coole. He was 19 and had recently returned from India, when he died on 14 May 1919 at Fort Pitt Hospital, Chatham, probably from an illness contracted abroad. His death is particularly poignant.

His father, Arthur Cook Coole, who came from Gloucestershire, was a solicitor who, together with Frank Haddock, started the local firm of Coole and Haddock in 1898. Arthur's first wife, Ellen, died in 1897 aged 51 and childless. Two years later, when he was 58, Arthur Coole married Sarah, an Australian, who at the age of 42 produced what must have been a longed for child. This boy, Arthur Evans born in January 1900, is recorded in 1911 as a boarder at Springfield Park School, his parents living nearby in a large house named Heatherleigh in North Parade, Horsham. When their only child, Arthur junior, died in 1919 his father and mother were 75 and 61.

The 32nd Sikh Pioneers were born of the Indian Mutiny in 1857 at Madhopore, being initially known as the Punjab Sappers. After various changes of title, in 1864 they were designated the 32nd Punjab Regiment of Bengal Native Infantry (Pioneers), dropping the word Native in 1885 and becoming the 32nd Sikh Pioneers in 1903. The Sikh Pioneers, together with other Indian troops, fought valiantly for the British Empire throughout the war. They were far from home and probably at times wondering what they were doing in such a wet cold place, but they were brave and loyal, suffering huge numbers of casualties and winning many gallantry awards including a number of VCs. The 32nd Battalion had seen active service in France throughout the war, and when Arthur Coole enlisted, probably in 1918, he was posted to their headquarters in Sialkot, Punjab, India.

There is very little information available about Arthur Coole and why he joined the Sikh Pioneers – he is recorded as being a British Army officer, but he must have been attached to the Indian Army, and may have had relatives who influenced him. He would not have been 18 until 1918. It may be that he joined up as a regular on leaving school and had intended to have a career in the army; but this is all speculation.

Arthur Coole is buried in Warnham churchyard.

Ian Douglas Dalrymple MC

Captain

2nd Battalion Highland Light Infantry
5th Brigade 2nd Division
Attached 2nd Battalion King's Own Scottish Borderers

Killed in action on Hill 60 on 5 May 1915, aged 26

Major Francis Bertram Dalrymple of the Royal Artillery, Ian's father, retired from the army in 1887. He and his wife Anna are recorded as living in Abergwili in Carmarthenshire in Wales when Ian was born in August 1888.

Ian Douglas was the fifth of six brothers. He also had two older sisters, Gertrude and Gwindoline Mary. By 1891 the family were living at Mays Mansion, now known as Mays Park in Warnham. Sadly, his mother Anna died in 1895 and his father remarried three years later to Alice Maud. They eventually settled in Bartley Lodge, Cadnam, Hampshire.

Ian Dalrymple at Charterhouse.

Ian was educated at Warren House Preparatory School in Eastbourne and from there he went to Charterhouse in Surrey. Like all his five brothers he was a member of Saunderites House. The photograph, extracted from a full house group, was taken in his final year.

Leaving Charterhouse in July 1906, he passed into Sandhurst in the November of that year and was gazetted to the 2nd Battalion Highland Light Infantry in March 1908. He served with the battalion continuously until he was wounded in November 1914. Rejoining the British Expeditionary Force in 1915 he was then attached to the 2nd King's Own Scottish Borderers.

On the day war was declared his battalion was stationed at Aldershot as part of the 5th Brigade of the 2nd Division. On 14 August they mobilised for war and landed at Boulogne and were soon engaged on the Western front. The Battle of Mons was the first major action of the BEF in the Great War. At Mons, the 2nd Division were part of the British army that attempted to hold the line of the Mons-Condé Canal against the advancing German First Army. Although the British fought well and inflicted disproportionate casualties, they were eventually forced to retreat due both to the greater strength of the Germans and the sudden retreat of the French Fifth Army. Though initially planned as a tactical withdrawal and executed in good order, the British retreat from Mons lasted for two weeks and took them to the outskirts of Paris before counter-attacking with the French Fifth and Sixth Armies at the Battle of the Marne.

The battalion was in action here from 5 to 12 September 1914 resulting in an Allied victory against the German Army. The battle effectively ended the month long German offensive that opened the war and had reached the outskirts of Paris. The battle of the Marne was an immense strategic victory for the Allies, wrecking Germany's bid for a swift victory over France and forcing it into a protracted two-front war. However two million men fought in the First Battle of the Marne and perhaps 500,000 were killed or wounded. British casualties were 13,000, 1,700 of them dead. No future battle on the Western Front would average so many casualties per day. The battalion was quickly involved in the Battle of the River Aisne where it soon became clear that neither side could move the other and since neither chose to retreat, the impasse hardened into stalemate and both sides began to build the trenches that would remain for the next four years. The final stage of this early period culminated in the stand made to hold Ypres as a barrier to the Germans reaching the sea. However the battle was also significant for the high number of casualties among the highly experienced and trained British regular army. Having suffered enormous losses for its small size, it now began to be to be replaced by fresh reserves which eventually turned into a mass conscripted army. The result was a victory for the Allies, although losses were particularly heavy on both sides and, indeed, in this battle in November Ian Dalrymple was injured twice and was sent back to Britain to recuperate.

Looking towards Hill 60 from the side of the railway.

On his return to the Western Front in April 1915 preparations were being made for the Second Battle of Ypres. Ian Dalrymple was now attached to the 2nd Battalion King's Own Scottish Borderers who were to be heavily involved in the successful capture of Hill 60. This engagement took place between 17 April and 7 May. Hill 60 is the name given to the high ground close to the village of Zillebeke, south

The Menin Gate.

east of Ypres. It is not a natural feature but was made from soil removed during the constructing of the railway line nearby. It had great strategic importance in the battle as it was 150 feet high and 250 yards long.

Captain Ian Dalrymple was killed on 5 May, just before the end of the attack. This account was recorded in the Charterhouse magazine, The Carthusian:

> *Captain Dalrymple fell on May 5th in France in an attack on Hill 60. A subaltern who was with him writes to his father: 'In the first 20 yards he was hit and fell down, but got up immediately and came on. Just as we got to the rise where the German trench is he fell again, but was able to get up and he charged up the slope to the parapet, where he fell for the last time. I think he and myself were the only ones of our company even to get as far as the parapet of the German trench. . . . I think your son was the very bravest man I have ever met, and I only hope when my time comes I may do as well'.*

Major Bertram Dalrymple, his elder brother, received information dated 21 May that, based on an eye witness account from an officer who was with him, there was now no doubt that he was killed around 10 pm on Wednesday 5 May. Lady Dalrymple received a letter from the War Office dated 2 June giving more details of his death.

We have been trying for the last three weeks to get some definite information about Jock, and I grieve to tell you that we have now received definite information that he was returning from an attack when heavy shells dropped in the vicinity, and he has not been seen since. Death was practically certain . . . I need not say how very much I grieve for you and at the same time I am authorised by the Military Secretary to express Lord Kitchener's sincere sympathy with you.'

His memorial is placed on Panel 38 of the Menin Gate.

Writing in the Warnham Parish Magazine, the Reverend Bowcott stated:

There are many in this parish who will have heard with profound regret of the death of Captain Ian Dalrymple. His name is among those gallant ones who have fallen in the service of their king and country. We knew him as a lad of charming ways. He lived well and died nobly. We sorrow for the loss of this young life, and we sympathise deeply with Major Dalrymple and his family.

Captain Ian Dalrymple was awarded the Military Cross for Gallantry. This was gazetted on 18 February 1915. He was also awarded three medals, the 1914-15 Star, the Victory Medal and the British War Medal in commemoration of his war service.

Ernest James Dinnage

44835 Rifleman

15TH (SERVICE) BATTALION (NORTH BELFAST)
ROYAL IRISH RIFLES
107TH BRIGADE 36TH (ULSTER) DIVISION
FORMERLY 2932 ROYAL SUSSEX REGIMENT

Killed in action near St Quentin
21 March 1918, aged 41

Ernest James Dinnage was born in Horsham in 1877, the son of James and Kate Dinnage (née Rowland), who were both from the local area. The census of 1881 shows him, aged four, living with his parents and one year old sister Beatrice, in Capel, Surrey. His father worked as a brickmaker, although ten years later he is described as a carter. By this time the family had increased to six children and were living in the Bishopric in Horsham, where Ernest was working as a shop boy.

In 1900 Ernest married Frances Pope from Frittendon in Kent. A year later the census records that the young couple now had their first child, Ethel, aged just two months old and that Ernest was working as a brickmaker, living in Littlehaven Lane, Roffey. His father James, now a foreman of a brickyard, together with his wife and six of their children lived only two doors away.

By 1911, Ernest and Frances, now with four children, Ethel, Douglas, Winifred and Phyllis had moved to 2 Station Cottages, Warnham, where his occupation is described as a clay miner at the brickworks. A fifth child, Bernard George was christened at St Margaret's Church, Warnham in 1912.

Brickmaking was an important industry in the area and the Warnham brickworks first began production in 1888 on land north of Station Road alongside the railway. The first cottages in the road where the Dinnage family lived, were built in 1898.

Ernest joined the army in Horsham initially serving in the Royal Sussex Regiment and his name appears in the Warnham Parish Magazine in January 1915 in the list of the men from the parish serving their King and Country. The photograph shows him and Frances, probably taken shortly afterwards and is from a family collection.

A moving letter also survives, written by Ernest to his sister Evelyn in June 1915, from the Soldiers' Christian Association Camp in Abbey Wood, Kent. He is

Ernest and Frances Dinnage.

barely six months into his army career, but is obviously concerned about his wife's despair at his absence:

> *'Frances says she will never get used to my being away from her, she feels very much down at times, poor dear'*

The 'Spring Offensive' began on 21 March 1918, when General Ludendorff ordered a massive German attack on the Western Front in an attempt to end the war before the imminent arrival of US troops into France, a move which came very close to winning them the war. Thousands of German troops were transferred from the Eastern Front, where Russian involvement had effectively ended, giving the enemy a short term advantage in numbers over the British and French.

The artillery bombardment on the British began in the early hours of 21 March, hitting targets over an area of 150 square miles, with over one million shells being fired in five hours and leaving nearly 20,000 British soldiers dead. There was dense fog that early morning which persisted for much of the day. So well hidden were the attackers and so devastating had been the preceding bombardment that all the forward outposts were immediately overwhelmed and in the course of the day the main positions were penetrated at many points. The German infantry went in at 9 am on a 50 mile front stretching from opposite Arras in the north to Laon in the south.

The 15th Battalion, Royal Irish Rifles were holding a position at the Racecourse Redoubt, south of St Quentin and faced an overwhelming onslaught from a German unit made up largely from Prussia. By nightfall, the Battalion had effectively ceased to exist, with most of the men either killed, wounded or taken prisoner. Ernest Dinnage, who at the age of 41 might normally have been considered to be too old to be in the front line. Together with at least four other Horsham men, he was killed on this first day of the German advance which took the enemy almost to Arras.

Rifleman Ernest James Dinnage has no known grave, but is commemorated with many of his fallen comrades at Pozières Memorial, Panel 74 to 76. He is also remembered on the Horsham War Memorial and on the memorial at Holy Trinity Church, Blunts Way, Horsham. He was awarded the Victory Medal and the British War Medal.

German Storm Troopers in the March 1918 Offensive.

Jonas Eames

G/57269 Private

2nd Battalion Royal Fusiliers
(City of London Regiment)
86th Brigade 29th Division
Formerly 21581 (Territorial Reserve) Battalion

Died on the Western Front
30 March 1918, aged 22

The Eames family moved to Warnham from Kirdford towards the end of the 19th Century. Jonas (senior) and Julia are first recorded as living at 3 Brickyard Cottages, Warnham where on 11 January 1896 their only child was born. He was christened Jonas on 23 February at St Margaret's Church in the same year. He attended Warnham School and was later joined there by his cousin Lucy, eight years his junior, who was living with the family sometime before 1911.

After leaving school Jonas followed his father into the Brickworks. At this time the family were living at 6 Station Road. However, a court case reported in the West

Station Road, Warnham.

Sussex County Times on 19 August 1916 states that Jonas Eames was now working as a railway porter. He was fined for using obscene language outside the quarters of Sergeant Major Edward Carter of the Royal Defence Corps. His defence was that he was very upset at the time. The account is somewhat ambiguous but it could be that this was linked to his being called up, as during the hearing PS Capelin told the Bench that the military authorities could not call the man up without the permission of the Railway Company. The Chairman intimated that the case would be referred to the Railway Company. Jonas was fined 5 shillings. The British government passed the Military Service Act in 1916. The act specified that single men aged 18 to 41 years old were liable to be called up for military service unless they were widowed with children or ministers of a religion. There was a system of Military Service Tribunals to adjudicate claims for exemption on the grounds of performing civilian work of national importance.

Jonas Eames enlisted in Horsham in 1916 and was eventually posted to the 2nd Battalion Royal Fusiliers (City of London Regiment). The 2nd Battalion, having previously been involved in the Gallipoli Campaign and then in Egypt, moved to France landing at Marseilles in March 1916. This battalion of the Royal Fusiliers was part of the 86th Infantry Brigade – sometimes known as the Fusiliers Brigade – of the 29th Division and was engaged in various actions on the Western Front until the end of the war. There is no detailed War Diary for Jonas Eames as is often the case for non-commissioned ranks, so it is only possible to discover the engagements detailed for his battalion during the time he was with them.

In the Autumn of 1916 the battalion was in action in the last campaigns of the Battle of the Somme at Le Transloy Ridges. This action was due to begin on 5 October but appalling weather meant the attack was not possible until two days later and lasted in dreadful conditions until 20 October. It was during this campaign that John Masefield had visited the Somme and had subsequently recorded his impressions:

> *I never saw such mud, or such a sight in all my days. Other places are bad and full of death, but this was deep in mud as well, a kind of chaos of deep running holes & broken ground & filthy chasms, and pools & stands & marshes of iron coloured water, & yellow snow & bedevilment. Old rags of wet uniforms were everywhere, & bones & legs & feet & heads were sticking out of the ground.*

In the spring of 1917 29th Division were engaged in three phases of the Arras Offensive around the River Scarpe between 9 April and 16 May. This was a combined operation with the French who planned the major Nivelle Offensive 80 km to the south. The aim of the British and Imperial attack was to draw the German troops away from this. Some limited success was achieved but the cost in casualties was severe.

A British machine gun post near Feuchy close to the River Scarpe in the first of the three battles here.

The Third Battle of Ypres was launched on 31 July 1917 and continued until the fall of Passchendaele village on 6 November. The offensive resulted in gains for the Allies but was by no means the breakthrough Haig intended, and such gains as were made came at great cost in human terms. The second battalion were involved at Langemark mid-August, at Broodseinde on 4 October and at Poelcapelle on 9 October. As winter approached the brigade took part in the Battle of Cambrai from 29 November to 7 December. The battle showed that even the strongest trench defences could be overcome by a surprise artillery-infantry attack, using the new methods and equipment, with a mass tank attack as a bonus. The German revival after the shock of the British attack improved morale but the potential for similar attacks meant that the Germans had to divert resources to anti-tank defences and weapons, an extra demand that the Germans could ill-afford to meet.

Having survived the gruelling and costly campaigns of 1917 this was the last active service seen by Jonas Eames. His death is recorded on 30 March 1918, 10 days before the 29th Division took part in the Battle of the Lys. No details are given for the manner of his death and there is no explanation for his memorial being placed in Cologne Southern Cemetery in Germany. More than 1,000 Allied prisoners and dozens of German servicemen were buried in Cologne Southern Cemetery during the Great War. There are now almost 2,500 Great War servicemen buried or commemorated in the Commonwealth plots at Cologne. It is possible that Jonas was taken prisoner or that his memorial there is linked to the fact that after the Armistice the Division was among those selected to march into Germany to occupy the Rhine bridgehead. All units crossed the Belgian-German border at Malmedy on 4 December 1918 and arrived in Cologne five days later. The Division crossed the Rhine by the Honhenzollern Bridge on 13 December. It remains a mystery.

Jonas was awarded two medals, the Victory Medal and the British War Medal in commemoration of his war service.

A poignant postscript is to be found in Ron Muggeridge's book *Warnham, A History*:

> *Next door to us . . . lived Mr and Mrs Eames. They lost their only son in the First World War and never really got over the loss . . . Also standing in the front room, was an enormous old fashioned pram which had been used for their son.*

CWGC Cologne Southern Cemetery.

Harry Edwards

10804 Second Lieutenant

12th (Service) Battalion
King's (Liverpool Regiment)
61st Brigade 20th Division
Formerly 1st Battalion
King's (Liverpool Regiment)
6th Brigade 2nd Division

Killed on the Somme 7 October 1916, aged 23

Alec Felix Edwards MC

200263 Captain

4th (Extra Reserve) Battalion
King's (Liverpool Regiment)
98th Brigade 33rd Division
Formerly 1/4th Battalion (TF)
Royal Sussex Regiment
160th Brigade 53rd (Welsh) Division

The father of these two young men, Felix Edwards, was born in 1858, the second to youngest child of the large family of Thomas and Mary Ann Edwards who lived in the School House, Kirdford. The census records of 1861 and 1871 show that Thomas was employed as a schoolmaster. Felix left school in 1872 at the age of 14 and worked as an agricultural labourer. This job eventually brought him to Warnham and by the age of 23 he was lodging with Tom and Mary Yates in Friday Street. He was married several years later and in 1891 he and his wife, Ellen, were living at 4 Wickersham Lane, Horsham where the records show that he was working as a Gardener/Domestic Servant indicating that his job was in the garden of a private house.

By 1893 Felix Edwards had worked his way up to head gardener, a responsible job requiring a good deal of horticultural expertise. The family were living in the Gardener's Cottage at Warnham Lodge where he was employed by Sir Henry

Harben. He had had very little formal education and all his knowledge had been learned by experience. Felix was held in high regard in the village by all classes. He was chairman of the Flower Show from 1921 until his death in 1937 and was also a prominent figure on the Sports Committee for 30 years or more. In his spare time he made cellos and probably played a string instrument. At least four of his children (Frank, Harry, Alec and Lizzie) played in the Warnham String Band, which accomplishment they most likely learned from their father.

Felix and Ellen had four sons and three daughters. The eldest boy, Francis (Frank) by 1911 was 24 and having finished his apprenticeship was employed as a carpenter and was still living at home with his parents, two younger brothers and three sisters. There are no records of Frank having been in the military and on a legal document concerning his brother's will, his address on 28 March 1917 is shown as 26 Carlisle Road, Norwich. He was by then 30 and would have enlisted or been conscripted by that time. It could be that he was not fit or, more likely, that his carpentry skills kept him on some war work in a reserved occupation. After the war he moved into a cottage on the Warnham Court estate at the side of the old A24 where he was employed as the estate carpenter for the rest of his working life. Like others of his family, he was a musician, and he was also an expert furniture maker and wood carver. In the window of the Caryll Chapel in Warnham Church are three beautiful figures he carved for his employer, Mr C J Lucas. Frank was a prominent member

Warnham String Band 9 April 1909. Alec and Frank Edwards are third and fourth from the left in the middle row. Their sister Lizzie is the lady cellist wearing a hat. Also in the picture is Alfred Comper Yates on the left with the double bass.

of the Cricket Club, playing and later umpiring for the club for over 40 years. He worked hard for the Sports Committee for many years, serving as secretary for a good deal of the time.

Alec, one of Frank's younger brothers, was born on 15 January 1896 and in 1911 was living at home and working as a gardener apprentice. He was 18 in 1914 and together with thousands of young men working in rural occupations eagerly and innocently marched off to war to join Kitchener's New Army with little idea of the horrors before him. He enlisted in Horsham joining the local battalion, the 4th Royal Sussex, soon to be known as the 1/4th. In July 1915 Alec, together with many men from the Horsham area and at least five others from Warnham, embarked on *HMT Ulysses* at Devonport arriving in Suvla Bay in the Dardanelles on 8 August. The battalion fought a hard battle here which is told in detail in the story of Jack Charman. Suffice it to say that Alec Edwards and William Miles, who had been a farm worker and lived with his parents in Friday Street, were both wounded very early on, transferred to hospital on Lemnos Island and invalided home. Being wounded most likely saved their lives and certainly would have removed them from the horrors of the futile and mismanaged battles on Gallipoli.

When the peninsula was evacuated in December 1915 the battalion was posted to Egypt and they remained in the Middle East for the next two years before moving to France in May 1918. In October 1916 Alec Edwards attended an Officer Training Course in Bristol and on 25 January 1917 he was commissioned into the 4th Battalion King's Liverpool Regiment. He served with the 4th Battalion for the rest of the war. In 1918 he was awarded an MC with the following citation published on 18 September 1918 in the Edinburgh Gazette:

> *For conspicuous gallantry and devotion to duty. This officer received orders to move up to the front line with his company. Here he found that the enemy had been driven back by a counter-attack, but a gap of 250 yards remained on the right. He made a thorough reconnaissance of this gap under intense fire, and by dawn had his company well dug in, filling the gap exactly as ordered. Quite 75 per cent of his men were under fire for the first time, and it was due to his energy and leadership that the task was successfully accomplished.*

Unfortunately it has not been possible to trace the date or place of this action but we do know that, despite their title of 'Extra Reserve', the 4th Battalion had been on the Western Front since 1915 and had taken part in a series of campaigns. The remark that most of his men were 'under fire for the first time' indicates that this battalion had suffered many casualties and had been reinforced with a large number of inexperienced new recruits, many of whom by this time would have been conscripts.

By the end of the war Alec had risen to the rank of Captain. For his years of active service in Gallipoli and on the Western Front, he received the 1914-15 Star together with the Victory Medal and the British War Medal in addition to his MC.

Alec's older brother, Harry, was born on 4 March 1893 soon after the family moved to Warnham. He left school at 13 and worked in the carpenter's shop at Warnham Lodge. In 1909 he joined the 1st Battalion King's Liverpool Regiment signing on for 12 years' service as a carpenter and a bandsman. He too had acquired some of the musical talent of this family and as a boy had played in the Warnham String Band with his brothers and sister.

Harry had an impeccable record in the army and rose steadily through the ranks from Private to Lance Corporal in 1912, Corporal in 1914 and Sergeant early in 1915. All the records show him as a hardworking and reliable soldier – on 4 September 1913 his conduct sheet describes him as 'Clean, smart, sober, honest, intelligent and a good worker' and his military character as 'Very Good'. But there was a secret. His enlistment papers show that when he signed on in December 1909 he gave his age as 18 years and 9 months when he was only 16 years and 9 months. Maybe his appearance – 6ft tall, 11 stone, and A1 sight and fitness was sufficient to bluff the army recruitment and medical officers. He was obviously a bright and attractive young man. And indeed his sponsor, Sir Henry Harben, (who gives his own trade as that of 'Knight') had not really studied the documents when he attested that the details were all correct. It is surprising that birth certificates were not required at recruitment, particularly in peace time when there was not the same pressure to increase the size of the army.

In August 1914 the 1st Battalion King's, stationed at Aldershot, were mobilised at the onset of war and immediately sent abroad. They sailed from Southampton on the *SS Irrawaddy* and landed in Le Havre on the 13 August. They were involved in the retreat from Mons but held ground on the Marne and earned praise for their stand at Villers-Cotterêts. The Allies halted the German advance in the First Battle of the Marne; the ensuing retreat, which prompted an Allied counter-offensive, ended at the Aisne. After both battles had been fought, the battalion moved north to Ypres, during the so-called 'Race to the Sea' and took part in the First Battle of Ypres in November 1914. So Harry and his companions had had a very lively and dangerous time for several months.

By this time the people of Warnham had really got into action with comforts and other goodies for wounded soldiers and for those in the front line. The February Parish Magazine printed a letter from Harry Edwards:

I wish to thank you all for your kindness in making my Christmas Day a real happy one. I received your parcel on Dec 24th and cannot tell you how pleased I felt in the knowledge that you remembered me. Warnham, I have heard, has given many sons to the country. At that, of course, I am not surprised; but still, it is awfully nice to hear that my own little village has responded so well. I hope you were able to have many of them home at Christmas or the New Year; for myself, it was spent in the trenches, and you made it by your thoughtfulness just as joyful as your own.

Sincerely your friend, H EDWARDS King's Liverpool Regt, on active service

Six months later Harry caused a little stir in the village in the summer of 1915 when he came home for a week's leave to marry his fiancée, Gladys Muriel Sheppard, on 8 June, as recorded in the Parish Magazine:

Troops going over the top – on the Somme.

We were all glad to see Sergeant Harry Edwards on a short visit home from the Front. It was to all an interesting occasion. He returned on a Sunday, and on the following Tuesday his marriage took place in the old parish Church, and he went back again to his work on the next Sunday. May God bring him back safely and grant him and his wife a long and happy life together!

We hear that Lord Derby sent out some band instruments to the 1st Bn King's Liverpool Regiment, and he has had the following interesting account of their playing. The instruments arrived a few days before the battalion left their billets to go to the trenches, and so they were able to get a few days' practice, and were also enabled to play in the square in the town in which they were billeted on French Day. The Mayor of the town [probably Béthune] *and the townspeople themselves were very pleased, and there was a great crowd listening to the music, and a great number of soldiers were able to partake in the enjoyment. It is rather curious that the town in which the band played was one which the Liverpool Regiment besieged in 1710. The Mayor presented a bouquet to the acting bandmaster, Sergeant Edwards, and when told of the incident which occurred in 1710 was so delighted that he begged an extract from the regimental records, so that it could be placed with the archives of the town in his keeping.*

The Sergeant Edwards referred to is our own Harry Edwards, son of Mr and Mrs Felix Edwards of Warnham Lodge gardens.

We also wish to congratulate Harry Edwards and his family upon the honour which has just been conferred upon him. In the list of awards conferred by the Czar, published in the daily press on Aug 16th occurs the following:

Medal of S. George, First Class[1] *– Acting-Sergt. H Edwards, 1st Batt. Liverpool Regiment.*

Harry was commissioned on 27 September 'For service on the field' and transferred to the 12th Battalion King's Liverpool. The Battle of the Somme is usually remembered for the appalling losses during the first few days at the beginning of July but *The Official History* shows that the Somme Campaign actually consisted of 12 separate battles fought between 1 July and 18 November. Despite the huge losses and the small amount of progress, Haig was heartened by the occupation of much of the Thiepval Ridge and determined to press on into the autumn. Throughout September the 12th Battalion had seen a lot of action. During the first half of October as part of the Fourth Army, they were deployed in the battle for the Transloy Ridges. The weather was rapidly becoming rougher with continuous rain. The main battle began on 7 October 1916, at 1.45 pm. South of Guedecourt, the 12th King's to the fore made progress of about 500 yards and into the western section of Rainbow Trench. The War Diary [WO 95/1359] records:

Attacked Rainbow and Cloudy trenches at 1.45 pm. Latter trench about 1,000 yds from our front line. Both objectives taken and several prisoners. Six officers hit, one of whom was killed. Spent all night consolidating.

That officer was Harry Edwards. His Colonel wrote to his grieving family and his young wife:

His death is a heavy loss to the Battalion. Although he had only been with us a short time he had done most excellent work, and was in command of a Company when killed. He was one of the most gallant officers I have ever seen (quite regardless of danger), and a very fine example to his men. You have the entire sympathy of myself and of the other officers in the Battalion in your great loss.

It was barely a month since Harry had received his commission yet he was now in command of a company. This reflects both the paucity of officers and the competence of Harry.

1. The St George Medal, a Russian honour, was awarded to NCOs for merit in combat – probably the equivalent of the Military Medal. It came in four classes, 1st Class being the highest. It was awarded for merit to other Allied soldiers as well as Russians. Quite how he came to earn it we do not know.

Thiepval Memorial to the Missing.

The Adjutant, Lieutenant J E S Plummer wrote to Harry's widow to tell her that her husband had been killed at 2.30 pm. On the evening of 7 October he and others had gone up and found the body and buried him just behind the trench which he and his company had captured. But he was not allowed to reveal the location because of censorship. Harry's body, so carefully buried, was never found and his name is recorded on the Thiepval Memorial to the Missing, on Pier & Face 1 D 8 B and 8 C. This huge memorial was designed by Sir Edwin Lutyens and contains 72,000 names of British and South African soldiers with no known grave who had been killed in the Somme area, over 90% of whom had died between July and November.

Despite the encomiums from his senior officers and his obvious valour and competence, the War Office sent a letter to Harry's father in 1917 *'. . . your son, the late 2nd Lt H Edwards, did not fulfil the conditions for the grant of the acting rank of captain whilst commanding a company. It is regretted therefore that as your son did not command a company for 30 days, the grant to him the acting rank of captain cannot be sanctioned.'* It seems he could do the work and die in the process but this could not be acknowledged because of the regulations.

In addition to his Russian medal and the 1914 Star, Harry was awarded the Victory Medal and the British War Medal. These were issued in 1920 and were claimed by his widow, Gladys, who by then had remarried and was living in Aldershot.

These two young men had received no secondary education and before the war were both in what would be considered fairly lowly jobs. In 1914-18 the majority of officers were graduates or public school educated, yet both the Edwards boys obtained commissions which is an indication of their ability and character. They must have been excellent soldiers and natural leaders to move up through the ranks despite leaving school at 14. What did Alec do when he returned to civvy street? By then he would have been too old to continue as a gardener's apprentice and the job would have seemed rather humdrum after all he had been through. He could have stayed on as a regular soldier and there is a slight indication on his records that this may have been the case. And, had he lived, what might his brother Harry have gone on to achieve?

Fred Edwards

T/206646 Private

2/4th Battalion (TF)
Queen's (Royal West Surrey Regiment)
160th Brigade 53rd (Welsh) Division

Killed in action in Palestine
27th December 1917, aged 22

Fred was a farm labourer, and belonged to a semi-nomadic farming family typical of the time. His parents George and Eliza came from just across the county border in East Sussex, and were married in Fletching in March 1890.

By the time of the census in April 1891 they were living in Brighton where George was working as a carman, someone who carried goods or produce around on a cart, either with or without the aid of a horse. Their itinerant lifestyle is borne out by the subsequent births of their four children. First was Charlie born 1892 in Nutley, then Fred born 1895 in Lewes, Richard born 1900 in East Grinstead and Edith born 1904 also in East Grinstead. It certainly appears as if they nearly put down roots in East Grinstead where they had a cottage to themselves on Shovelstrode Farm, but by 1911 the family had moved to Yard Farm in Ewhurst, just 7.5 miles from Warnham. During that intervening period Fred's elder brother Charlie died, although exactly when and how is not known, but it must have been a terrible blow for the family, and perhaps precipitated their move away from East Grinstead.

The 1911 census shows that Fred then aged 16 was a farm labourer. We do not know what happened to him between then and the outbreak of war, but on enlistment in Guildford he gave his residence as Warnham, so presumably he was labouring on one of the many farms in the area.

Fred joined the 2/4th Battalion, Queen's (Royal West Surrey Regiment), nicknamed 'the Mutton Lancers' on account of their Lamb and Flag cap badge. The 2/4th was a Territorial Force so Fred may well have joined them some time before he saw action. However, in 1916 aged 21 his war started in earnest as he made his informal Army Will on the 24 July 1916, leaving everything to his mother, now living back in the East Grinstead area. We can also reasonably infer from the Will that he was not married.

Fred was almost certainly initially posted to Egypt, but then as part of the Palestine Campaign saw action in and around Jerusalem, fighting the Ottoman Empire and its allies. On 11 December 1917 the Egyptian Expeditionary Force under General Allenby occupied Jerusalem. The regimental War Diary tells how they had marched their way there via Bethlehem, on standby to fight at the Mount of Olives. This had to have been a surreal experience for a farm hand from Sussex, and must have felt like being on a 20th Century Crusade.

After the capture of Jerusalem the EEF had to defend it against strong opposition, and the 'Battle of Defence of Jerusalem' officially raged from 26 to 30 December 1917. It was during a particularly strong enemy offensive on the 27 December that Fred was killed. He was buried in the Jerusalem War Cemetery, grave reference Q.54. Fred was posthumously awarded the Victory Medal and the British War Medal.

Surrender of Jerusalem.

Clifton Brown Grant

Captain

99th Company, Machine Gun Corps
99th Brigade 2nd Division
Formerly 22nd (Service) Battalion
(Kensington) Royal Fusiliers
(City of London Regiment)

Killed in action Delville Wood
27 July 1916, aged 22

In September 1916 the Vicar wrote in the Parish Magazine: *We all wish to express our sympathy with Mrs Grant and her family in the loss of her son, Capt. Clifton Brown Grant. This gallant young officer was killed in action in Delville Wood on July 17th* [should be 27th] *All who knew him speak of his devotion to duty and of the splendid soldierly qualities which were his.*

Clifton Brown Grant was born in Kiltarlity, Inverness-shire, on 6 July 1894, the youngest child of John and Jessie Grant. He had one older brother, Ian, and three older sisters, Jessie, Annie and Mary. His parents were Scottish, his father from Moray and his mother from Nairn, and the four older children were born in Strathglass, Inverness-shire. John Grant was an Estate Factor which is the Scottish equivalent of a Land Agent and at the time of the birth of their youngest child they were living in Knockvoid, a tiny hamlet in the rural parish of Kiltarlity 12 miles from Inverness where John was running a large estate. This role was a senior position as right-hand man to the landowner and the Grant family lived in some comfort, employing a cook, a housemaid and a nurse for the children.

Probably in order to obtain a higher position, John Grant brought his family to the south of England sometime in the late 1890s and took a job as a Land Agent in Slaugham where they lived at Eastlands Farm. In 1904 they moved to New Park, Nuthurst where John became Land Agent to Sir Edmund Giles Loder at Leonardslee receiving a salary of £350 per annum. By this time the two eldest children had left home, Annie and Mary were still living with their parents and the family were employing a cook and a housemaid but had dispensed with the governess. That same year Clifton, who was now 10, was admitted as a pupil at Christ's Hospital.

Soon after 1911, John Grant retired, and the family moved to Warnham where they made their home at The Firs which is No 2 School Hill on the corner of Bell

Clifton Brown Grant, in 1907, at the age of 13 as a very junior member of Barnes 'B' – a house at Christ's Hospital.

Road. John had retired rather early as he was still in his 50s and it may be that his health was failing as he died early in 1915. Soon after the death of her husband, Jessie moved to Brook Cottage, Bolney.

Clifton, who must have been a bright boy to gain a place at Christ's Hospital, proved to be a good pupil. On leaving school at the end of the Easter term 1911, his report gave him 'Good' grades throughout and placed him 1st in class for History and 4th for Maths. His school records show that he worked for a spell as a clerk on the Southern Railway and it is likely that this job was a stop gap, as he soon became a full time student at Wye College, Kent. At this time Wye College, as part of the University of London, was prominent in the area of agricultural practice and research and a leading centre for rural business and management. Perhaps Clifton was intending to follow his father as a Land Agent, or maybe he intended to go into farming. We do not know whether he had finished his course by 1914 but it seems likely that he joined the army at the very beginning of the war when he was 20.

After initial training he was commissioned 2nd Lieutenant in the 22nd Battalion Royal Fusiliers and went to France on 17 November 1915 seeing some action with them during the next few weeks. Two days before embarkation he had made a will at Southampton leaving everything to his mother. On 29 February 1916 Clifton was gazetted as temporary captain in the Machine Gun Corps and on 21 March 1916 he was given command of the 99th Machine Gun Company, his early promise at school being reflected in his rapid promotion.

The attack on Delville Wood in July 1916, as part of the Battle of the Somme, was designed to remove all Germans from that area. It started on 15 July and the infantry moved in after heavy shelling. Conditions were appalling – the trees having been uprooted restricted the depth of trenches giving minimal protection. On his History Learning website, Chris Trueman records the words of Captain S

J Worsley MC: We stood and lay on putrefying bodies and the wonder was that the disease did not finish off what the shells of the enemy had started. There was hand-to-hand fighting with knives, bombs and bayonets, cursing and brutality on both sides such as men can be responsible for when it is a question of 'your life or mine', mud and filthy stench; dysentery and unattended wounds; shortage of food and water and ammunition.

It was as bad for both sides; a German officer described it:

Delville Wood has disintegrated into a shattered wasteland of shattered trees, charred and burning stumps, craters thick with mud and blood and corpses, corpses everywhere. In places they were piled four deep.

There was some criticism of the lack of thought which had been given to the use of machine guns as the practice of sending the gunners in with the first wave of infantry had led to high casualty rates, which gave rise to the Machine Gun Corps being given the nickname 'The Suicide Club'. But in an article on the subject of machine guns on the Western Front, Paul Cornish comments on changes which had been made:

A case in point was the intelligent use of machine guns in the assault on Delville Wood on 27 July 1916. The gun teams of 99th Machine Gun Company were not sent forward with the first wave of the attack, but moved up with a supporting battalion. Infantrymen were seconded to the machine gunners to carry ammunition and water, enabling a reserve of trained gunners to be maintained.

Digging in at Delville Wood.

In addition each gun team was accompanied by at least one selected rifleman, to protect it against enemy snipers. Once the far edge of the wood had been reached, the machine gunners assisted in repelling the inevitable German counter-attacks.

Christ's Hospital 1914-18 War Memorial above seats in the Quad.

Some lessons had been learned but that did not save our young Captain who was killed on that same day and is buried in Serre Road Cemetery No 2 (Plot XX.A.8). His grieving mother collected his medals after the war and the £184-6-8d he had bequeathed to her. This mainly consisted of accrued back pay at 12/6d per day. He had not appointed an executor and so Letters of Administration were obtained by the services of Horsham solicitors, Coole & Haddock. Mr Coole was the father of Arthur Evans Coole, another war casualty. Captain Grant's name is also on the memorials at Christ's Hospital and Wye College.

The County Times of 12 August 1916 records:

Writing to Mrs Grant, 2nd Lt Christopher Stone, whose home is at Field Place, testifies to the gallant behaviour of Captain C B Grant in the fighting in Delville Wood on 27th July. 'It was' he writes 'a terrible day and place and all who were there spoke in glowing terms of Capt Grant who was here, there and everywhere, helping everyone, unperturbed and cool as ever, although he knew before he started that it was almost certain death. Of his nine or ten officers, only one came back. Capt Grant was beloved by all the Battalion He combined extraordinary ability in his work with a wonderful coolness to danger and charm of manner. I needn't tell you what a fine and gallant fellow he was.'

The chaplain of the Battalion, the Rev Ernest S John, writes: 'I have asked many who were near him about him and he seems to have been absolutely magnificent. He knew no fear. A stretcher bearer who saw him hit says his death was quite instantaneous and that he felt no pain.'

The award of Mentioned in Despatches is Gazetted on 4 January 1917 and it is likely that this was in recognition of his bravery at Delville Wood. This, the lowliest award in the military, is the only one other than the highest, Victoria Cross, which can be awarded posthumously. Had he lived he would most likely have been recommended for an MC or DSO. In 1921 his mother received his campaign medals, the 1914-15 Star, the Victory Medal and the British War Medal.

Reginald Walter Grant

Captain

8TH (SERVICE) BATTALION
QUEEN'S OWN (ROYAL WEST KENT REGIMENT)
72ND BRIGADE 24TH DIVISION
FORMERLY 3RD (MILITIA) BATTALION
QUEEN'S OWN (ROYAL WEST KENT REGIMENT)

Died in Paddington 26 November 1918, aged 42

Reginald was born into an affluent family on 6 May 1876 in Gipsy Hill, near Croydon in Surrey. His baptism record at Christ Church in Norwood gives his name as Walter Reginald, and he was also known as such at the age of 14 whilst at Brighton College. But by 19 he had become Reginald Walter, and remained that way for the rest of his life.

Reginald's father, Alexander Grant, made his money as a merchant in Mexico, probably in relation to a ranching business there. Later official records of Reginald describe him as a 'Gent' or 'living on own means' so it is clear the family were financially secure. Not surprisingly therefore when Reginald completed his private education at Brighton College he joined the military as an officer.

In 1896, aged 19, Reginald enlisted in the 3rd (Militia) Battalion Queen's Own (Royal West Kent Regiment) as a second lieutenant. This was what we would now call a Territorial Army unit. These were part-timers whose role was to support the Regular battalions in times of war. As a 'Gent', Reginald was able to join the militia as a junior officer without any formal military training. Just over a year later he was promoted to Lieutenant.

When the Second Boer War broke out in 1899 the 3rd Battalion was mobilised and all the men were asked if they would volunteer for overseas service. There was an enthusiastic unanimous response, and so right at the beginning of the new century on 4 January 1900 the Battalion left Maidstone to the sounds of a military band and cheers from a patriotic crowd. They arrived at the Royal Albert Docks and set sail for Malta where they were to perform Garrison duties, freeing up regulars for active service in South Africa.

Stonyhurst – now Slaughter Bridge House.

Reginald's stay in Malta must have been extremely easy. Most of their time was taken up with military exercises and practice, with the occasional celebrations and parades for events such as the relief of Ladysmith, the Queen's birthday and a royal visit by the Duke and Duchess of Cornwall and York (later to become King George V and Queen Mary). Being an officer he would no doubt have eaten and boarded well. After sixteen months his sojourn in Malta came to an end and in June 1901 he arrived back in England, returning home to his mother's house in Norwood. For his service in Malta he received the Queen's Mediterranean medal.

In September 1906 Reginald married Florence Mabel Schilling at All Saints Church, Upper Norwood. On the marriage certificate Reginald describes himself as a merchant, and his father is noted as being deceased. So it seems Reginald had by then taken over some or all of his father's interests. Less than a year later their first and only child Dorothy Joan was born in Lewisham. At some point between Dorothy's birth and the 1911 census Reginald and Florence moved to Warnham, and lived at Stonyhurst on the Guildford Road, now known as Slaughter Bridge House.

At the outbreak of war in August 1914 when Reginald was 38 years old, he re-enlisted with his old regiment, thinking like everyone else that the war could be won by Christmas. He was assigned to one of the new volunteer service battalions, the 8th, and was promoted to temporary captain in September 1914. This new battalion was initially raised in Maidstone, but moved to Shoreham and then to billets in Worthing by December 1914. They stayed there (within easy reach of

Warnham) until April 1915 when they returned to Shoreham, and then finally moved on to Blackdown near Aldershot (now Deepcut Barracks) in July 1915. From there the now fully trained volunteers made final preparations to join the British Expeditionary Force. Unlike Reginald's previous service with the Reserves, this time he was clearly going to experience combat.

The 8th Battalion landed in Boulogne as part of the 24th Division on 30 August 1915. Their first major engagement with the enemy was to be the Battle of Loos in Northern France near the Belgian border, the largest conflict in the war for the BEF up to that point. When the battle started on 25 September it soon became clear that General Haig's optimistic plans were not being realised. Artillery was not as effective as it needed to be, there were problems in deploying poison gas, and communications were difficult. The reserve divisions including the 24th were stationed too far away from the conflict so when they were called into action they arrived on the battlefield tired, poorly briefed and being mostly new recruits, totally inexperienced at fighting under heavy artillery bombardment, sniper and machine-gun fire. They were so badly briefed in fact that they did not know what was expected of them and their presence on the first day of battle was ineffective. Those gains made by the BEF during the day were substantially lost during the night when the

Battle of Loos – British infantry of the 47th (2nd London) Division advance through the gas cloud on 25 September 1915. A photograph believed to have been taken by a soldier of the 1/5th London Regiment.

Germans counter-attacked. The following day, 26 September, saw the British mount a major offensive yet again, but the German guns, trenches and barbed wire had not been neutralised as planned. The Royal West Kent 8th Battalion, including Captain Grant commanding 'D' Company, were instructed to take the Hulloch quarries. But with the German defences intact they were caught with nowhere to go in no-man's-land. They were mown down by machine gun fire from the front and side and stood no chance. With heavy losses they retreated back to the British line. Captain Grant was badly injured, shot in both thighs.

The 8th Battalion suffered 24 officer casualties; 13 killed, six badly wounded and found by the Germans in no-man's-land, and five who were invalided back to England, including Captain Grant. Some accounts state that only one officer survived the battle, so it may be that four of the five that made it home did not live long. Of the other ranks in the 8th Battalion, 550 were lost. In all close to 60% of the 8th Battalion died at the Battle of Loos.

Captain Grant had survived the battlefield but the rest of the war was to be one long physical and mental struggle for him. He spent a month in an officers' hospital in London and then went home to Warnham to convalesce, with monthly physical check-ups by the military. This went on until May 1916 when, despite still being declared unfit for service, he turned up at the War Office asking for orders. He was told to report to the 9th Reserve Battalion in Shoreham, which he did on 4 May. By 24 May however he had again been declared unfit and was sent home for light duty. By now it seems his physical wounds had healed, but the trauma of Loos had left him with persistent shell-shock, and no doubt what we would today call 'survivor guilt'. He clearly wanted to return to the fray despite his condition.

His monthly medicals continued to declare him unfit until he failed to attend one in August 1916. Somehow he had persuaded the Regiment to send him to Salonica. Yet again he only lasted a few weeks before being sent back to England as unfit. He was assigned to the 3rd Reserve Battalion but was sent home to Warnham for rest. During the course of 1917 and 1918 he was further assigned to various training battalions and administrative roles but his medicals still noted that he was unfit for any form of active service, to the extent that he was even unable to march. His condition was in fact deteriorating, and in August 1918 he was admitted to the Maudsley Neurological clearing hospital who subsequently declared him permanently unfit for service in September of that year. His doctor noted that he was suffering from *'loss of memory, sleeplessness and depression and an inability to work, attributable to military service. He is old for his years and is physically broken down'.*

On the 26 November 1918 at the age of 42 Captain Grant died from Influenza and Pneumonia, and was buried in Paddington Cemetery. In his wife's words, he *'had only been out of Neurasthenic hospital at Denmark Hill about 6 weeks and was too weak to fight the flu'*.

Captain Grant was posthumously awarded the Victory medal, British War medal and the 1914-15 Star. He was also awarded the Silver War Badge, an acknowledgement that his inability to serve was a direct result of injuries received. This is at odds however with the War Office's attitude to paying him a 'wound gratuity'. This should normally have been paid for a debilitating injury attributable to active service, but despite several attempts to claim it, the War Office deemed him ineligible, presumably because his physical wounds had healed. To the further discredit of the War Office, because of some overpaid billet allowance they held up settlement of his salary to his widow, who was clearly suffering financial hardship and begged them on several occasions to settle his finances.

Florence never re-married, and died in Berkhamstead in 1938. Their daughter Dorothy married a distinguished army officer in 1933, Major Francis Cockburn Curtis who went on to become a Brigadier and was made a CBE at the end of the Second World War.

Arthur Eldred Hards

G/17844 Private

12th (Service) Battalion (2nd South Down)
Royal Sussex Regiment
116th Brigade 39th Division
Formerly 3560 Private
1/4th Battalion (TF) Royal Sussex Regiment

Killed on the Somme 10 October 1916, aged 24

Arthur was born in Warnham in 1892 and baptised at St Margaret's Church on 31 July. He was the first child of Eldred and Jane (née Wales) who had married just two years earlier and were living at Goose Green. Eldred was a brickmaker who was born and brought up in Grub Street, Horsham by Arthur's grandparents Robert and Charlotte, along with four of Arthur's aunts and uncles. Eldred and Jane went on to have two more children Albert and Edith, but then sadly Jane died in 1899.

By 1901 Eldred and his three children were living with his widowed mother at Burford Road, Horsham. Later that year Eldred married Emma Smithers and over the next few years they had five more children, one of whom died as a baby in 1904. So in 1911 Eldred, Emma and seven children were living at Prospect Place, Horsham, now Milton Road. Eldred was no longer a brickmaker but employed as a farm labourer. His sons Arthur and Albert were also labourers, but had followed in their father's footsteps and were working in the brickfields.

In 1915 Arthur joined the 1/4th Battalion the Royal Sussex Regiment, but did not go with them to Gallipoli and after initial training was transferred to the 12th (Service) Battalion (2nd South Down) Royal Sussex Regiment which landed in France in March 1916.

The 11th, 12th and 13th Battalions were three South Down battalions raised at Bexhill in late 1914 by Lieutenant Colonel C Lowther MP and a committee which were taken over by the War Office on 1 July 1915. The battalions were known as Lowther's Lambs, forming three-quarters of the 116th Brigade of the 39th Division which took part in the little recognised Battle of the Boar's Head on 30 June 1916. This offensive was launched 30 miles north of the Somme, at Richebourg l'Avoue near Béthune with the intention of occupying the enemy and discouraging them from transferring troops to the Somme area where the massive offensive was due to start the next day. The Boar's Head attack was led by the 116th Brigade, Lowther's Lambs, many of whom were slaughtered as the venture failed, the 13th Battalion being all but wiped out. Company Sergeant Major Carter of Arthur's battalion, the 12th, won a posthumous Victoria Cross, the country's highest award for gallantry. The day is remembered in the phrase 'The Day Sussex Died' and was described by one young soldier as 'a butcher's shop'.

The Battle of the Somme lasted from its bloody beginning on 1 July until 19 November 1916 with total casualties on both sides of over one million. In fact, the Somme was a series of battles including the Battle of the Ancre Heights, 1-18 October 1916. On 7 October the 39th Division relieved the 18th Division and was one of six divisions to gain three major successes with the capture of the Stuff Redoubt, the Schwaben Redoubt and Regina Trench, reputedly the longest in the German front line. Having survived the carnage of Boar's Head, Albert's luck ran out when on 10 October, before the battle was won he was in the line near Auchonvillers, north of Albert, where he was killed aged 24.

He is buried in the Auchonvillers Military Cemetery, Grave Reference II J 6; the Commonwealth War Graves Commission's printed record gives his age as 26 instead of 24. He was awarded the Victory Medal and the British War Medal and is commemorated on Horsham's War Memorial.

Frederick Charles Hayler

S3/030286 Private

ARMY SERVICE CORPS

Died at Aldershot 28 January 1915, aged 22

At the time of the 1911 Census, Charles and Jane Hayler were living at 16 Church Street, Warnham with their younger son, 14 year old George, who had just started work as a gentleman's valet. Charles was a cowman; he and Jane had been married for 20 years and had another son, Frederick, who was 19. On his gravestone he is given the name of Charles F, but on his army records he appears as Frederick Charles. Presumably he was called Frederick to avoid confusion with his father. There is no trace of this family on either of the two previous Censuses in 1901 or 1891.

Charles Hayler had been born in Horsham and his son, Fred, in Broadbridge Heath. When he left school, Fred trained as a butcher and in 1911 was lodging with John and Ruth March in Worthing and working as a butcher's assistant. In November 1914, Fred joined up and was posted to the Army Service Corps (ASC) in Aldershot as part of the Third New Army (K3). The ASC were responsible for the transport and supply of ammunition and stores to the troops both in the UK and abroad and their training establishment was at Aldershot. Despite being described in his medical as having 'good' physical development, it could be that his 'slightly flat right foot' and skills as a butcher (though only described as 'fair') kept him out of the infantry at this stage. A year or two later he may well have been sent out to France as happened to the obviously sick Willie Wood in 1917. Sadly this poor young man had barely eight weeks in uniform before he succumbed to scarlet fever and died in the isolation ward in Aldershot on 28 January 1915 at the age of 22. The Vicar wrote in the Parish Magazine:

> *Greatly to our sorrow we have lost another of our young friends. It was a great shock to us all to hear that Fred Hayler had died of scarlet fever at Aldershot on Thursday, the 28th after a very short illness. Only a few weeks ago he came to tell us that he had joined the Army Service Corps. He was a good lad, liked by all who knew him. Full of hope and promise he was so happy in the thought that he was going to do something for his country. He was in our choir as a boy and*

he loved his Church. We grieve for this young friend of ours, and we sympathise with his parents and with his brother.

Fred Hayler is buried in Warnham Churchyard. Towards the end of the war Charles and Jane moved to 130 Ham Road, Worthing. Their younger son, George had now joined the army and was serving in Palestine. He survived the war.

Thomas James Higgins

202296 Private

13TH (SERVICE) BATTALION
ROYAL SCOTS (LOTHIAN REGIMENT)
45TH BRIGADE 15TH (SCOTTISH) DIVISION
FORMERLY 4TH BATTALION
QUEEN'S OWN (ROYAL WEST KENT REGIMENT)
4TH BATTALION ROYAL SUSSEX REGIMENT

Died from wounds in France
2 August 1918, aged 18

At the time of his death, Thomas Higgins gave as his address the home of his parents, John and Margaret, in Rowhook. His mother had been born in Warnham and no doubt it was his family connections that led to his name being added to the Warnham War Memorial. The hamlet of Rowhook is on the boundary of Warnham Parish and over the years has been variously described as being part of Warnham, Broadbridge Heath and Slinfold.

John Higgins was born in Herefordshire in 1873 one of six children of James, an agricultural worker and his wife Mary. He is recorded in 1891 at the age of 18 lodging with Thomas and Caroline Hibby in Mountain Ash, Glamorgan and working as a labourer. This was only a few miles from his home outside Hereford and it could be that the coalfields of Merthyr Tydfil offered more employment than did rural Herefordshire. Somewhere along the line he met his wife Margaret and they were married in 1896. Margaret was the eldest daughter of James and Ellen Stanford, living in Goose Green – one of the many branches of the Stanford family living in and around Warnham in the late 19th century. In 1891 Margaret, then 17, was living in at Kingsfold Place and working as a housemaid for the Withington family.

Quite how John and Margaret met we do not know but they moved around during the first few years of their marriage. Their first child, Arthur was born in Warnham, their second, Thomas James, was born in 1899 in Thornton Heath, Surrey and a year later the family were living in Glamorganshire, where they had two rooms in a shared house at 108 Woodfield Terrace, Mountain Ash. John was working as a labourer in a coalmine. Their third child was born there but a year or two later the family moved back to Sussex settling in Rowhook where three more children were born and John was now working as a general labourer.

The surviving war records of Private Higgins are tatty and mostly illegible, nearly all of the papers too faint to read or badly damaged by bombing in the Second World War but from the few little bits of information which can be gleaned, this boy shows up as a lively lad and something of a rebel. Seeking some excitement and a chance to break away from his job as a cowman, young Thomas enlisted in Horsham in the Army Reserve on 11 December 1915, giving his age as 18 years and one month, when he was only just 16. No checks appear to have been made and he was mobilised into the 4th Battalion Royal Sussex Regiment on 15 May 1916.

Thomas Higgins experienced his preliminary training with the Royal Sussex but on 19 October 1916 for some unknown reason he was transferred into the 4th Battalion Royal West Kent Regiment and on 1 November left with them to join the British Expeditionary Force in France. During the next few weeks someone in the battalion became suspicious about his age and on 4 December the Infantry Record Office in Hounslow wrote to the RWK Depot Office in Maidstone sending copies of his enlistment documents and saying that they had written to ask his mother to forward her son's birth certificate. The next thing we know is that on 2 December he is sent back to England being 'Under Age'.

However, although only just 17, he was not discharged from the army and on 31 January 1917 he was transferred to the 13th Battalion Royal Scots. During the next year while in Britain, mainly in Edinburgh, he gathered a few black marks. On 26 February he was absent from the 7 am parade, and on 8 March he was put on a charge for using improper language on parade. For each offence he received three days CB (Confined to Barracks). On 18 August he was late for the 9 am parade, on 30 October he was accused of 'Irregular Conduct' on church parade, and on 22 March he was absent from the 1.40 pm parade, all these misdemeanours earning some more days CB. He left England to join the battalion in France on 4 April 1918.

From April 1918 the 13th Battalion was involved in a number of engagements. Perhaps having more serious things to do and very little time to waste helped Thomas not to get into any more scrapes. In July and August, as part of the 15th Division, the 13th Battalion took part in the Second Battle of the Marne. The battle has been credited as signalling 'the turn of the tide' and certainly brought some cheer to the Allies. The Marne was considered to be 'down south', being some way south of the Somme and to the west of Paris. During the beginning of July German activity around Soissons and Reims indicated that a major attack was imminent and the French began shifting troops to the danger points. After some persuasion Haig agreed to send two, and later four more, British Divisions into the area. The Germans did in fact attack on 15 July but the French were ready for them. The French were reinforced by two divisions of fresh American troops and two days later the Germans withdrew across the river. The Allies together with the Americans continued to pursue the enemy through the Ardre Valley where it was said that 'the ripe corn standing two feet high helped and hindered both sides and casualties were huge'. The Allies were finally victorious on 4 August and the German Generals were overwhelmed, their plight exacerbated by deprivations at home and their desperate shortage of military manpower.

For the part they played over these few days the 15th (Scottish) Division which included the 13th Royal Scots received many plaudits from the French High Command. In a letter to General Haig, the French General wrote: . . . *by their dash and courage and their devotion, they have excited the admiration of the French troops in whose midst they fought.*

Thomas Higgins was seriously wounded in this campaign on 31 July and taken to No 63 Casualty Clearing Station at Senlis. CCSs were part of the casualty evacuation chain, further back from the front line than the First Aid Posts and Field Ambulances. They were manned by troops of the Royal Army Medical Corps together with trained women nurses, with attached Royal Engineers and men of

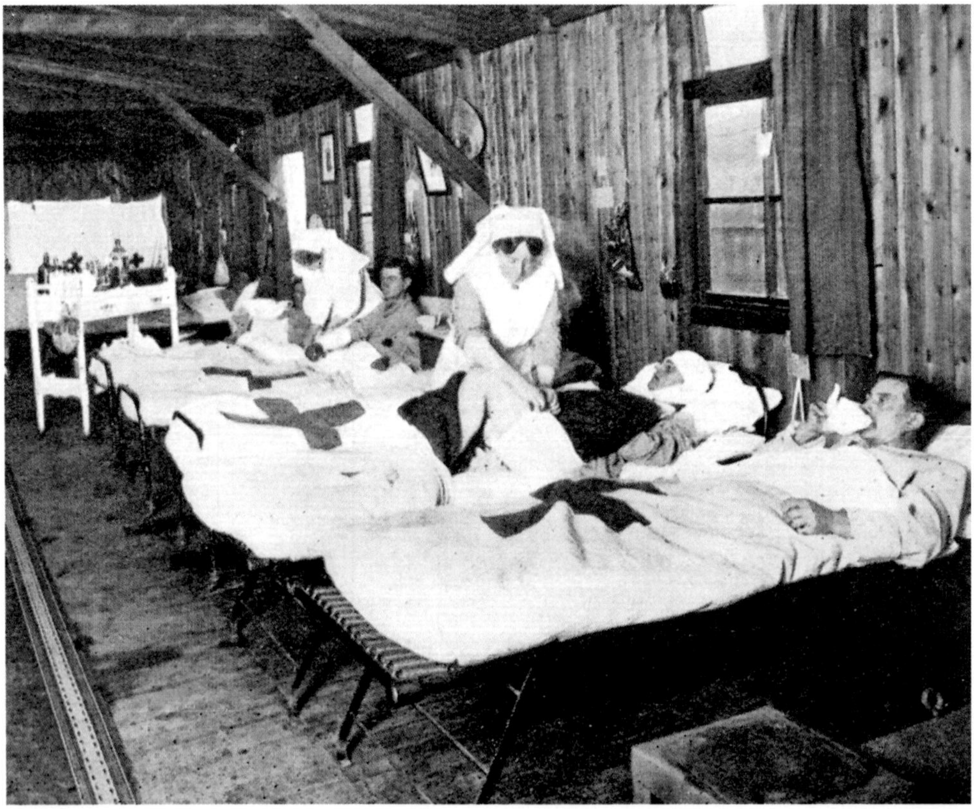

A Casualty Clearing Station.

the Army Service Corps. The job of the CCSs was to treat a man sufficiently for his return to duty or, in most cases, to enable him to be evacuated to a Base Hospital. A CCS was not the place for a long-term stay.

CCSs were generally located on or near railway lines, to facilitate movement of casualties from the battlefield and on to the hospitals. Although they were quite large, CCSs moved quite frequently, especially in the wake of the great German attacks in the spring of 1918 and the victorious Allied advance in the summer and autumn of that year. Many CCSs moved into Belgium and Germany with the army of occupation in 1919. The locations of wartime CCSs can often be identified today from the cluster of military cemeteries that surrounded them.

The British 63rd Casualty Clearing Station was at Senlis for twelve days in August 1918 and it was here that Thomas Higgins died on 3 August. He is buried in Senlis French National Cemetery (Plot II.E.87). There are now over one hundred 1914-18 British war casualties commemorated in this French military cemetery. The majority belonged to the 15th (Scottish) and 34th Divisions, who fell in July and August 1918. Thomas was awarded the Victory Medal and the British War Medal for his active service in France.

William Valentine Kemp

20705 Private

1st Battalion Essex Regiment
88th Brigade 29th Division
Formerly 3/7569 Norfolk Regiment

Died at sea at Gallipoli 13 August 1915, aged 18

Both Henry William Kemp and his wife Sarah Jane came from Norfolk to the Parish of St Andrew's in Nuthurst, West Sussex, towards the end of the 19th Century. Their elder son, Henry Laurence, was born in Roffey. However in the following year, 1897, they were living in Warnham where their second son, William Valentine, was born. He was christened on 28 March 1897 at St Margaret's. At this stage Henry Kemp was working as a domestic coachman, but little more is known of their time here. By the time of the 1911 Census Sarah Kemp is described as a widow. She had been born in Sculthorpe in north Norfolk and had moved back to Fakenham nearby, perhaps to be near her family. Both the boys went with her. Henry Laurence was working as an American oil carter and William Valentine as a printer's labourer.

When war broke out William Valentine Kemp, only 17, enlisted at Tottenham in Middlesex. He joined the Norfolk Regiment as a Private soon after. It appears that he first served in France from 3 December 1914, but in early 1915 he was transferred to the 1st Battalion Essex Regiment. The reason for this is not known but it is possible that he was injured.

In January 1915 the Essex Regiment moved to Banbury and came under orders of the 88th Brigade of the 29th Division. On 21 March 1915 they sailed from Avonmouth for Gallipoli, going via Egypt and Mudros. The battalion took part in Sir Ian Hamilton's major attack in April 1915. They landed at Cape Helles on 25 April and engaged in various actions against the Turkish Army including the First, Second and Third Battles of Krithia, the Battle of Gully Ravine, and the Battle of Krithia Vineyard. Private Kemp may have been involved in these attacks and indeed in the final assault which began on 6/7 August. He was drowned on 13 August, only 18 years old. His body was never recovered and his memorial has been placed on Panel 144-150 or 229-233 on the Helles Memorial at Gallipoli. He is also remembered on the war memorials at Fakenham, Norfolk.

Private William Valentine Kemp was awarded three medals, the 1914-15 Star, the Victory Medal and the British War Medal in commemoration of his war service.

The war memorial in the town of Fakenham, Norfolk.

James William Miles

200247 Lance Corporal

1/4TH BATTALION (TF) ROYAL SUSSEX REGIMENT
160TH BRIGADE 53RD (WELSH) DIVISION

Killed in action in Palestine
6 November 1917, aged 25

Frank Alfred Miles

G/7473 Private

8TH (SERVICE) BATTALION
QUEEN'S OWN (ROYAL WEST KENT REGIMENT)
72ND BRIGADE 24TH DIVISION
FORMERLY 1732 1/4TH BATTALION (TF)
ROYAL SUSSEX REGIMENT

Died of wounds in Béthune 16 April 1917, aged 20

At the outbreak of war James William (always known as William) was living with his family in Friday Street. His father, also James William, was born in Itchingfield and his mother, Margaret Jane (known as Jane) was a Warnham girl. Also in the house were his two sisters and younger brother.

The mother of James William Senior had died when he was quite young and his father, William, had married a widow, Eliza Brooker, who had brought an assortment of children with her – an 18 year old illegitimate son (one of two children she had given birth to who had her maiden name of Steer), and four Brooker children, two boys and two girls from her first marriage to Sam Brooker. In 1871 they are recorded as living at Parbrook where William was a farm worker and with the addition of two more children from this marriage the house, probably a farm worker's cottage, was soon overflowing. It must have been something of a relief to his eldest son, James William (father of our soldiers) to move out into the small household of his employer where he and a young co-worker both lodged with Walter and Ann Peskett at Southlands Farm, Adversane.

By 1891 James William Junior has married his wife Jane and they had set up house in Goose Green. Two children were born there – James William (William) in 1891 and Celia in 1894. They moved for a year or two to Slinfold where Frank was born in 1897 and then into 49 St Leonards Road in Horsham where Daisy the youngest was born in 1901. James, the father, worked for some time as a navvy and then reverted to agricultural work and the family moved back to Warnham where they lived in Friday Street. Having lost a child in infancy, they were hit very hard in 1917 when they lost both their sons in the war.

James William (our soldier) – who was always called William in an attempt to avoid some of the confusion caused by the 19th century fashion for naming sons after their fathers – on leaving school started work on a farm and became a stockman. As a teenager he was active in the village, was a member of the committee of the Athletic Sports and, with his friend, Alfred Comper Yates, became a keen bell ringer. At the outbreak of war at the age of 22, he enlisted at Horsham with the 1/4th Battalion Royal Sussex Regiment together with many of his local friends. After training with the battalion in Cambridge and Bedford, he went with them to Gallipoli in July 1915. They arrived on 8 August and William was wounded at Suvla Bay in mid-August in the battle in which Jack Charman was killed. He was taken to hospital on Lemnos which was the main military hospital for the peninsula and later transported back to England for convalescence.

Wounded troops being evacuated from Suvla Bay.

The County Times in October 1915 printed a letter from Private A F Mansbridge of the 1/4th Sussex written on 14 September. The following extract gives an impression of the life of these young men and tells of the very poor communication. In France letters and parcels arrived from home within several days. It seems Private Mansbridge had arrived with the second wave of troops of the 1/4th Battalion who had not yet seen action. The first batch, including the Miles brothers, had arrived from Alexandria on 8 August.

> *A few more lines to let you know I'm still alright. I haven't gone up to the firing line yet but expect to very shortly. We left Alexandria over a week ago, and are now on an island* [Lemnos] *properly cut off from the outside world. My chum, Miles,* [William Miles] *from Warnham has been wounded. He is in a hospital here. He had almost recovered and then got dysentery very badly too, the doctor looked pretty straight about him so they told me. I went over to see him on Sunday, but he had been moved to another tent, I couldn't find out which one . . . There are quite a number of our chaps in the camp I'm in so I am more at home here as the saying is. I expect you hear more of our casualties than we do, but there will be a lot of Horsham lads missing at the finish . . . Grapes grow in the fields here, also tomatoes and melons and cotton. It's a job to get water though. I get about three washes a week unless I go bathing, but it's a little too cold for me, being only a novice at bathing in open water. It's no good sending anything out to me as I've given up any hopes of receiving any letter or anything else from home. All the fellows are the same. A few stray ones come along sometimes though. I'm about fed up with writing and getting no replies so this is the last I'm sending before I hear from someone. We had a rumour of peace. I wish it was all over today. I guess we shall appreciate old England home if we ever get there. It's rougher here than in France I might tell you.*

Captain F W Paddon MC.

In December 1915 the 1/4th were evacuated from the peninsula and sent to Egypt where they became part of the Egyptian Frontier Force and indeed stayed in the Middle East until 1918 during which time most of the men were given no home leave. After his recovery, William joined them there and for most of 1916 they had a relatively uneventful time. Their main assignment was to keep the Turks from invading from the East and to guard the vital artery of the Suez Canal. In December 1916 the battalion took part in a campaign to drive the Turks from the Sinai desert. Apart from this they had a fairly quiet period in the desert and were able to enjoy themselves some of the time. They wrote home that camels were tricky creatures and not so tractable as the horses and cows they had left in Sussex, though Captain F W Paddon MC, a Canadian serving with the 1/4th Sussex, seems to have his under control.

The 1/4th moved on to Palestine early in 1917 and took part in all three battles of Gaza. It was in Egypt that William had met up again with his old friend from Warnham, Alfred Comper Yates. But their enjoyment was short lived as tragically William and Alfred were both killed in the Third Battle of Gaza on 6 November 1917. This is recorded in more detail in the story of Alfred Comper Yates. Both soldiers are commemorated in the 'Great War Memorial Book of Church Bellringers' held in the ringing chamber of St Paul's Cathedral where they are erroneously described as being from the Horsham rather than Warnham.

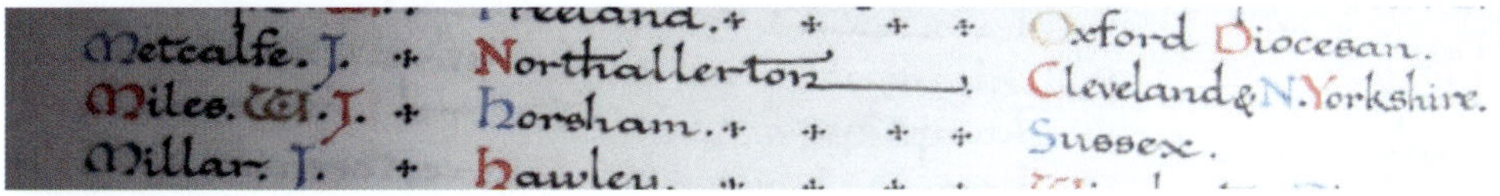

William Miles' entry in the Great War Memorial Book of Church Bellringers.

The Vicar wrote in the Parish Magazine in January 1918:

> *Yet three more names we have to add, alas, to the list of those who have fallen in the war. Two of these, Alfred Yates and William Miles, had lived all their lives among us. They were of us; bright, warm-hearted lads whom it was good to know. We shall miss their cheery faces. We are proud of them, for we feel that they died as they had lived – ready and anxious to do their best. A memorial service was held for them on the 6th December. We think of the families upon which the sorrow has fallen so heavily and we offer them our sympathy in their trouble.*

1/4th Royal Sussex on the march in Palestine.

A Group of 4th Royal Sussex at Bedford before leaving for Gallipoli May 1915.

William was awarded the 1914-15 Star together with the Victory and British War Medals and he is buried in in the Beersheba War Cemetery (Plot G 64) together with his friend Alfred Yates and 1,240 other British and Commonwealth soldiers. The cemetery is on the edge of the Negev Desert, 75 km south-west of Jerusalem.

The second son of the Miles family, Frank Alfred, born in Slinfold early in 1897, and baptised there on 13 March, was only 17 in 1914. He too enlisted in the 4th Battalion Royal Sussex at Horsham in August 1914 when he was two years under age, no doubt wanting to keep up with his older brother. After training in Cambridge and Bedford he also went with the battalion to Gallipoli. This must have been an anxious time for James and Jane and their two daughters and it would have been a great relief after hearing the terrible stories of the slaughter at Suvla Bay, to know that both their sons had survived, though William had been wounded.

As we know, William after recuperation rejoined the Royal Sussex in Egypt, but for some unknown reason, Frank transferred to the 8th Battalion Queen's Own (Royal West Kent Regiment). While his brother was fighting in the Second Battle of Gaza, he was involved in hostilities in France. The 8th Battalion became part of the 72nd Brigade of the 24th Division and after some time in Shoreham and Worthing, left for Boulogne on 30 August 1915. Frank was still in Gallipoli at this time and probably joined them early in 1916.

We do not know exactly where Frank Miles was wounded but have accounts of heavy and concentrated shellfire being poured on to the 8th Battalion, reaching even what had been felt to be sheltered positions. On 15 April 'C' Company HQ, which was sited in a tunnel, received a direct hit from a German shell destroying the dugout and killing or severely wounding those within. On the 16th there is a report of deaths in a trench which had recently been taken from the Germans and was being heavily bombarded. There were other bombardments and skirmishes taking place all around and in one of these Frank Miles was mortally wounded. Béthune at this stage in the war was still relatively unscathed and was serving as a respite and hospital centre. Frank was taken to the 33rd Casualty Clearing Station in Béthune where he died of wounds on 16 April and he was buried in Béthune Town Cemetery (Plot VI.D.18). For his service in the Balkans and on the Western Front he received the 1914-15 Star together with the Victory Medal and the British War Medal.

Again the Vicar, conscientious over these deaths, wrote in the Parish Magazine of July 1917:

> *We omitted to record last month the death in action of Frank Miles. He was killed while fighting in France. He was one of our own boys, a good lad, well spoken of by all who knew him and he was a good soldier. A memorial service was held for him here. We thought of the lad whom we had known and we committed his soul to the safe keeping of His Heavenly Father. Our sympathy is with the parents and the family.*

This death was the first of the two great blows for James and Jane who lost both their sons within six months.

George Henry Miller

TF/6527 Private

1/5th (Cinque Ports) Battalion (TF)
Royal Sussex Regiment
Pioneer Battalion 48th (South Midland) Division
Formerly 1/4th Battalion (TF)
Royal Sussex Regiment
160th Brigade 53rd (Welsh) Division

Killed in action at Battle of Ancre
14 November 1916, aged 18

George and Louisa Miller moved into Warnham at the end of the 19th Century. George was born in 1857 in Roffey near Horsham and Louisa was from Ifield. They lived at 4 Sunnyside, Friday Street (now numbers 46-54). George was employed as a brickfield worker. Also living there was a nephew, Charles, who worked as a garden boy.

Their son, George Henry, was born some time in 1897 and there is reference to a second living child in the 1911 Census, but no record of him/her living at this time with the family. George attended Warnham School and was then employed in the gardens at Warnham Court by Mr C J Lucas, JP until war broke out.

George Henry Miller can have been barely 18 years old when like a number of others from the village he enlisted in the 1/4th Battalion Royal Sussex Regiment which mobilised on 5 August as part of the Home Counties Division. After a period of training the battalion was attached to the Mediterranean Expeditionary Force. In 1915 they were posted to Cambridge in preparation for the journey to the Eastern Mediterranean and Gallipoli. George arrived in the Balkans on 14 September 1915 but it seems that he was very soon stricken with dysentery and sent to Malta to recover. On leaving there for Liverpool he contracted enteric fever and spent several months in hospital and in convalescent homes.

Sunnyside today – now 46-54 Friday Street.

On his recovery Private Miller was transferred to the 1/5th Battalion Royal Sussex which had been fighting in Flanders throughout 1916. This was a pioneer battalion. Men were often assigned to the Pioneers because of their reduced medical category and given George Miller's history of illness since Gallipoli, this seems very possible. These men carried out a whole range of defence works duties. These included road and railway building/repair, moving ammunition and stores, loading and unloading ships and trains and even burial duties. During the war there was a much heavier reliance on field work. Engineers alone could not meet the heavy demand, while rifle men were always needed at the front. Therefore, pioneer battalions were raised to meet the needs of both and trained to support engineers and infantry.

Pioneers sweeping mud from a road near St Julien.

The battalion took part in the Battle of the Somme from 1 July onwards. George Miller arrived in October as the last engagements of the Somme were being fought along the River Ancre. His battalion was involved in the Battle for Ancre Heights which took place between 1 October and 11 November, a fierce struggle which was frequently interrupted by terrible weather. The final Battle of Ancre began on 13 November. Private George Henry Miller was killed while with a working party on the second day. The objectives of the battle were not achieved; only in the marshy lowlands near the river were gains made, and these at great cost. On 19 November, with winter rain again pouring on the battlefield, offensive operations were called off. So ended the Battle of the Somme.

In the Gazette it was reported that writing to his parents Captain Rose said that Miller was killed while with a working party, death being instantaneous. He was a good lad and he (the Captain) was very fond of him and sympathised sincerely with the parents. The WSCT also recorded that his death was the result of a shell.

George Henry Miller is buried in Plot E 21 in Martinpuich British Cemetery

He was awarded two medals, the Victory Medal and the British War Medal in commemoration of his war service.

William Charles Frederick Morris

137060 Gunner

12TH SIEGE BATTERY
ROYAL GARRISON ARTILLERY
FORMERLY 1832 3/1ST LONDON
HEAVY BATTERY ROYAL GARRISON ARTILLERY

Died of wounds in Rouen
20 December 1916, aged 27

In 1881 the headmaster of Warnham School, living in the School House, was William Morris, a certificated elementary school teacher born in Walcote, Leicestershire. He was in fact the first headmaster and had opened the new school in 1873, gradually building up the number of pupils and remained there until his retirement. In 1881 he was 36 and his wife, Harriet, was 28. Ten years later they are recorded, still in the School House, with the addition of one baby boy, William Charles Frederick, born in 1890. This little boy seems to have been an only child, most unusual for Victorian times. Also in the household was the headmaster's niece, Anne Billson, aged 28, who was working in the school as an assistant teacher.

The Old School in Warnham which opened in 1873.

By 1901 William had retired from school mastering, although he was only 56. He and his wife and son were living at 17 Wellesley Road, Low Leyton, Essex. William died in 1910 and the widowed Harriet moved with her son to 63 Leybourn Road, Leyton, Essex. Here they shared a fairly substantial house with Harriet's younger sister, Florence and her husband and son, Arthur and Clifford Orton. William was now 21 and working as an assurance clerk, probably in the City of London.

In the summer of 1914, when he was 24, William married his 22 year old girl friend, Annie Elizabeth Jones, a shorthand-typist, maybe in his firm. William enlisted that same summer, at Offord Road, North London and joined the Royal Garrison Artillery. Annie continued to live with her parents and younger sister at 17 Belgrave Road, Wanstead.

Having joined up as a Gunner in the Royal Artillery, young William spent a few months training in England. At the time of his death he was recorded as being part of the 12th Siege Battery, Heavy Battery Royal Garrison Artillery. This unit went out to France on 8 March 1915 but as William did not receive the 1914-15 Star he must have transferred to the 12th some time in 1916. What happened to him from early 1915 until his death 21 months later it has not been possible to trace but as he died from wounds in December 1916, he may well have been fighting in the Somme battles. The Siege Batteries were equipped with heavy howitzers and were most often employed in destroying or neutralising the enemy artillery as well as putting destructive fire down on strongpoints, dumps, stores, roads and railways behind enemy lines.

British Troops moving a gun.

Rouen was some miles behind the line and was used to accommodate men, supplies and hospitals much of which was stationed on the southern outskirts of the city. These included a base supply depot and the 3rd Echelon of General Headquarters. Almost all of the hospitals at Rouen remained there for the whole of the war. They included eight general, five stationary, one British Red Cross and one labour hospital, and No 2 Convalescent Depot.

Several of the dead from these hospitals were buried in other cemeteries, but the great majority were taken to the city cemetery of St Sever and in September 1916 it was found necessary to begin an extension. It seems that William Morris was taken to one of these hospitals in Rouen after he was wounded and that he died there. The young Annie had lost her husband and his widowed mother, Harriet, had lost her only child and all they had left was his Victory Medal and the British War Medal. William lies in the St Sever Cemetery Extension, Rouen (Plot O.111.J.1).

John Edward Campbell Muggeridge

242006 Private

1/6th Battalion (TF)
South Staffordshire Regiment
137th Brigade
46th (North Midland) Division

Killed at Lievin 22 April 1917, aged 32

In 1871 Moses and Harriett Muggeridge were living at Little Malt Mays, Warnham with their five children, the eldest of whom was Harriett. She married a William Muggeridge by whom she had two children, Florence and James. By 1881 they were living at Durfold Farm House, Warnham where William worked as an agricultural labourer. William died in 1890 aged 46 as did Harriet's mother aged 66, leaving Harriett a widow and the mother of four children, one of whom was John Edward Campbell, born on the 1st May 1884 in Warnham, where he was later baptised.

In 1891 Harriett was registered as a farmer and head of the family at Ridge Farm, Honey Lane, Rowhook where she was joined by her father Moses, two brothers and Harry Welch, all four being agricultural labourers. In 1911 Harriett, now 60 years old, was still working as a farmer at the same place, helped by three of her four sons, John, William and James. There were also two grandsons, probably James's sons as he was a widower, and Harriett's father Moses aged 85, a great age for those days.

When war broke out in 1914 John was 30 and living in Ockley. At some time he enlisted in the Army, but we don't know where or on which date. We do know he joined the 1/6th Battalion, South Staffordshire Regiment, a Territorial Force unit of the North Midland Division. The Division suffered heavy casualties in the 1916 Battle of the Somme and the attack on Gommecourt leading to the sacking of its commander by General Haig. His replacement set about improving the Division's tarnished reputation which was achieved in 1918 when it made a daring and successful crossing of the St Quentin Canal, a feat which was recognised as a Battle Honour.

The 1/6th South Staffs War Diary for Wednesday 18 April 1917 records that they were manning a support trench in Lievin, south east of Béthune in northern France. On Thursday they were in the front line, on Friday they were holding the line and being shelled by German guns, but there were no reported casualties for the month to date. Patrols were sent out on Saturday 'but no special incidents occurred'. On Sunday 22 April preparations were made for an attack the next day and, although the diary records no casualties, the Commonwealth War Graves Commission records that John died on that Sunday. The attack took place on Monday, but was unsuccessful. The War Diary records the death of two other ranks together with seven wounded and one missing in the attack, but the April summary records just one other rank killed, 32 wounded and one missing, at odds with the daily records. The contradictions serve to remind us of the confusion, and even chaos that could occur in the heat of battle and its aftermath.

John is buried in the Canadian Cemetery No 2, Neuville Saint Vaast, plot 6 A 22. He was awarded the British War Medal and the Victory Medal.

Charles Munday

4/2820 Private

1/4th Battalion (TF) Royal Sussex Regiment
160th Brigade 53rd (Welsh) Division

Died of dysentery in Egypt 18 May 1916, aged 32

Charles Munday came from a family very much rooted in Warnham and the local area. His father James was born in Rudgwick, Sussex in 1851 and in 1871 he married Mary Nightingale of Tanners in Warnham. The men of both their families were described in 19th century censuses as general or agricultural labourers and moved with their families around the Sussex and Surrey borders finding employment in various farms. The young couple lived at Wotton in Surrey and at Cider Mill Farm in Warnham, bringing up eight children (of whom seven survived) including Charles, their youngest son, who was born in Horsham on 5 February 1884. Parish records show that unusually, he was not baptised until he was 24 years old, on 3 January 1909 at St Margaret's Church, Warnham.

Chapel Cottage.

The Census returns of 1901 and 1911 record him as working as a general labourer and living at home with his parents, James and Mary, at 1 Byfleets Lane, now Chapel Cottage. Before he enlisted in the Army he was working in the gardens at Graylands near Warnham, the home of Duncan Boyd Wallis, whose story is told elsewhere in this book.

Charles's name appears in the Warnham Parish Magazine in 1915 as one of the local men who had volunteered for Active Service and, as he was a young bachelor with no family responsibilities, by responding to the call up campaign he was probably caught up in the patriotic mood of the day as well as the prospect of a change from uneventful rural village life.

Like many others from the village, he joined the 1/4th Battalion of the Royal Sussex Regiment and was part of the ill-fated campaign in which the Allied forces landed at Suvla Bay on the Aegean Sea, on 8 August 1915, to launch a fresh attack against Turkish and German forces on the Gallipoli Peninsula. A fuller account of the campaign can be found under the entry for Jack Charman.

Private Munday was lucky to survive the landing as he was saved from drowning by two sailors who jumped into the sea as he was sinking for the second time. He narrowly escaped death sometime after, when a bursting shell killed his mate who was right at his side in a trench. Although Private Munday was fortunate to survive the horrors of the fighting at Gallipoli, he was one of the hundreds of thousands of soldiers who contracted dysentery, which caused epidemic sickness on all sides because of the insanitary conditions. Disease was rife through the hot summer and bitingly cold winter on the Peninsula, with polluted water and swarms of flies carrying deadly bacteria from unburied corpses to the soldiers' food.

Due to heavy casualties from combat, disease and severe weather conditions the 1/4th Battalion were evacuated from Gallipoli to Egypt in December 1915. It was there that Charles Munday died on 18 May the following year, from 'syncope following dysentery', according to a newspaper report of his death, submitted by his parents and printed in the West Sussex County Times in 1916. 'Syncope' is the medical term for fainting, or loss of consciousness and it seems likely that Private Munday never recovered his health after his gruelling experiences in Gallipoli.

He was awarded the 1914-15 Star, the British War Medal and the Victory Medal, which were applied for by his mother in 1919.

His name appears under the heading of Territorials on a handwritten 'Roll of Honour' dated May 1915, now in the WSRO. Such a list was usually reserved for those who had given their lives for their country 'Being the names of those of the Parish of Warnham Sussex who are actively serving their King and Country'.

Albert John Nightingale

175891 Sapper

254TH TUNNELLING COMPANY,
ROYAL ENGINEERS

Killed in action near Cambrai
30 November 1917, aged 33

Albert John Nightingale was born in Warnham in 1884, the son of John Nightingale and his wife Mary, who died at the very young age of 22 the following year. Her burial on 15 May 1885 is recorded in the Warnham Parish Registers, which contain many entries relating to this very old Warnham family going back to the late 16th century.

The census of 1891 shows John, an agricultural labourer and widower of 39 living with his only child, Albert John, aged six years old in Friday Street, Warnham. Ten years later, however, father John was still living in Friday Street, working as a labourer, but Albert, now aged 16, must have left home, as there appears to be no trace of him in the census of 1901, his whereabouts and subsequent history up to 1911 being unknown.

Albert appeared again in the census return of 1911 where he was recorded as a clay miner in a brickworks and living in shared accommodation at Shakespeare Avenue, Willesden in London with his wife and daughter. When he was only 19 he had married his wife, Gertrude, who was three years older than him and came from Guildford. They now had a daughter Emily who was five years old and had also been born in Guildford. The census returns are the only reference to this marriage and Albert's service records have no mention of a marriage, wife or family, even giving his status as being single, so his relationship with Gertrude may not have been formalised by marriage, or the couple separated, with no further contact.

On 21 August 1916, Albert enlisted at Westminster, London, in the Royal Engineers. Service records show that he was living just off the Harrow Road and that his occupation was given as a miner, although his experience in the brickworks was probably limited to digging out clay, rather than tunnelling and extracting mineral or coal. His rank was that of a Sapper, the same as a Private in the Army and his pay was at the rate of 2/2d a day.

He joined the 254th Tunnelling Company, arriving in France barely six weeks after he had enlisted and it is likely that they were operating in the Givenchy area of northern France, involved in tunnelling operations in the Flanders and the Ypres sector.

Sappers were military engineers who were trained in the basic applications of the Corps of Royal Engineers of the time, such as constructing defensive positions, bridging, mining and setting explosives. By the end of 1917, when Albert was killed, the offensive tunnelling operations of earlier years, such as mining to lay explosives and digging trenches was no longer strategically essential, so the tunnellers were used to dig out extensive networks of deep dugouts to shelter the British troops, something that had been lacking until that date, contrasting with the well-established network of German dugouts and bunkers. The work was still largely carried out on the front line and would have been in claustrophobic and dangerous conditions. Working in waterlogged ground, the tunnellers had to dig particularly deep in order to construct shellproof dugouts. The threat of a tunnel collapse, entombing the soldiers, was ever present, especially as a result of German mining and artillery, and it was hoped that a new weapon, the tank, which was being employed in large numbers for the first time at the Battle of Cambrai in November 1917, would break the deadlock of trench warfare.

The 254th Tunnelling Company were operating in the Cambrai region and Sapper Albert Nightingale was wounded in August and killed in action on 30 November 1917, aged 33. On that day, in retaliation to the British tank offensive ten days earlier, the German forces led a massive counter attack, using intensive artillery fire and new ‘stormtrooper’ units. Casualties on both sides during the battle were over 40,000 but the trench stalemate had been broken for the first time since 1914.

Albert’s service records gave The Stores, Warnham, as his ‘discharge’ address, where his aunt, Fanny Carter lived and worked as a cook. This establishes a strong thread of evidence that the Nightingales were associated with the Society of Dependents, or ‘Cokelers’, a religious sect who lived and worshipped in the areas of Warnham, Loxwood and Northchapel. They owned and ran Warnham Stores which was a large, general shop business, with a bakery, joinery and drapery in the centre of the village in Church Street.

In 1919, the official Army records for the next of kin for Sapper Albert Nightingale show that his father John had moved to Broadbridge Heath, while his aunt, Fanny Carter, still lived at Warnham Stores and his grandmother, Mrs Holloway, lived in Holly Cottage, Toat Hill, Slinfold. The form and declaration was completed and signed by Henry Piper, the Minister of the Dependents, a well-known and respected elder of the sect in Warnham.

Photograph of Warnham Stores and staff. There is no evidence of how Alice Carter (wearing apron in middle of right hand group) may have been related to Fanny Carter, Albert's aunt.

Albert's aunt, Fanny Carter, was the person to whom his personal effects were to be forwarded, but official records show that there were none to be passed on. Albert was awarded the British War Medal and the Victory Medal, and Fanny acknowledged receipt of them in March 1922.

Sapper Albert John Nightingale is buried at Vlamertinghe New Military Cemetery, Belgium: Grave Reference IXA 30.

Cadwaladr James Ottley

G/2191 Private

7th (Service) Battalion
Queen's (Royal West Surrey Regiment)
55th Brigade 18th Division

Killed in action in Flanders
21 January 1916, aged 20

The Ottley family were Londoners, most of the men working as general labourers in the 19th century but Charles Ottley, born in Battersea in 1864, improved his future by learning to be a carpenter when he left school. He later found a job in Sussex, married a girl from Slinfold and set up house in Goose Green. Charles and his wife Margaret filled the little cottage with a large family. They had ten children, including twins and at least the two eldest, Christopher Charles and Cadwaladr James (born in Warnham on 31 May 1894) became carpenters. The 1911 census describes them as Estate or Domestic Carpenters so they most likely were employed by one of the big estates in Warnham.

Cadwaladr, who was born in Warnham on 18 September 1895, did not use his rather difficult, and frequently misspelled, old Welsh name and was generally known as Jim. The County Times of 26 February 1916, when reporting his death, says that before the war Jim had worked as a gardener, first for Mr Maudsley of Warnham Court, then at Broomhall and later under Felix Edwards at Warnham Lodge. This conflicts with the census record which clearly shows Jim, his brother Christopher and their father all as carpenters.

Kitchener's call for his New Army raised 100,000 volunteers in two weeks. On 28 August the situation in France led to his call for a second 100,000 volunteers, referred to as the K2 battalions. Jim enlisted in September 1914 and was posted to the 7th Battalion Queen's (Royal West Surrey Regiment) where he joined 'B' Company. The 7th, a Service Battalion, became part of 55th Brigade. Around this time his parents and younger siblings had moved from Goose Green and were living at 4 Percy Road in Horsham. Christopher, his older brother by one year, had enlisted in the Royal Sussex Regiment at the beginning of the war, but he survived,

After many months of training, 7th Queen's left Codford in Wiltshire, one detachment via transports to Southampton and then to Le Havre aboard the *SS Mount Temple.*

The main body of the battalion travelled to Folkestone via trains and sailed on the *SS Victoria* arriving in Boulogne on 27 July 1915. Their strength was 33 officers and 947 other ranks, including Jim Ottley.

In early August 1915 the battalion was on the fairly quiet stretch of frontline that in 11 months' time would be the scene of bitter fighting. For now it was to be the battalion's learning ground. In spite of the relative peace, the battalion still suffered some casualties in the four remaining months of 1915. The next few months over the winter and spring were to serve as the build-up for the great Battle of the Somme.

The war diaries for January 1916 [WO 95/2051/1] tell of a quiet time for the battalion though there was spasmodic shelling and some casualties. They were relieved on 7 August and spent the next week safely and relatively comfortably in billets in Ville-sur-Ancre. On 15 August they returned to the line in the sub-sector of Bécourt and for the next few days there was an exchange of trench mortars and mines. On the morning of 20 August the enemy fired three mines and four heavy trench mortar bombs but there were no casualties. On the next day the writer records the enemy being active with field guns and trench mortars. The battalion was relieved on 23 January and returned to the billets. The diary writes of much constructive work being undertaken by the battalion during this moderately quiet period – digging a new communication trench 160 yards long and burying a cable of 1,200 yards. It records one officer wounded, three other ranks killed and seven wounded. One of these must have been the 20 year old Jim Ottley who seems to have been very unlucky to have lost his life on 21 January when things were fairly quiet.

His platoon commander, 2nd Lieutenant G S Dandridge, writing to his parents two days later, said:

> *It is with much regret that I have to tell you how your son was killed. A nice quiet lad, very willing with his work, much liked by both officers and comrades and any who came in contact with him, I myself am most sorry to have lost him from my platoon. The men of the section to which he belonged were so much attached to him that they have written a little note among themselves to send you their sympathy for your and their loss. He was killed while on guard duty two nights ago by a rifle grenade, the grenade bursting so close to him that it mortally wounded him and he died in a few minutes. He was hit in the right side very severely, the same grenade also wounding another of my men, but only very slightly. They are beastly things and if ever they fall close they usually do some damage. I offer my sincerest sympathy and sorrow and know that you will keenly feel this loss.*

The 'little note' referred to was printed in the County Times in February 1916. By modern standards it reads as being over sentimental and emotional, but it reflects the feelings and views of the time and the constant effort to justify the wasteful and seemingly pointless carnage.

> *Private Ottley's comrades in No 8 Platoon, in a letter to his father said: He was always a good soldier and it must be some consolation to you in your great bereavement to know that he died in the service of his king and country . . . Your son always appeared to be a God-fearing man. I, the writer, can truthfully say this, because it has been my good fortune to be one of his colleagues and on several occasions we had quiet conversations. What better death for an ardent soldier of God, of King and of Country could there be, than to die on the battlefield whilst pursuing a work, a titanic struggle . . . We miss him greatly. He was always so popular with all, ever ready and willing to obey those superior. It did not seem to be true when marching back to billets, after having been relieved from the firing line, that we had left 'Little Jim' slumbering peacefully in the graveyard behind the trenches. His wounded body lies alongside many brave lads who in the prime of life were called upon to make the great sacrifice. Heroes everyone, who, like Jim, were cheerful under difficulties and great hardships and calm in the face of danger. His life has not been taken in vain. Although his part is done we who are left are more determined to carry on and finish the great task which has swallowed up so many of our comrades.*

On 26 January, the sergeant of the stretcher bearer section of the 7th Queens, enclosed photographs found on the deceased and wrote

> *'We all wish to express our sincere sympathy with you.'*

The Rev L Jeeves in a letter of regret and sympathy said:

> *I went up to the trenches and buried him this morning in the quiet spot where with other heroes, he was laid to rest. Two of the senior officers were present together with a large number of his comrades. He was always a good soldier and it must be some consolation to you in your great bereavement to know that he died in the service of his king and country.*

The County Times also printed a little poem sent to them by 'his sorrowing Dad and Mum in loving memory of little Jim':

A devoted son, a faithful friend,
One of the best that God could lend:
He bravely answered duty's call.
His life he gave for one and all.
But the unknown grave is the bitterest blow,
None but an aching heart can know.

Let us hope they were comforted by the fact that he was later remembered in a marked grave when he was reburied nearby in the Norfolk Cemetery, Bécordel-Bécourt (Plot I.A.32) though it was still a long way from home and unlikely that they ever visited. Jim was awarded the 1914-15 Star together with the Victory Medal and the British War Medal.

The Vicar wrote in the Parish Magazine:

It is with profound regret that we have just heard of the death in action of J W Ottley [should be C J Ottley], *better known amongst us as Jim Ottley. The Chaplain, his Lieutenant and some of his comrades have written, all bearing the highest testimony to the character of this young friend of ours. We knew him well, and we were all drawn to him by his gentle, unassuming ways as a boy in school. As a member of our choir and as a soldier he had but one idea, and that was to do his duty to the best of his power. We are sorry for our loss and we offer our sincerest sympathy to his parents and to his brothers and sisters.*

Horsham War Memorial.

A memorial service was held in Warnham on 9 February and Jim Ottley is also commemorated on the Horsham War Memorial.

Frederick Picton

52825 Private

21ST (SERVICE) BATTALION (6TH CITY)
MANCHESTER REGIMENT
91ST BRIGADE 7TH DIVISION

Killed in Belgium 24 October 1917, aged 19

Frederick was born in Great Missenden in Buckinghamshire in 1898, the sixth child of William and Kate Picton. His father William was a labourer for a pheasant breeder at the time, and both he and Kate were born and brought up in Missenden. However, sometime in 1904 or 1905 the family now with nine children moved to Warnham where William was employed as a gamekeeper.

William and Kate had at least two more children in Warnham and their large family lived at Old Barn Cottage in Kingsfold. In 1911 Frederick was 13 and still at school in Warnham, whilst his two older brothers Frank and Albert were farm workers, which is almost certainly the line of work Frederick was to take up shortly after.

Passchendaele, November 1917.

The Parish Magazine notes that at the beginning of the war a Picton from Kingsfold enlisted. We do not know whether this was Frederick or one of his older brothers, but from Frederick's high service number it was probably not him. However from the records we find that he enlisted in Chester so must have moved away from the area, which would explain how he came to join the Manchester Regiment. Unfortunately what we do know for certain is that he was killed in Belgium in 1917. He died just two days before the start of the Second Battle of Passchendaele in which his Battalion was involved, so probably during pre-offensive manoeuvres.

His name is recorded in Belgium on the Tyne Cot Memorial to the missing, so his body was never found, or his grave was lost. Although Frederick had moved away from Warnham his family still lived in the parish, and they ensured his name was added to the Warnham war memorial. Frederick was posthumously awarded the Victory Medal and British War Medal.

Tyne Cot Memorial.

Thomas Peter Reed

PS/1148 Colour Sergeant

19TH (SERVICE) BATTALION (2ND PUBLIC SCHOOLS)
ROYAL FUSILIERS
98TH BRIGADE 33RD DIVISION
FORMERLY OF THE ROYAL MARINES

Died at Warnham 11 April 1915, aged 57

The West Sussex County Times of 17 April 1915, under the heading *A Sergeant's Funeral* reported the burial in Warnham churchyard of Sergeant Thomas Peter Reed of Serapis Cottage, Durfold-hill, Warnham. He was 57 and died of pneumonia on 11 April 1915 while on leave from his unit, the 19th (Service) Battalion (2nd Public Schools) Royal Fusiliers.

Thomas Reed was born in 1858 at Widdington, Essex to a single mother, Susan Barker, and was baptised Thomas Peter Barker on 26 December 1858. His mother married Charles Reed in late 1859 at Widdington but Thomas retained his Barker surname until he enlisted in the Royal Marines sometime between1871 and 1881. He served in the Egyptian campaign in the 1880s, for which he obtained the medal. He was a first class instructor of musketry at Hythe and retired with the Royal Navy Long Service and Good Conduct Medal, for which 15 years' service was the qualifying term. On 13 August 1893 Thomas married Harriet Ann Hunt at Bow. He was a Marine pensioner and worked as a mail clerk with the Patent Agency. At the outbreak of war he promptly re-enlisted and joined the 19th Battalion Royal Fusiliers at Epsom, Surrey. With the rapid expansion of the army from 1914 onwards there was a pressing need for NCOs to lick the volunteers into shape to face the challenges to come. Thomas Reed, with his Royal Marines service, was ready-made for that task. Sadly, he died of pneumonia leaving a widow.

His commanding officer, Lieutenant-Colonel W W Gordon wrote to his widow:

> *I cannot tell you how shocked we all were to hear of your husband, Colour Sergeant Reed's death. I need hardly say that I appreciate very highly the excellent work your husband did in this battalion. All ranks are greatly grieved at your loss and also the loss to the battalion he served so well.*

The battalion was represented at the funeral by a Major, a Company Sergeant Major and two Privates. A splendid cross bore the inscription: *'From Colonel W Woolrige Gordon and the Officers 19th (Service) Battalion Royal Fusiliers'*. It is now broken and lying on the ground north-east of the church, displaying little text. There was also a beautiful wreath from the NCOs and men of 'E' Company. The Vicar, the Reverend Prebendary Bowcott, officiated at the graveside. Mrs Reed was the chief mourner together with various Warnham residents.

He is recorded on the War Memorial as 'CSM Thomas Reed, Royal Fusiliers'. CSM is an abbreviation for Company Sergeant Major, not the Colour Sergeant rank mentioned in his Colonel's eulogy. A CSgt is the senior sergeant in a company; a Colour Sergeant is of lesser importance than a CSM. It is most unlikely that a commanding officer would have used an incorrect rank in writing a condolence letter to a widow. Also, if Thomas Reed had been a CSM his death would have required the presence of the Regimental Sergeant Major at his funeral. The CSM at the funeral was probably Thomas's own. It is most likely that those compiling the War Memorial entry confused CSgt with CSM, something easily done if you are unfamiliar with military ranks and their subtleties. Thomas was not eligible for the War Medal as he had not served overseas in a theatre of war.

As a postscript, the 19th Battalion Royal Fusiliers was raised by the Public Schools and University Men's Force at Epsom on 11 September 1914, one of four Public Schools Battalions. All four battalions were not taken over by the War Office until 1 July 1915. The 19th Battalion was disbanded in 1916, when most other ranks were commissioned, so helping to fill the greatly expanded army's pressing need for leaders. Thirty four men of the battalion were posted to the 12th Battalion Royal Fusiliers in which Cecil Burchett and Albert Charman also served. Sadly these two Warnham lads were both killed – Cecil at Messines in June 1917 and Albert at Passchendaele later that year. Charles Eric Lucas of Warnham Court also served with the 19th Battalion and survived the war.

Albert Wilfred Richards

S.S.4476 Able Seaman

HMS Prince of Wales
Royal Navy

Died 25 June 1916
RN Hospital Plymouth,
aged 20

Albert, or Bertie as he was known to his family, was born in Warnham on 18 May 1896 at Little Chickens Farm, and baptised in St Margaret's Church the following month.

Albert's father James was a farm labourer who was born in Hampshire but settled in Warnham. James married Albert's mother Harriet Francis in Warnham in 1888. She was Warnham born and bred, as were her parents before her. Both James and Harriet had been married before though and already had children from their first marriages, so Albert was born into a rapidly growing family, finally acquiring ten full and step siblings. He was the second youngest of them all.

By 1911 at the age of 14, Albert had left school and found work locally as a domestic gardener. He had probably decided not to follow his father into farm work, but evidently wanted more adventure than just gardening, as before long he had run away to sea. On 7 October 1913 aged 17 he signed up for five years short service with the Royal Navy, but lied about his date of birth by six months so as to appear to be 18. His service record describes him as being 5ft 4in tall with a 35in chest, dark brown hair with brown eyes and a fresh complexion. He also had a distinguishing mole on his left arm.

Albert underwent three months of Naval training at Portsmouth before joining *HMS Prince of Wales* on 4 January 1914 as an Ordinary Seaman. *HMS Prince of Wales* was a London class pre-dreadnought battleship, and in August 1914 her entire class was formed into the 5th Battle Squadron (with the similar Formidable class ships), taking part in the operations to protect the British Expeditionary Force as it crossed the channel. *HMS Prince of Wales* served as the flagship of the squadron, for Rear-Admiral Bernard Currey. She was then used to transfer part of the Portsmouth Battalion of Marines to Ostend during an unsuccessful naval attempt to defend that channel port.

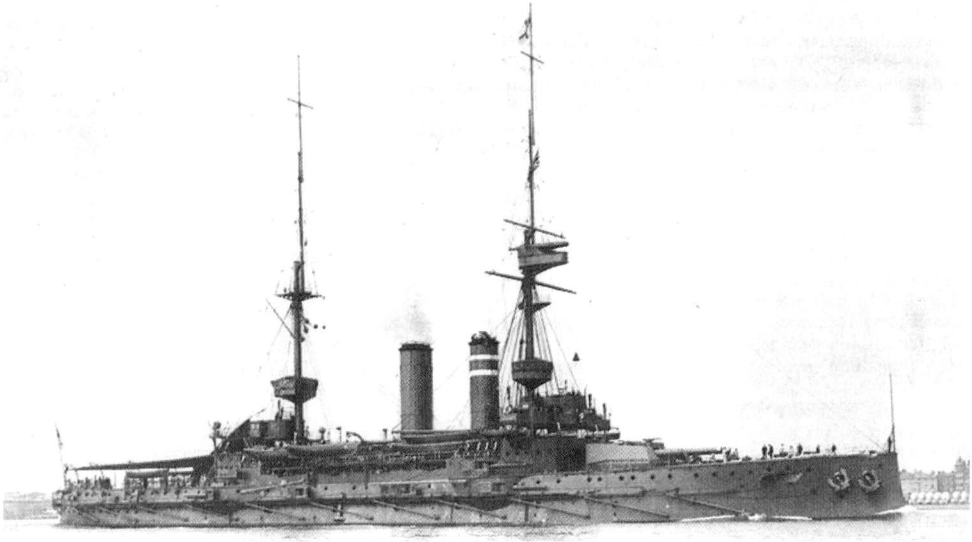

HMS Prince of Wales in 1912.

By February 1915 she was one of only four battleships left with the Channel Fleet. A War Council meeting of 19 March decided to send *HMS Prince of Wales* to the Dardanelles. She arrived in time to take part in the Gallipoli landings on 24 April, helping to transport 1,500 men of the 3rd Australian Brigade.

She was soon moved again. In May 1915 the Italians came into the war. One of the conditions of their entry was that the British would provide them with a battleship squadron to help counter the threat of the Austro-Hungarian Fleet. On 15 May 1915 *Queen, Prince of Wales, Implacable* and *London*, left the Dardanelles, arriving at Taranto in Italy on 27 May.

The Austro-Hungarian threat never materialised but *HMS Prince of Wales* remained in the Adriatic. By August 1915 Albert had obviously proved his worth as he was promoted to Able Seaman. He could easily have ridden out most of the war in the Adriatic as *Prince of Wales* did not leave until April 1917, but in January 1916 Albert was taken ill and sent to hospital in Malta.

In February 1916 he was moved to the transfer station Fort St Angelo in Malta (known as *HMS Egmont*) from where he was sent back to a Naval Hospital in Plymouth. On 25 June 1916 he died from Musculo-skeletal Miliary Tuberculosis, primarily focused in the hip joint. This is a rare form of TB, possibly precipitated by an injury. He was buried in Ford Park Cemetery, Plymouth.

Albert was posthumously awarded the 1914-15 Star, British War Medal and Victory Medal.

Arthur Rush

5371 Trooper

4TH (ROYAL IRISH) DRAGOON GUARDS

2ND CAVALRY BRIGADE 1ST CAVALRY DIVISION

Died from wounds at Mons
24 August 1914, aged 21

Arthur is an enigmatic character, and it has taken some detective work to uncover what little is known of his story.

The listing of 'UK Soldiers died in the Great War' compiled by the government in the early 1920s states that he was born in Kingsfold (part of Warnham Parish), and that he enlisted at Horsham. Unfortunately there is no record of anyone with that name having been born in or around Kingsfold at that time. The only other clue as to his identity comes from The Commonwealth War Graves Commission record of his death which says that his aunt was a 'Mrs Emily Barker of Southwater', presumably his next of kin.

That Arthur was associated with Southwater is confirmed by his name appearing on the original Roll of Honour inside Southwater Church. Emily Barker, whose maiden name was Chantler was born and bred in the area and lived at the Station Stores with her husband, Thomas, until the 1940s. Thomas came from Kings Lynn in Norfolk and his siblings did not move to Sussex, so it would appear Arthur had to have been a blood relative of Emily. Given that her maiden name was not Rush, Arthur's mother therefore must have been one of Emily's sisters.

Emily Barker, née Chantler.

Emily had several sisters, but the only one to have had a child at the time Arthur was born was Patience. Patience was the eldest child in the Chantler family, born in Shipley in 1868. The head of the family was Albert, a farm worker. In 1891 at the age of 23, like many girls in her position Patience was a general domestic servant, working for a couple living in Hampstead. We can only guess what happened during her time in London because we next hear of her two years later when she gives birth in Kingsfold to an illegitimate child called Albert Arthur Chantler on the 20 January 1893. At the time she was working as a barmaid, quite possibly at the Wheatsheaf in Kingsfold. Neither his birth certificate nor his private baptism record in Horsham specify the father.

Albert Arthur Chantler was to become Arthur Rush. It was not unusual for people to be known by their middle name, especially if the first one is a well-used family name handed down, but there are any number of explanations as to where he acquired the surname of Rush, so we can only speculate. What we do know is that no further record of Patience has yet come to light. Neither Patience nor her son appear in the 1901 census, and she has not been found in the 1911 census either. There is no sign of her being married or having died, she just seems to have disappeared.

By 1911 at the age of 18 Arthur had acquired the surname Rush and was a Private with the 4th Royal Irish Dragoon Guards at their barracks in Preston, near Brighton. On the face of it this seems a little unusual. Then as now the Guards was a prestigious body to join, and it would have been more normal for someone of agricultural stock to have joined the Royal Sussex Regiment. It may be that he demonstrated particularly strong horsemanship skills, or perhaps a benefactor had used influence to pull some strings, we will probably never know.

When the United Kingdom declared war on Germany on 4 August 1914 the 4th Dragoon Guards were stationed at Tidworth Camp in Wiltshire, as part of the 2nd Cavalry Brigade under the command of Brigadier General Henry de Beauvoir de Lisle. The regiment crossed to France on 15 August as part of the British Expeditionary Force, and Arthur's official entry into the war began on 16 August.

The 4th Dragoon Guards were involved in the very first engagement with Germany just a week later on 22 August, the day before the first battle of the war at Mons. At 6.30 am they ambushed a patrol of German lancers outside the village of Casteau near Mons. When the Germans retreated, a troop of the Dragoons, led by a Captain Hornby, gave chase with sabres drawn. The retreating German patrol rejoined a large force of lancers, whom the Dragoons promptly charged and scattered. Captain Hornby is credited with being the first British soldier to kill an enemy in the Great War, fighting on horseback with sword against lance. After a pursuit of a few miles, the Germans turned and fired upon the British, at which point the Dragoons dismounted and also opened fire. Drummer Edward Thomas is reputed to have fired the first shot of the war for the British Army, hitting a German trooper. It may well be that Arthur Rush played a part in this skirmish.

The following day, 23 August, saw the start of the Battle of Mons when German artillery attacked the Allied line. Despite heroic and well-disciplined defence by the British they were heavily outnumbered and had to retreat. At some time during this retreat on 24 August Arthur succumbed to wounds and died, just eight days after landing in France.

Arthur's body was never found or his grave was lost. He is named on the La Ferté-sous-Jouarre Memorial in France which commemorates 3,740 officers and men of the British Expeditionary Force who fell at the battles of Mons, Le Cateau, the Marne and the Aisne between the end of August and early October 1914 and have no known graves. Arthur was posthumously awarded the Victory Medal, British War Medal and 1914 Star.

La Ferté-sous-Jouarre Memorial.

Dorothy Lottie Salmon

VAD Nurse

HANTS 208 BRCS

Died on 8 May 1918, aged 19

Dorothy Salmon is the only woman whose name appears on the Warnham War Memorial, but very little evidence exists about her war experience and the cause and location of her death.

The Warnham Parish Magazine of June 1918 contains the following paragraph:

> *It is with great regret that we heard of the death of Dorothy Salmon, elder daughter of Mr and Mrs Salmon of Robert's Lane that occurred on 8th May. We did not realise at the time that she had died in the service of her country, otherwise this notice would have appeared before. She had gained her certificates of qualification as a VAD nurse and contracted the illness from which she died while discharging her duties in a military hospital. Much sympathy is felt for her parents.*

Dorothy Lottie Salmon was born in Witley, Surrey in December 1898 and baptised in June 1899 at All Saints Church. Her parents were John James and Rosina Salmon, née Francis. Census records show that her father was a gamekeeper, who was born in Wolferton, Norfolk, and that he was the son of a gamekeeper, also called John. Dorothy was probably given her middle name after her grandmother and aunt, both of whom were called Charlotte.

Her mother, Rosina Francis was born in Babcary, Somerset. She worked as a domestic servant and the 1891 census shows that she must have met Dorothy's father, John James while they both worked at Sandringham House in Norfolk, the home of the Prince of Wales, later King Edward VII.

The census return states that Albert Edward, Prince of Wales was the head of the household and that he and his wife Alexandra, Princess of Wales were in residence at Sandringham House on Sunday 5 April 1891. The entry also lists an extraordinary collection of royalty – besides Edward and Alexandra were the Duke of Cambridge, the Princesses Victoria and Maud and Princess Margaret of Prussia. Supporting these were equerries, private secretaries, ladies-in-waiting and a huge number of household and estate servants as well as servants to visiting guests.

Rosina Francis was listed as a kitchen maid and John James Salmon as a steward's man. They were married in 1894 in Norfolk and according to the census of 1911 had five children, two of whom died in infancy.

By 1901, John and Rosina were living with Dorothy Lottie aged two and her younger sister Rosalie, seven months old at Witley (Lea Park) Lodge, in Surrey, where John had followed his father by working as a gamekeeper. After life as servants on the royal estate at Sandringham, the young couple had moved to a country estate of breathtaking ostentation, the creation of the infamous Whitaker Wright, described in the census entry as a 'Director of Public Companies'. Whitaker purchased Lea Park Estate, near Godalming from the Earl of Derby. He installed an observatory, a theatre, a velodrome, a private hospital and vast stables, but the most bizarre construction was a glass-domed ballroom underneath the lake in the grounds. His lavish building works provided employment for hundreds of local workers.

He was a speculator specialising in overseas mining ventures whose fortunes rose and fell as he floated companies, rigging the market in their shares until the inevitable collapse in 1900, which bankrupted and ruined many shareholders and associated businesses. He eventually was brought to trial in 1904 and was convicted of fraud, but committed suicide by swallowing a cyanide pill immediately after the trial in a court anteroom.

After his death, the Lea Park estate was divided up and sold off, so the Salmon family moved once more and by 1911, was recorded as living in Keeper's Cottage, Robin Hood Lane, Warnham. John was working as a gamekeeper for the Lucas family on the Warnham Court Estate and another child, John had been born, baptised at St Margaret's Church in October 1905. Keeper's Cottage was one of a pair at the end of Robin Hood Lane and Dorothy's brother John remained there until 1957, also working as gamekeeper for the Estate. In 1957 the two cottages were converted into one house and renamed 'Salmons'.

Dorothy was only 15 years old when war was declared in 1914, but at some date between then and her death in May 1918 at the age of 19, she joined the Hampshire Unit 208 of the British Red Cross Society, being awarded a certificate of qualification as a 'VAD nurse'. The information on the War Memorial and the entry in the Parish Magazine about her death are the only details which survive as no trace of her service has been found in Red Cross records.

Voluntary Aid Detachments were created after 1909, when the War Office gave the Red Cross and the Order of St John and Jerusalem the responsibility of providing additional medical aid to the Territorial Forces Medical Services. These detachments were organised by county branches. Volunteers, both men and women, were trained in first aid and nursing. At the outbreak of war in 1914 the Red Cross and the Order of St John and Jerusalem joined together to form the Joint War Committee.

Throughout Britain auxiliary hospitals and convalescent homes were administered with VADs undertaking general nursing duties and administering first aid, alongside qualified nurses. VADs also worked in military hospitals abroad and provided medical services behind the front lines, although at first, age restrictions were in place. In addition, clerical and kitchen duties were performed by VADs and as many men were engaged in military service, women VADs took on the roles of ambulance drivers, civil defence workers and welfare officers besides helping wounded soldiers write letters home and undertaking many caring duties.

Many vivid accounts of working as a VAD nurse in the Great War have been written, the most notable probably being the best-selling *Testament of Youth* by Vera Brittain, published in 1933.

Although we know that Dorothy died in 1918 we have been unable to trace her grave. Her parents and sister are buried at Warnham.

Grave of John, Rosina and Kathleen Salmon at Warnham.

Frank Simmonds

G/25363 Private

11TH (SERVICE) BATTALION (LEWISHAM)
QUEEN'S OWN (ROYAL WEST KENT REGIMENT)
122ND BRIGADE 41ST DIVISION

Killed in action at Passchendaele
20 September 1917, aged 22

According to the Rev Bowcott's tribute in the January 1918 Parish Magazine, Frank Simmonds was a relative newcomer to the village. The Vicar is writing about three deaths – Alfred Yates, William Miles and Frank Simmonds.

> *They were of us; bright, warm-hearted lads whom it was good to know. We shall miss their cheery faces. We are proud of them, for we feel that they died as they had lived – ready and anxious to do their best. Frank Simmonds had not been so long in the Parish, but he had been long enough for us to see that he was an earnest, conscientious man, bent upon doing his duty to all. A Memorial Service was held for them on the 6th of December. We think of the families upon which the sorrow has fallen so heavily, and we offer them our sympathy in their trouble.*

Frank Simmonds was the youngest of the seven children of William and Mary Simmonds. William was born in Trotton in 1838 and spent some years as a regular in the Royal Navy. At the end of his years of service he retired on a Naval pension and returned to live with his mother and sister in Minsteadgate House, Stedham, a couple of miles from Midhurst. At the age of 33 he married Mary Randell from Hampshire. Mary was 22 and already had a one year old son, Henry, whom she brought with her. Henry became the eldest of seven children, and adopted the surname of Simmonds. William started work as a shepherd and the family lived for a year or two in Chithurst and then moved to 2 Durrants, Iping. These places are all within three or four miles of each other and are a cluster of attractive little villages along the River Rother to the west of Midhurst.

The family stayed at Iping for some years, moving from No 2 to No 8 Durrants, during which time their older boys grew up and left home. In 1899 Mary died, leaving her 61 year old husband with two teenage daughters and two little boys to look after, the youngest being Frank who was only four. In 1903 William died and his daughters were left to look after their little brothers. By 1911 Frank, now 17, was living in Chithurst with his sister Minnie and her husband Henry Baker and was working as an under carter on a farm. A year or two after this, Frank moved to Warnham where he had probably obtained a better job as an agricultural worker.

The 11th Battalion West Kents was formed in Lewisham on 5 May 1915 and it could be that Frank enlisted at that time, perhaps attracted by this enticing advertisment.

> The Queen's Own Royal West Kent Regt.
> 'The Regiment that never loses a trench'
>
> The 11th Battn. is in Comfortable Billets at Lewisham (within easy distance of London by train or tram). The Headquarters are on the Private Banks Ground. This is one of the finest Cricket Grounds in the South of England. Boxing, Cricket, Football and all conceivable kinds of SPORT are encouraged, and many excellent Smoking Concerts (cigarettes free) arranged for the amusement of the men.
>
> COME AND BRING YOUR PALS
>
> You can ENLIST together, PLAY together, TRAIN together and FIGHT together.
>
> Any further particulars can be obtained from Lieut. G F Pragnell, Private Banks Ground, Catford SE. Phone Lee Green 631.

After training in England and now part of the 41st Division, they landed in France in May 1916. They were sent to Ploegsteert Wood and their first major action was the Battle of Flers Courcelette on 15 September. The Battalion suffered heavy casualties from artillery and machine gun fire but reached their objective near what is now Bulls Road cemetery. After this baptism of fire, how many of them will have thought back to the recruitment advertisement they had seen a few months previously?

Destroyed German trenches at Passchendaele.

In October the 11th Battalion took part in the attack on Le Sars and Warlincourt and then spent the winter of 1916 in and out of the trenches in the Spoil Bank sector near St Eloi. By June 1917 they were back near Ploegsteert preparing to take part in the attack on the Messines

Ridge. In August they moved a few miles to the north and in September the Battalion fought in the Battle for the Menin Road, as part of the Third Battle of Ypres, known colloquially as Passchendaele. More detail of this operation is given in the story of William Wood.

Both William Wood and Frank Simmonds were killed on the same day fighting with the same unit and it was likely that they knew each other and perhaps reminisced at times about Warnham. Frank, who was awarded the Victory Medal and the British War Medal, is buried in the Ypres Reservoir Cemetery (Plot VIII.C.31).

Passchendaele today.

William Alfred Spink

L/10426 Private

1st Battalion Queen's Own
(Royal West Kent Regiment)
13th Brigade 5th Division
Previously 7th and 10th Battalion
Temporarily 56439 Private
Royal Fusiliers Labour Corps

Killed in action near Hazebrouck France
16 April 1918, aged 29

William's unfortunate story started before he was born. His parents Shadrach, a railway porter and Mary Isabella had married in Stepney in 1883, and their first child Shadrach Sayer, William's elder brother was born the following year. After Mary became pregnant with William in 1888 but before he was born in December, Mary and Shadrach separated. William's father went back to Norfolk where he had been born and took William's brother with him.

William was born in Leytonstone on 8 December 1888 and baptised at the Parish Church on 4 January 1889. By 1891 he and his mother were living in Leytonstone, and according to the census she was 'living on own means', which is not very informative and could be interpreted a number of ways. His father and brother were in Norfolk, helping out on the family farm.

Unusually and tragically we know a fair amount of what happened to William between 1891 and the next census in 1901, due to proceedings at the Old Bailey in 1903: the trial of one Severino Klosowski, alias George Chapman for the murder of Mary Isabella Spink plus others.

Mary Spink and George Chapman were living as man and wife in Hastings by early 1897. In the autumn of that year Mary, young William and George moved back to London to run the Prince of Wales beer house in Finsbury. Quite soon after, Mary became very ill and was confined to her bed, then on Christmas Day 1897 she died. What we learn from the court proceedings of 1903 is that George Chapman went on to have further relationships and two of his subsequent 'wives' died in very similar circumstances. It was proven that all three had died from antimony poisoning. George Chapman was found guilty of pre-meditated murder and hanged at Wandsworth Prison on 7 April 1903.

Naturally the trial was a major media event and papers all over the country told the story. There is even credible circumstantial evidence that George Chapman was Jack the Ripper.

William was only nine at the time of his mother's death and he may have carried on living with her killer for a while, although there is reference to Dr Barnardo's having been involved with his case during 1898. In any case he was admitted to Hornchurch Cottage Homes as an orphan over a year later in May 1899. This institution was the Children's home attached to Shoreditch Workhouse.

William must have had some knowledge of his father's origins because on his release from Hornchurch in June 1903 at the age of 14 he was sent directly to Aylsham Workhouse in Norfolk. William's father knew about the death of his wife from the trial of Chapman, but he and his eldest son had moved to Eastbourne and clearly made no attempt to find and look after William. Unsurprisingly therefore when William arrived in Aylsham he was almost immediately sent to work as a house-boy for one Reverend Hutt in Bingham, Nottinghamshire, and was not taken on by his grandparents at the family farm in Norfolk. Presumably neither William nor the authorities were aware of this family connection.

By all accounts William was happy working at the rectory; this was his first taste of living in a normal household. As far as he was aware he had no living relatives so those living at the rectory became his surrogate family. Miss Ellen Richardson was the housekeeper, and evidently got on well with William as he later named her his next-of-kin in his Army Will. William stayed at Bingham rectory for seven years and returned there regularly for annual holidays and military furlough.

By 1911 William was living and working at Warnham Court as an odd-job man, so in all probability he came directly to Warnham from Bingham around the age of 22. He stayed at Warnham until late 1913, and then moved to Bromley to become a manservant for Charles Eric Hambro, the Chairman of Hambros Bank and a former MP. However, he must have made a lasting impression at Warnham Court as we know the owner, Charles J Lucas, wrote to military records at least twice to enquire after William during the war when William's communications to them ceased.

At the outbreak of war William enlisted immediately at Bromley on 13 August 1914, joining the 3rd (Reserve) Battalion the Queen's Own (Royal West Kent Regiment) based in Maidstone where he received his initial training. According to his service record he was 5ft 3in tall, with fair complexion, fair hair and light grey eyes.

On 25 August 1915 he was posted to the 7th Battalion Royal West Kents to serve with the British Expeditionary Force in France. Almost certainly he would have fought in the Battle of the Somme in July 1916. In October 1916 he was wounded by shrapnel to the left buttock and sent to hospital in Chichester for a month, before returning to the front in January 1917, this time with the 10th Battalion.

In February 1917 his regiment was engaged with the enemy at Givenchy, and pulled off a successful text-book raid now known as 'the Royal West Kent Givenchy Raid'. Unfortunately William was injured again by shrapnel in this action, this time to his right hand. He was sent initially to the Metropolitan Hospital who discharged him to the Chelsea VAD Hospital in Belgravia for convalescence on 27 March 1917. During this hospitalisation he was also diagnosed with partial deafness in both ears, which must have been a common occupational hazard. Chelsea discharged him on 16 April 1917, and he was able to return to Bingham Rectory as a Reserve in the Royal Fusiliers Labour Corps, possibly working in munitions.

William must have hoped he could sit out the war in Nottinghamshire as a reservist but on 9 October 1917 he was posted back to the Royal West Kents to join the 1st Battalion. His battalion moved to Italy in December 1917 to strengthen Italian resistance, and it was here that William served for a short while in the 13th French Mortar Battery. The regiment returned to the Western Front in April 1918 to help repulse the German Spring Offensive in Northern France. The 1st Battalion dug in close to the Nieppe Forest, preventing any further German advance toward the strategic town of Hazebrouck. Here they suffered continual bombardment from artillery and gas; on 16 April 1918 William was reported missing presumed dead.

There is no grave for William, but his name appears on the memorial at Ploegsteert in Belgium. He was posthumously awarded the British War Medal, the Victory Medal and the 1914-15 Star. Back in Warnham in 1919, a committee was formed to decide whose name should appear on the newly commissioned war memorial. William's name was put forward by Major Stone, seconded by Mr Osbourn and passed unanimously.

Just as William's story started before he was born, it also continued after his death. Ellen Richardson his friend from Bingham and his nominated next-of-kin died on 30 May 1920 before she could take possession of his medals. Legally they then belonged to her sister, but there is no evidence she claimed them.

William's brother Shadrach married in 1911 and settled in East Preston, West Sussex. He was therefore living in East Preston with his family while William was working just 24 miles away at Warnham Court. Neither knew of the other's whereabouts and maybe even of their existence. Shadrach also served in the war with the Army Veterinary Corps, and fortunately survived. Much later Shadrach's descendants discovered William's story and he was brought back into the family picture. They are proud to be linked to this brave man, as is the village of Warnham.

Christopher Reynolds Stone DSO MC

Major

22ND (SERVICE) BATTALION (KENSINGTON)
ROYAL FUSILIERS
(CITY OF LONDON REGIMENT)
99TH BRIGADE 2ND DIVISION
FORMERLY 16TH (SERVICE) BATTALION
(PUBLIC SCHOOLS)
MIDDLESEX REGIMENT
(DUKE OF CAMBRIDGE'S OWN)

Survived the War

Christopher Stone was an author, correspondent, soldier, broadcaster and collector – undoubtedly a man of action. He was born at Eton on 19 September 1882 and was educated at Eton College, moving on to Christ Church, Oxford. In 1906 he published a book of sea songs and ballads. Three years later he married Alice Emilia Chinnery, whose daughter he had tutored, and who was 17 years his senior. She was the widowed mother of Esmé F Chinnery, soon to distinguish himself as a military aviator early in the Great War and whose story is told elsewhere in this book. Their private means allowed them to live in a large house at Witley in Surrey, staffed by eight servants, including a chauffeur – a sign of the times. Sometime just before or during the War they moved to Field Place, Warnham, birthplace of the poet Shelley.

Christopher Stone enrolled as a Private in the 16th (Service) Battalion (Public Schools) Middlesex Regiment, raised in London on 1 September 1914. He was commissioned in 1915 and joined the 22nd Battalion, Royal Fusiliers which had been raised by the Mayor and Borough of Kensington in September 1914 at the White City. The Mayor and the Borough bore the costs of running the battalion of a thousand men until it was taken over by the War Office in July 1915 when those costs were reimbursed. The battalion was quartered at Roffey camp, Horsham from October 1914 until June 1915 where they forged lasting links with the townsfolk. In November of that year the battalion was posted to France.

The Battle of the Somme opened on 1st July 1916 with a massive attack on the German positions which developed into a series of actions including the Battle of Delville Wood (named Devil's Wood by the troops, with good reason). It had been

22nd Battalion Royal Fusiliers – Guard Duty at Roffey Camp.

won and lost and was recaptured on 27 July followed by ferocious German counter attacks which the 22nd Royal Fusiliers helped to repel. A key role was played by Captain C B Grant who commanded the 99th Brigade's Machine Gun Company and who was killed that day, as were many others. Captain Grant's story is told elsewhere in this book. Suffice it to say that the wood was held. On 4 August the battalion withdrew from the wood but remained in the Somme area until, after other ferocious and costly battles, the action was closed down on 19 November 1916. One feature of this campaign was that tanks were used for the first time in September but there were too few to be decisive and had the disadvantage of warning the enemy of their existence, giving them a chance to prepare their response in future battles.

On a lighter note, prior to Delville Wood and in a letter to his wife, Lieutenant Stone described the former German dug-out that he now occupied. It was constructed for long term use having wallpaper, cheval glass and an electric bell. This all seems incredible, but is confirmed by another witness who occupied a similar dugout.

The September 1916 Warnham Parish Magazine published this citation for the award of the Military Cross to Christopher Stone, the 22nd Battalion's Signalling Officer:

Lt.Christopher Reynolds Stone, for gallantry and devotion to duty, especially on two specified occasions – On the night of 1-2 August 1916 as there was no telephonic communication between Battalion Headquarters and companies in the line, he personally laid a line, carrying the wire drum himself. The shell fire was so intense that a front line company that had been relieved was unable to move out. Snipers also were reported to be in the wood. He was out on the wire all night, mending it whenever a break occurred. On the night of 2-3 August he again laid a duplicate wire and remained out all night, repairing breaks under heavy shell fire and during a German Infantry attack. By his devotion to duty it was possible at a critical time to telephone to companies in the front line that news had been received from the rear of a projected hostile attack. This message was received by front companies five minutes before hostile attack. Had there been no telephone, a message could not have reached them in time.

In the spring of 1917 the Battle of Arras had lasted a mere five days from the 9-14 April and was adjudged a success, albeit with heavy losses. The battalion's War Diary for April was being compiled by Captain Stone MC who was now promoted, decorated and appointed battalion adjutant, in effect, assistant to the commanding officer. The battalion saw action later that month in the little remembered battle of Oppy Wood which left the battalion crippled. The 22nd Battalion was disbanded in February 1918, chosen by drawing lots to reduce the brigade by one battalion, in line with Army policy. Their former commanding officer in a eulogy said they had 'never lost a yard of trench'. Major Stone went on to be appointed to the post of Aide-de-Camp to the General Officer Commanding the 2nd Division, in effect his personal assistant; a position he relinquished in March 1919. The London Gazette of 31 May 1918 records his award of the Distinguished Service Order but unfortunately extensive searches have failed to reveal the citation.

Hostilities between Germany and the Allied Powers came to a stop with an armistice on 11 November 1918, formalised by the Treaty of Versailles signed on 28 June 1919 and the survivors came home. The Warnham response was in 1919 to establish the Warnham Comrades Club with Major Stone as its treasurer. In July 1919 he joined the committee of the newly formed 22nd RF Old Comrades Association. In November 1919 he attended a service at St Mary's Church, Horsham to honour the men of the battalion who had died in the War and at which he read a Lesson. Major Stone then led a march to the cenotaph in the Carfax at which he laid a wreath.

In 1923 Major Stone wrote the history of his old battalion, which is still in print. His brother-in-law, the author Compton Mackenzie of 'Whisky Galore' fame had started *The Gramophone Magazine* and Christopher Stone became its London Editor. Ever enterprising, in 1927 he convinced a sceptical BBC that playing records on air would be well received, and so it was, thanks to his relaxed conversational style. Nonetheless he wore a dinner jacket when broadcasting. So he entered history as Britain's first disc jockey. Sometime around 1920 he moved from Field Place to Peppers Farm near Steyning then to Old Manor in Warnham.

In1934 Stone joined the commercial station Radio Luxembourg for a remarkable £5,000 a year, getting himself barred by the BBC in the process. Three years later, as Uncle Chris, he presented the first children's programme, *Kiddies Quarter Hour* on Radio Lyons. Christopher Stone later rejoined the BBC but caused a major row in 1941. On 11 November, of all days, he wished King Victor Emmanuel of Italy a happy birthday on air adding *'I don't think any of us wish him anything but good, poor soul'.* Good wishes towards the head of state of a country we were at war with was not well received. The BBC's Senior Controller of Programmes was sacked and tighter Government control over all broadcasts ensued. His reputation was apparently untarnished in that he was invited as a 'popular broadcaster' (nowadays he would be called a celebrity) to launch the appeal in 1945 for £250,000 to rebuild the Dover Memorial Hospital.

Stone was an avid record collector and by the mid-1930s he already owned over 12,000. When he turned 75 in1957 the *Melody Maker* magazine praised his pioneering work: '*Everyone who has written, produced or compered a gramophone programme should salute the founder of his trade.*'

Christopher Stone died on 22 May 1965 at Haslemere in Surrey.

Christopher Stone in 1945.

Duncan Boyd Wallis

Lieutenant

3RD BATTALION CONNAUGHT RANGERS
ATTACHED 2ND BATTALION
ROYAL MUNSTER FUSILIERS
3RD BRIGADE 1ST DIVISION
FORMERLY 18TH (SERVICE) BATTALION
(PUBLIC SCHOOLS) ROYAL FUSILIERS

Died of wounds at Chocques near Béthune
23 July 1915, aged 24

Duncan Boyd Wallis's family did not originally come from Warnham. His father, Henry, was born in 1840 in Orsett in Essex. At the age of 21 he went to Natal in South Africa and during this time he married Edith Grice. Henry Boyd Wallis made his fortune in the Kimberley Diamond Mines and returned to England in 1881 and settled, as a man of independent means, first in Wimbledon and then in Holland Park, West London. This became the family's permanent London residence, but in1894 they purchased Graylands in Langhurst, near Warnham. Here Henry became an active member of St Margaret's Church.

Graylands.

The Boyd Wallis boys. Left to right – Percy, Duncan, Gordon, Bertram and Harry.

Duncan Boyd Wallis was born in London on 23 July 1891. He was christened at St Jude's, Kensington in November that year and at the age of three came to live in Warnham. He had three older brothers and three older sisters and in 1897 a much younger brother arrived. The family lived in some style at Graylands with a governess, Lizzie Mays, and five other servants.

Duncan attended Cheltenham College and from there went to Pembroke College Cambridge to read engineering. When war broke out in August 1914 he was living at 11 Gibbons Road, Bedford and working as an apprentice engineer for W H Allen at the Queen's Engineering Works in Bedford.

On 2 September 1914 he applied to join the 18th (Service) Battalion Royal Fusiliers and was posted as a Private on 14 September. This was a unit formed by the Public Schools and the University Men's Force and many of the recruits were later commissioned as officers.

He did his initial training with them but on 2 January he applied for appointment for a commission in the 3rd Battalion Connaught Rangers and was discharged from the Royal Fusiliers as being granted a commission three days later. He was passed fit on 7 January 1915 and gazetted as a Second Lieutenant with his new regiment.

In the Spring of 1915 Duncan Boyd Wallis was attached to the 2nd Battalion Royal Munster Fusiliers. The Battalion had landed with the Expeditionary Force in 1914, fought all through the war on the front line being brought up to strength thirteen times, so great were their casualties. They fought at Mons, and in November in the First Battle of Ypres. During the winter they were busy maintaining the trenches and rebuilding their depleted numbers. There followed the Second Battle of Ypres near Neuve Chapelle where again they suffered devastating losses in May 1915. It was at this stage that Duncan joined the Battalion in the field on 28 May having sailed for France two weeks earlier.

The summer was relatively quiet as the Battalion moved to the Loos sector once again to rebuild and recover their strength and to prepare for an attack with the French which eventually began on 25 September. The French were to attack from

Chocques Military Cemetery.

Champagne aiming to seize open country in that area and the British offensive was centred at Loos. A number of minor skirmishes and shell attacks brought some casualties in July and August. Unfortunately one of these was Duncan Boyd Wallis who was shot in the head near Vermelles, a small village behind the lines, on 18 July. He was moved to the No 1 Casualty Clearing Station at Chocques, but he did not recover from his wounds. He died on 23 July, his 24th birthday, and was buried in Chocques Military Cemetery (Grave reference 1.b.20).

He was awarded three medals, the 1914-15 Star, the Victory Medal and the British War Medal in commemoration of his war service.

Charlie Winchester

SD/752 Private

16th (Sussex Yeomanry) Battalion
Royal Sussex Regiment
230th Brigade 74th (Yeomanry) Division
Formerly 11th (Service) Battalion
(1st South Down) Royal Sussex Regiment

Killed at Richebourg near Béthune
14 October 1918, aged 27

Private Charlie Winchester was born in 1891 in Ashburnham, East Sussex, one of the eight children of Mark and Lucy Winchester (née Ballard) who were both from that area.

According to the 1901 census, Mark and Lucy were living in The Street, Ashburnham, near Battle, with Charlie (written as 'Charley'), their eldest son Herbert, aged 25, a woodman and carpenter and Ada who was four years old.

Ten years later, the census of 1911 shows Charlie working as a domestic gardener at Westhumble, near Dorking, Surrey. He was a boarder at 3 Burford Cottages, sharing hostel-like accommodation in two rooms with 'tight cubicules' (sic) with five other young men, also listed as gardeners. It is likely that he was employed at Burford Lodge, a large country house and estate near Box Hill, the home of Sir Trevor Lawrence, a politician and horticulturist who was the pre-eminent orchid grower and collector in 19th century Britain. Orchids were the ultimate status symbol for any Victorian horticulturist and the collection at Burford Lodge was considered one of the finest in existence, with around 3,000 different species, varieties and hybrids growing in the extensive glasshouses.

In the census of 1901, one of the young gardeners gave Ashburnham, Sussex as his place of birth, so he may have recommended Charlie to apply for a place at Burford Lodge. Successful horticulture in Victorian times depended largely on a huge labour force, mainly of boys and young men who were paid very little. In addition to basic food and communal lodgings, they received, if they were lucky, some training in gardening techniques. The maintenance of the stoves and fires to keep the orchid hot houses warm, the constant attention to the control of air temperature and opening vents and windows provided endless work for the young gardeners many of whom were a long way from home.

Charlie's name is on the Warnham war memorial, so at some time after 1911 he must have moved to Warnham. There is no information about where he was living, or the sort of work he had found, but it is very likely that he was working at Warnham Court and living in the bothy there. Charles Lucas the owner was also a very keen orchid grower and a member of the RHS Orchid committee and would have employed this man because of his previous experience and training.

Charlie joined the army before conscription was introduced, his name appearing under the heading 'Territorials' on both the handwritten Roll of Honour in May 1915 and the Parish Magazine. His service number (SD/752) is consistent with those numbers assigned alphabetically, from A-W during the Horsham enlistments and initially he joined the 11th Battalion of the Royal Sussex Regiment. The battalion arrived in France in March 1916 and their first engagement, together with the 12th and 13th Battalions, was the Battle of Boar's Head on 30 June, a disastrous diversionary attack at Richebourg about five miles north east of Béthune, in an attempt to draw German troops away from the Somme as told in the story of Alfred Hards. In August the 11th Battalion moved south to the Somme where they suffered terrible casualties at Beaumont Hamel and Thiepval. In November 1916 they transferred to Passchendaele and by the end of 1917 there were very few of them left. We have no proof that Charlie was with the 11th Battalion at that time but do know that the remnants of the battalion were absorbed into other battalions in February 1918 and this could have been when he transferred to the 16th.

The 16th Battalion had been deployed in Egypt and Palestine from January 1917 where they saw a great deal of fighting and suffered many casualties. On 1 May 1918 the battalion embarked on the *HMT Caledonia*, part of a convoy of fast ships rushing troops from Egypt to Europe. The weather was rough and quarters crowded and the ships arrived in Marseilles on the 7th. Two days later the troops entrained for the north and the journey occupied the following three days. An eye witness recorded:

> *It was a pleasant journey for us all, especially those who had now been three years in the East without leave home. The green fields and trees and running streams of France made our slow progress an experience which all ranks enjoyed despite the rather hard and cramped quarters marked Chevaux (horses) 8, Hommes (men) 14.*

After Egypt the battalion's first posting was on the Somme where during September they were involved in some bitter and costly fighting near Peronne. At the end of the month they were ordered to move further north to become part of the final push. On their departure from the Somme a letter from General Sir H Rawlinson, commanding the Fourth Army thanked the 74th Division for their work:

> *The 74th Division has taken a prominent part in the successful advance of the Fourth Army during the past month and much to my regret has been ordered to another part of the British front. The work of this Division during a period of severe and continuous fighting is worthy of the best traditions of the Yeoman stock of Great Britain.*
>
> *Brought to this country from a hot climate, where they took part in a very different method of warfare, the 74th Division has quickly adapted itself to the altered conditions and has fought with a determination and courage which is beyond praise.*

We were now in what has become to be known as the final phase of the war. During September some of the ground previously lost to the Germans was regained and from 26 September the Allies, greatly strengthened by the Americans, launched a concerted attack along the whole line from the Meuse to the Sea. The strategy of attacking on all fronts meant the enemy could not afford to relocate their troops where they were most needed and eventually they were not strong enough to hold their ground. But it was no walk-over and bitter fighting in bad conditions with huge casualties continued throughout October.

With scarcely a chance to draw breath the 16th Battalion, its numbers greatly depleted and its troops battle weary, moved north from the Somme to Chocques just east of Béthune, where they entrained on a light railway for Locon. En route the train broke down badly at a small bridge over a stream and had to be man-handled back on to the rails. They spent the next few days in and out of the line in a series of small costly battles around bombed-out farms, ruined and looted villages and woods reduced to tree stumps. By the 10th they were manning the line along the railway by a row of ruined houses called Quinquibus. On arriving at Quinquibus on 10 October in the pitch dark they began by burying soldiers who had been killed the previous day. Troops were very thin on the ground and exhausted and were subject to continuous bombardment over the next few days. 'C' Company was in the thick of the fighting and the situation was made worse by terrible weather, an inadequate front line of trenches, which were either too shallow or poorly protected and lack of visibility caused by smoke shells being fired by the enemy.

The Battalion was in an exhausted state, with barely enough men to hold the line when on 14 October 1918, Charlie was killed in action at Richebourg during the final advance. Ironically this may have been the second time he had fought in a bitter battle at Richebourg as the 11th Battalion were there in March 1916. He was 27 years old and died a mere month before the ending of the hostilities. He was buried at Cambrin Cemetery, Pas de Calais, Grave number Q14.

Private Charlie Winchester is commemorated on no less than four war memorials, as besides Warnham (where he is listed as 'Charles'), his name appears on three others in East Sussex – Bexhill on Sea, Ashburnham Place Parish Church and Ninfield Church. On two of these he is described, almost certainly erroneously, as having been in the Royal Horse and Royal Field Artillery.

In October 1920, his older sister Mary applied for his British War Medal and his Victory Medal on behalf of her mother. The family were living at Bexhill on Sea and must have made extraordinary efforts to ensure that Charles was remembered in so many of the Sussex locations with which he had been associated in his short life.

William Charles Wood

G/12467 Private

11TH (SERVICE) BATTALION (LEWISHAM)
QUEEN'S OWN (ROYAL WEST KENT REGIMENT)
122ND BRIGADE 41ST DIVISION

Killed in action at Passchendaele
20 September 1917, aged 32

Private William Charles Wood of the Royal West Kent Regiment, is commemorated together with his parents in Warnham churchyard on a wooden 'headstone' made of oak which has held up amazingly against the weather for the past 90 years. William's father, Robert, was born in Woodmancote in 1847, son of a groom and started work as a garden labourer at Woodmancote Place. He married around 1876 and, with his wife Lucy, moved to Roberts Cottages in Roberts Lane in Warnham which was to be his home for many years. Roberts Lane probably named after Robert Agate the original owner of the farm in that area before it was incorporated into the Warnham Court Estate, is now called Robin Hood Lane. The Wood family lived in the second of the pair of cottages at the very end of the lane.

Roberts Cottages.

Robert and Lucy had at least six children, of whom William Charles, born in Warnham on 30 September 1885, was second to youngest. Lucy died in 1904 when she was 53 and Robert worked for 49 years in Warnham Court Gardens.

On leaving school William trained as a gardener and eventually moved away from home and by the age of 30 was living in The Bothy, Weardale Manor, Brasted Chart, Near Westerham, Kent working as a gardener for Philip Stanhope, 1st Baron Weardale, who built that enormous mansion, since demolished.

It is questionable whether William should have been sent abroad at all. His medical examination, dated 8 December 1915, declared him 'Fit for Home Service' at which time he was put in the Army Reserve. The medical officer had detected a mass of cartilage on his 4th rib, flat feet and bandy legs, together with several other weaknesses. Despite being far below A1, he was mobilised at Sevenoaks in March 1916 into the Royal West Kent Regiment. His battalion, the 11th, was part of the 41st Division and arrived in France in May 1916. After his initial training William joined them in November, serving in France and Flanders. On 13 February 1917 he received a severe gunshot wound in the neck and was taken to the No 13 General Hospital in Boulogne. Three weeks later he was transported back to England on the *SS Princess Elizabeth*.

William spent 45 days in a military hospital in Nottingham after which he was transferred on 28 April to a military depot for a recommended 'course of special drill and marching'. The death toll had been so high and the shortage of troops so acute, that this young man who was most likely not at all fit, was sent back to France on 26 May 1917.

William was 32 when he was killed in the Battle for the Menin Road on 20 September 1917. This battle was part of the Third Battle of Ypres otherwise known as Passchendaele. The name Passchendaele usually conjures up a picture of heavy rain with horses, guns and men all struggling through the deep mud and it was the case that much of Third Ypres (which started in July and continued until November) was fought in these conditions. But there was a brief spell of drier weather in the middle of September and Haig decided to go into the attack once more, this time along the Ypres-Commines Canal. On 20 September, after a massive bombardment, the Allies (two Australian Divisions together with the 23rd and 41st British Divisons) attacked and managed to hold their objective of about 1,500 yards despite counter-attacks. The attack was considered to be a great success and caused panic to German commanders who had thought their well-prepared defences were impenetrable. But the cost was 21,000 casualties, two of them from Warnham, William Wood and Frank Simmonds. Only seven officers and 95 other ranks of the 11th Battalion came out unscathed. The Second and Fifth Army casualties of these four months of battle were horrendous – 2,118 officers and 33,713 other ranks killed, 452 officers and 19,036 other ranks missing and a total of 172,994 wounded. It was no great victory and the only gain was a small piece of land approximately 50 miles square.

It is to be hoped that the worry and hindrances caused to the enemy by these actions contributed towards the conclusion of the war a year later. In his book *Ypres*, Norman Gladden makes the stark comment:

Exhausted troops resting at Passchendaele.

> *Our new line was now on the far side of the ridge. Certainly the day's advance was more than sufficient to justify the paeans of victory which we knew would fill the newspaper headlines at home. It was so easy to overlook the price paid in lives.*

William is buried in Hooge Crater Cemetery (Plot XIX.C.1) and remembered on the wooden gravestone in Warnham churchyard. He was awarded the Victory Medal and the British War Medal and is also commemorated among 'The Lost' on the Brasted website. The Vicar wrote in the Parish Magazine:

> *The sad announcement that Willie Wood of Robin's Lane had been killed on the Western Front in action on Sept. 20th brought sorrow to all who knew him. He was a good lad, with a high-minded sense of duty, and it is not too much to say that everybody liked him. He was for some years a member of our choir, and his Church with Her Services had a real meaning for him. A memorial service was held for him on Nov. 14th. His father and the family wish to record their sense of gratitude for the sympathy shown to them. May God support and strengthen them.*

Percy Woodman

26599 Private

2/7TH BATTALION (TF)

ROYAL WARWICKSHIRE REGIMENT

182ND BRIGADE 61ST DIVISION

Died in hospital at Lincoln as a result of gas 5 September 1918, aged 19

The Woodman family were a long line of agricultural workers who had lived in Warnham for many years, Percy's grandfather, George, having been born here in 1817. George married a laundress, Mary Owen, and they set up home in Church Street where they had at least seven children, and possibly more judging by the uncharacteristic gaps in ages in the Census records. Their fifth child, George, born in 1868, was married in 1893 and with his wife Ellen set up home in Goose Green where they had three children, the youngest of whom was Percy, born on 2 January 1899. By this time George had changed from working as an agricultural labourer and was now a road foreman.

At the time of the Great War there were only a handful of small cottages in Goose Green, most of them crammed with large families of working people. For many years the Woodmans had as their neighbours the Ottleys and no doubt the children from these families played together in the fields and woods around that hamlet, though the Ottleys moved to Horsham in 1916. As told elsewhere in this book, the Ottleys' son Jim was killed in France in 1916 and so this tiny settlement lost two of its boys in the war giving an illustration of the high proportion of deaths in every community.

Both Percy and his older brother joined the army. Arthur was 18 in 1915 and served throughout the war with the 11th Battalion King's Royal Rifle Corps surviving the hostilities.

Percy, who was two years younger, joined the 2/7th Battalion Royal Warwickshire Regiment in 1917. The 2/7th, a Territorial Battalion, was on the Western Front throughout 1917 and 1918 and it was likely that Percy went out there early in 1918. These will have been anxious times for George and Ellen, with their two sons both on the front line, and they might have been relieved to hear that Percy was wounded, rather than killed, and had been brought back to England to be in hospital in Lincoln. But his injuries were the result of gas and he died on 5 September 1918 at the age of 19. There is no record of how long Percy had been in the hospital at Lincoln. To have him so far away when he was obviously critically ill would have been an additional grief to this family who would not have had the opportunity or the resources to visit him often, if at all.

Poison gas was one of the most feared of all weapons in the Great War and even towards the end of the war, by which time each side had developed more sophisticated gas masks and better warning systems, the insidious nature of its use made it a stealthy and unpredictable force. The first gas attacks were made by the French in 1914 using tear gas grenades in a desperate attempt to stop the German advance. Both the Allies and the Germans continued to use gas and developed a variety of poisons (chlorine, mustard gas, phosgene) throughout the war with terrible consequences for those caught up in this terror. Sometimes the wind would suddenly change and the gas blew back into the lines of the perpetrator. Depending on the nature of the poison gas and the degree of protection given by the gas mask, victims sometimes died within a few hours. Others lived for several weeks or months or even years, often blinded or badly disabled and unable to work ever again.

We have no record of where Percy was gassed or when it was. The 2/7th had been involved in the fighting in 1918 during the German spring offensive in the Ypres Salient and we know that gas was used in a number of places on the Salient. He may have been in hospital for some weeks before he died. The effects of gassing were devastating and painful, and Percy was a victim of this horror.

It is hoped that it might have been a small comfort to his parents to receive the Victory Medal and the British War Medal on his behalf. Percy was buried in Warnham churchyard on 10 September 1918, and the Vicar wrote in the Parish Magazine:

Percy Woodman's grave in the churchyard, now broken.

To all who knew our young friend, Percy Woodman, the tidings of his death was a matter of profound regret. He succumbed to the effects of gas received in action on the Western Front, at a Lincoln hospital to which he had been brought from France. His sufferings were great, but he bore them all with admirable patience. He was a good, quiet lad, and it is certain that he did his duty well. He was laid to rest under the shadow of the old Parish Church in which he had been a choir boy. We offer our heart-felt sympathy to his parents and the family. They wish to record their grateful thanks to all the friends for their sympathy and for the flowers which they sent.

Albert Worsfold

T/27471 Driver

HQ Company Army Service Corps

2nd Division British Expeditionary Force

Killed at the Aisne, 14 September 1914, aged 24

Albert was the only son of William and Isabella Worsfold of Little Haven, Horsham where he was born in 1890. The family soon moved to 9 Brickyard Cottages, Warnham Station, also known as Station Cottages. William, a brickyard labourer, was widowed when Isabella died in 1898 aged 37, leaving a son, Albert, and two daughters, causing William to engage a housekeeper, Caroline Styles, a widow who lived in with her son. In 1901 William married Caroline and adopted her son. By 1911 the family was living at Mount Road, Cranleigh, Surrey and William was working as a labourer scavenger while his son, Albert, and his adopted son, William, were both employed as labourers. The family had gained a one-year old grandson, Ernest.

Two years earlier, on 2 April 1909, Albert had enlisted at Aldershot in the Army Service Corps to spend two years in the Regular Forces and 10 years in the First Class Army Reserve. Acceptance for army service depended on passing a medical examination and receipt of a satisfactory reference. Albert trained as a driver, a farsighted choice given how motor transport was to expand. On completing his two years' regular service on 1 April 1911 he transferred to Section 'A' of the First Class Army Reserve. This required the passing of another medical examination and the signing, by a Colonel no less, of a Sobriety Certificate attesting to Albert's trustworthiness and the fact that he had never been under the influence of alcohol during the whole two years of his Army service. On 31 March 1912 Albert was released from his Section 'A' commitments when he transferred to Section 'B' of the Army Reserve. On 1 September 1913 Albert married Alice Hilda Parsons, a domestic servant from Cranleigh, Surrey, at a ceremony witnessed by her brother Norman and her sister Amelia.

On 4 August 1914 the United Kingdom declared war on Germany. As a Regular Army Reservist, Albert was mobilised at Aldershot just two days later, showing a degree of planning by the authorities in anticipation of the war to come. Albert landed in France on 15 August to serve as an ASC Driver with the Headquarters Company of the ASC Divisional Train, of the 2nd Division of the British Expeditionary Force.

The ASC's role was to supply food, equipment and ammunition to the front line troops using mechanical and horsed vehicles, railways and waterways. Typically, they delivered supplies to battalion quartermasters, a task which frequently took them near or right up to the front line. As the Army expanded so did the ASC which, at its peak, mustered over 300,000 men. The ASC are spoken of as the unsung heroes of the war and though they were not directly involved in fighting, they met the needs of those who were and who won the ultimate victory. 'Unsung' meant only four mentions in the Official History of the War. Nor is there a memorial dedicated to the ASC, who suffered many casualties, one of whom was Driver Albert Worsfold.

The County Times of 8 July 1916, under the heading *Forgotten Heroes of the Army Service Corps*, printed a poem from Captain L R Whiting, an ASC soldier serving in France, lamenting the Corps' lack of glamour and emphasising its vital function:

When honour is divided and victory is won.
Don't think the only hero is the man behind the gun.
What corps of men work harder than the happy ASC .
With their labourers, clerks and butchers, not to mention bakery?

While Tommy's in the trenches, and Jack is on the sea,
They labour at the bases, and their work is hard maybe.
But you never hear them grumble, though they toil through night and day,
To prepare the food for others who are fighting in the fray.

The baker at the oven toils hard throughout the day,
To give Tommy bread, not biscuit, to cheer him on his way.
It is brought to him by transport, sometimes motor, sometimes horse,
And helps to keep him happy and prevent the heavy loss.
So when the boys come marching home just think of what I say :
The ASC have helped to rob the Kaiser of 'The Day'.

The 2nd Division's first major action was at the Battle of the Aisne, 12–18 September 1914, which was preceded by the battles of Mons and Le Cateau from where the BEF had to retreat to the River Marne. With Paris threatened, the French and British Armies under General Joffre halted the German advance and caused them to retreat to strong defensive positions across the River Aisne, destroying bridges as they went. The Royal Engineers, under heavy fire, repaired enough bridges to allow the infantry and cavalry to cross the river and attack the enemy. On 14 September the Guards Brigade of the 2nd Division were entrenched at Soupir Farm and the 4th Dragoon Guards had captured nearby Bourg-et-Comin, just south of Moussy-Verneuil, the most likely place of Albert's death as he delivered supplies.

The battle was indecisive; the BEF suffered 13,500 casualties to add to its losses in previous battles. As a result, both armies extended their front lines until they reached the sea and with little change they remained unaltered until late 1918 near the war's end.

Albert was an 'Old Contemptible', an insult attributed to the German Kaiser. Although it was never authenticated, the story went that he referred to the BEF as a 'contemptible little army'. The British troops turned this remark into a matter of pride in that very British way. They knew they weren't contemptible, they fought well and suffered heavily in helping to halt the German advance. Albert was one of Warnham's early fatal casualties. He was awarded the 1914 Star given to those who had served in France and Belgium between 5 August and 22 November 1914. Albert's Star came with a clasp given to those who had been under fire within the range of mobile enemy guns during the period, lending support to the surmise that Moussey-Verneuil was the place of Albert's death. He also received the War Medal and the Victory Medal. Albert is also commemorated on the Cranleigh War Memorial. He is listed on the splendid Memorial to the Missing at La Ferte-sous-Jouarre, Seine et Marne, commemorating the 3,888 men of the BEF who fell at Mons, Le Cateau, the Marne and the Aisne and whose graves are not known. At the time of his death Albert's widow was living at Park House Green Cottages, Ewhurst Road, Cranleigh.

George Worsfold

69295 Private

2/2nd (City of London) Battalion
London Regiment (Royal Fusiliers)
173rd Brigade 58th Division
Formerly T/1448 Army Service Corps

Killed in action near Amiens
24 April 1918, aged 26

The Worsfold family came to Horsham from the Kirdford and Wisborough Green area. In 1861 George's grandfather, William and his wife Matilda were living at Quannels House, Plastow (Plaistow) with their six children, including George's father, also called William, who had been born there in 1854. Young William, an agricultural labourer married Elizabeth Sarah Farley in 1877 and they set up home in Five Oaks where their first child, Mary Jane, was born in 1878. They had a second daughter in 1886, but two years later Elizabeth died.

The following year William married Sarah Scutt and in 1890 she gave birth to another little girl. In 1891 William and Sarah moved to Church Street, Warnham where William now worked as a bricklayer's labourer. While in Church Street, their only son, George was born in 1892. A year or so later the family moved to Broadbridge Heath where three more daughters were born. For several years they all lived in 6 Garden Cottages, Sullington (probably where Sullington Mead now is). This area takes its name from the time when Broadbridge Heath was part of the Manor of Sullington. The family later moved to St John's Cottages and William returned to working on a farm, while his wife was the school cleaner.

In 1911 George was still living at home and working as a gardener. As a Territorial he was mobilised at the outbreak of war and became one of the First One Hundred Thousand, joining the 3rd Labour Company of the Army Service Corps as a driver. He was sent to France on 5 October but we do not know where he served. ASC personnel were attached to various units, providing supplies and ammunition to the fighting troops. They also worked at the docks supplementing the local dockers who needed assistance with the sudden and massive flow of cargo of all varieties arriving at the Channel ports. A few months later he was transferred to the Royal Fusiliers and joined the 2/2nd Battalion London Regiment (Royal Fusiliers). This battalion, together with many others, was re-organised when manpower was short and ended up in 1916 combined with the 3/2nd Battalion, the whole being renamed the 2/2nd.

On the morning of 9 April 1918, denied a decisive result in the south, where the enemy had come within ten miles of Amiens, the Germans switched their efforts northwards and launched an attack on a 12 mile front from Givenchy and Festubert through almost to Armentières and wider. This was the start of the Battle of the Lys. Although the Germans were held back at Givenchy, they had success further north and were encouraged to drive on. Their advances caused great alarm to the British High Command and on 12 April Haig sent out his 'Backs to the Wall' message.

The Germans then turned their attention to the area around Amiens which had been held by the British 8th Division, now very tired with its infantry reduced by half and replaced by hastily trained young recruits with no previous battle experience. Intelligence obtained from captured German prisoners indicated that the Germans were planning to drive towards Amiens with the intention of taking the town, assisted by their new tanks. Hasty reinforcement work was carried out but the Official History reports that the trenches were shallow, the wire was poor, and there were no communication trenches, dug-outs or shelters except in the cellars in the centre of the village. With the great prize of Amiens in its sights, in the early hours of 24 April the German army, taking advantage of the fog, weakened the British defences by mustard gas and high explosive rounds and with supporting tanks broke through to capture the village of Villers-Bretonneux. This strategically

British tanks in a ruined village.

situated village, gateway to Amiens, is on the south side of the River Somme about ten miles east of Amiens and about ten miles south of Albert.

The action is recorded in the War Diary [WO 95/3001/4]:

> *24th South of Bois de Hangard. Enemy attacked. Heavy barrage and gas bombardment at 3 am. Attack developed at 6 am. Btn held front line all day in spite of flanks falling back. Heavy fighting throughout the day. British and French counter-attacked at 10 pm and restored line in parts on the left flank. Situation on the left flank obscure in Bois de Hangard. Casualties – 6 Officers, 210 Other Ranks*

The 173rd Brigade, including 2/2nd London, brought in to assist the 8th Division, were in the front line of this attack, and although they repulsed the enemy infantry, they sustained heavy losses and were forced by the tanks to retreat. Although tanks had already been used in the war with varying success, this was recorded as the first battle in which tanks were used by both sides. Later that night, the Allies, greatly strengthened by Australian reinforcements, counter-attacked, drove out most of the enemy and captured the remainder inside the village. The next day Villers-Bretonneux was given back to its inhabitants. Three Australian brigades took part in this battle, together with one depleted and exhausted British brigade, the 173rd. It was a huge success for the Australian forces against a numerically superior German force and is the site of an impressive Australian memorial. The battle of Villers-Bretonneux went down in history as one of the most important successes of the war, preventing the enemy from advancing to Amiens in their drive to the coast.

George Worsfold, mourned by his parents and his six sisters, was killed in this battle on 24 April. He is buried in the Crucifix Corner Cemetery, Villers-Bretonneux (Plot VII.B.7). His name is on the war memorial at Broadbridge Heath. He was posthumously awarded the 1914 Star together with the Victory Medal and the British War Medal.

War Memorial at Broadbridge Heath.

Army organisation

The Army is a generic term for armed forces serving on land. In August 1914 the British Army consisted of the Regular Army, numbering 250,000 well-trained soldiers many serving overseas, largely in India, and the Territorial Force (TF) which was of similar strength but part-time and serving at home. The Regulars and the TF were grouped into Divisions. The make-up of the Division and its chain of command remained largely unchanged throughout the war.

The Division was a large self-contained unit of about 19,000 men having its own cavalry, artillery, engineers, signals, transport and medical services. Its infantry was organised into three brigades, each consisting of four battalions. Each battalion, numbering over 1,000 men, was organised into four companies, each company into four platoons and each platoon into four sections. The command structure was as follows:

Division (Div)	Major-General
Brigade (Bde)	Brigadier-General
Battalion (Bn)	Lieutenant-Colonel
Company (Coy)	Major or Captain
Platoon	Lieutenant or 2nd Lieutenant
Section	Sergeant or Corporal

Most soldiers were Privates, the lowest rank, but sometimes the titles Gunner, Sapper, Trooper, Rifleman or Driver were used according to their role. A Private could be appointed Lance Corporal taking over a section as required in battle. More senior ranks could move upwards likewise.

The regiment has gone unmentioned because it was not an operational unit but rather the parent body, with its own depot, to which each of its battalions owed allegiance, often inspiring a fierce pride in its members. Battle honours were awarded to regiments and emblazoned on their colours.

Early in August 1914 three infantry divisions of the Regular Army with one cavalry division and supporting troops were sent to France, quickly followed by two more infantry divisions. This constituted the first British Expeditionary Force (BEF) which fought heroically and suffered heavily alongside our French and Belgian allies to stem the German advance. During the following few weeks the BEF was reinforced by divisions of regular soldiers recalled from India and Africa and by Territorials.

In the summer of 1914 as war threatened it had become obvious to the government that the professional British Army, even with the addition of the TF, was far too small and would be no match for that of Germany. It had to expand rapidly and early in August Lord Kitchener launched his famous recruiting drive which drew in a flood of volunteers. The Call to Arms led to the formation of Service Battalions to accommodate the new recruits and these were affiliated to existing regiments. Local connections were sometimes recognised in battalion titles. The thirty divisions raised this way were grouped into five armies. These were known as Kitchener's New Armies (K1, K2, K3, K4 and K5). The size of the TF also increased and its members were soon serving in France with over one million passing through its ranks during the war. The TF had its own named divisions which often attracted pride and loyalty. At the same time the Artillery, the recently formed Royal Flying Corps and other vital service corps grew dramatically.

A large influx of soldiers from the TF, the New Armies and overseas troops rapidly swelled the BEF which in 1916 would be expanded still further by the arrival of conscripts. The title BEF continued to be used for British, Imperial and Commonwealth Forces deployed in Europe for the duration of the war. Fresh titles were created for our forces in other theatres of war – the Mediterranean Expeditionary Force (MEF) to invade the Gallipoli Peninsula and the Egyptian Expeditionary Force (EEF) to protect the Suez Canal, the lifeline to India.

By 1915 the high number of casualties and the addition of TF, New Army and Overseas troops into the BEF had blurred the clear-cut lines of pre-1914 organisation. It was decided to create a new formation designated the First Army commanded by a Lieutenant-General or General and made up of a number of divisions. The Second, Third, Fourth and Fifth Armies followed in time, Kitchener's Armies supplying some of the manpower. Within those five Armies, two or more divisions could be grouped into a Corps so that two or more Corps would make up an Army. Each Army was deployed on a different sector of the Front.

As the war progressed the number of casualties and changing requirements led to the establishment of new units including the Tank Corps, the Machine Gun Corps, the Royal Defence Corps and the Labour Corps. In 1916 a pool of 112 Training

Battalions was created to supply front line units. Artillery and other vital service units also had to expand substantially. Almost 5 million men from the UK served in the Army and manpower demands were such that in 1916 conscription was introduced. This expanded army with its Dominion and Empire troops was commanded by Field Marshal Haig from its GHQ in Montreuil-sur-Mer.

The high rate of casualties combined with increasing demand for munitions workers caused a manpower crisis at the end 1917 and in January 1918, after considerable wrangling, the War Cabinet ordered the army to scale down the number of battalions, causing great consternation among the 140,000 men of the 141 disbanded infantry battalions. Co-ordination of the British and French forces had proved to be problematic and soon after the start of the German spring offensive in 1918 the French General, Marshal Foch, was given overall command of the British and French Armies. The American Expeditionary Force (AEF) was subsequently accommodated into this unified structure which saw the Allies through to ultimate victory.

Those who served

Some names, for which we have been unable to verify military service, appear on a hand-written Warnham Roll of Honour held by West Sussex Records Office or in the Parish Magazine. It is possible some of these names are misspellings and duplicates but are included here for completeness.

Warnham addresses, if known, refer to where an individual is associated, not necessarily where they were living during the war.

Fuller details on each person are available on the Warnham Society website at www.warnhamsociety.org.uk

NAME	Address	Rank	Service/Unit
ARCHER F.			Army
ARCHER G.T.	Geerings	Able Seaman	Royal Navy
ARNOLD G.T.	Corner House	Private	Army Service Corps
ASHTON F.			Army
ATTWATER F.	Rose Cottage, Dog & Duck Inn	Private	Labour Corps
AYLING F.H.	School Hill		Royal Flying Corps
BAINES J.T.	Westbrook	Captain	Welsh Regiment
BAINES M.T.	Westbrook	Captain	Royal Air Force
BAKER E.	Ends Place Farm		Army
BARNETT F.	Dawes, Northlands	Sergeant	King's Own (Royal Lancaster Regiment)
BARRETT F.			Army
BATES W.G.H.	Father-in-law at Daux in 1911	Captain	Leinster Regiment
BAZELEY C.	1 Wild Goose Cottage	Private	Tank Corps

BENNETT A.H.	Friday St.	Private	The Queen's
BICKNELL A.J.	Garmans Cottage	Private	Machine Gun Corps
BIRCHMORE W.	Cradles Cottage	Private	Royal Sussex Regiment
BLACKWELL A.		Trooper	6th Dragoon Guards
BOOKER A.P.	Stoneleigh, Church St.	Private	Machine Gun Corps
BOOKER E.J.	Church St.	Private	Labour Corps.
BOOKER F.S.	Church St.	Private	Royal Sussex Regiment
BOOKER W.J.	9 Lower Gables	Private	Labour Corps
BOOTH S.	Warnham Court Stables	Private	Army Service Corps
BOUSFIELD/BUSFIELD J.			Army
BOWLES W.E.	Station Cottages	Private	Royal Defence Corps
BRANCH J.	Sussex Oak	Private	Labour Corps
BRANCH R.W.	Warnham Court Gardens	Private	Suffolk Regiment
BRONSDON G.L.	Holmhurst	2nd Lieutenant	Royal Engineers
BROOKER P.			Army
BROWN A.E.	Northlands		Army
BROWNING J.	12 Station Cottages	Private	Royal Engineers
BROWNING M.	Rowhook Farm	Private	Labour Corps
BROWNING P.	12 Station Cottages	Private	Royal Sussex Regiment
BURBERRY B.N.	Kingsfold		Royal Navy
BURCHELL T.W.	Warnham Place	Private	The Queen's
BURCHETT C.	Old Barn Cottages Kingsfold	Private	Royal Fusiliers
BURCHETT C.	Kingsfold	Corporal	Royal Field Artillery
BURCHETT H.	Ridgbrook	Lance Corporal	1st County of London Yeomanry
BURCHETT V.J.	Ridgebrook Cottage, Kingsfold	Private	Royal Marines
BURNETT F.			Royal Navy
BURRAGE G.	Farthings Farm	Private	Middlesex Regiment
BURRAGE H.	Garden Cottage, Church St.		Royal Navy
BURRAGE T.A.	Garden Cottage, Church St.	Private	Royal Marine Artillery
BURTENSHAW J.H.	18 Station Cottages	Sergeant	Royal Sussex Regiment
BURTENSHAW M.F.	18 Station Cottages	Private	The Buffs
BUTCHERS W.G.H.	Bell-houses		Army
BUTTERFIELD A.E.			Army

CANNON G.	Friday St.	Private	Army Service Corps
CAPON C.M.	The Bungalow, near Warnham Lodge	Private	Army Ordnance Corps
CHANDLER E.E.A.	6 School Hill	Private	Royal Fusiliers
CHANDLER P.	probably 4 Warnham Cottages, Station Rd.		
CHAPMAN W.	Goose Green		Army
CHARMAN A.	Denn Farm, Ends Place, and Kingsfold	Private	Royal Fusiliers
CHARMAN A.	Sands Farm	Private	Royal West Kent Regiment
CHARMAN C.W.	Friday St.		Army Service Corps
CHARMAN J.E.	2 Cherry Tree Cottages, Friday St.	Private	Royal Sussex Regiment
CHARMAN M.	Oak Cottage, Church St.	Driver	Royal Engineers
CHARMAN P.G.	Oak Cottage Church St.	Private	Labour Corps
CHARMAN R.	Oak Cottage, Church St.	Driver	Royal Engineers
CHATFIELD C.R.	9 Station Rd.	Pioneer	Royal Engineers
CHENNELL C.	Benland Cottage	Sergeant	Royal Sussex Regiment
CHENNELL G.	The Gardens, Kingsfold	Driver	Army Service Corps
CHENNELL T.	Tickfold Cottage, Kingsfold	Lance Corporal	Army Service Corps
CHINNERY E.F.	Field Place	Captain	Royal Flying Corps
CLARK E.	Rowhook	Lance Corporal	Military Foot Police
COBBY W.	Northlands		Territorial Force
COMPER A.C.	3 School Hill	Corporal	Royal Sussex Regiment
COOK J.	1 Friday St.	Driver	Army Service Corps
COOLE A.E.		2nd Lieutenant	Sikh Pioneers
COOPER A.C.	Grayland's Farm	Sublieutenant	Royal Naval Volunteer Reserve
COOPER J.	Rowhook	Gunner	Royal Field Artillery
COPPARD G.	Mandora, Friday St.	Private	Suffolk Regiment
COX F.	Friday St.	Private	Grenadier Guards
COX T.W.	10 School Hill	Sapper	Royal Engineers
COX W.A.	Friday St.	Sapper	Royal Engineers
COX W.J. MM	7 Sunnyside, Friday St.	Sergeant	Machine Gun Corps
CROWHURST A.J.	Mill Pond Cottages	Driver	Royal Field Artillery

CROWHURST H.V.	Mill Pond Cottages	Gunner	Royal Field Artillery
DALRYMPLE I.D. MC	Mayes House	Captain	Highland Light Infantry
DAVEY A.H.	Friday Street		Army
DAVEY T.H.	Stone Farm	Gunner	Royal Horse Artillery
DEARDEN R.	Bell Rd.	Trooper	2nd County of London Yeomanry
DENNIS H.E.	Durfold	Lieutenant-Commander	Royal Naval Volunteer Reserve
DENYER A.E.T.	Myrtle Cottages, Kingsfold	Driver	Royal Engineers
DEWDNEY J.T.	2 Bay Cottages, Friday St. & Geerings	Private	Durham Light Infantry
DIBLEY G.	Friday St.		Army
DINNAGE E.J.	2 Station Cottages	Rifleman	Royal Irish Rifles
DOYLE P.J. MM	New Cottage, Friday St. Woodside Cottages Friday St.	Corporal	Royal Engineers
DRAPER H.D.	Little Daux	Private	Royal Garrison Artillery
DUFFIELD G.			Army/Territorial Force
DUMBRILL C.H.	10 Friday St	Private	Labour Corps
DUNSTALL A.E.G.C.	Serapis, Durfold	Bombardier	Royal Field Artillery
DUNSTALL W.E.	Serapis, Durfold	Private	Army Veterinary Corps
EAMES J.		Sergeant	Royal Field Artillery
EAMES J.	16 Station Cottages & 2 Friday St.	Private	Royal Fusiliers
EDWARDS A.F. MC	The Gardens, Warnham Lodge	Captain	King's (Liverpool Regiment)
EDWARDS F.		Private	The Queen's
EDWARDS H. Medal of St George 1st Class	Warnham Lodge	2nd Lieutenant	King's (Liverpool Regiment)
ETHERIDGE S.	Friday Street	Private	East Surrey Regiment
EVANS J.			Army
FAIRS F.C.	Roberts Cottage, Roberts Lane	Company Sergeant Major	Royal Field Artillery
FARLEY H.	The Cottages, Rowhook Hill	Private	Labour Corps
FARLEY S.	1 Cherry Tree Cottages, Friday St.	Driver	Royal Field Artillery

FARNES A.T.	Tanners Cottage	Trooper	19th Hussars
FARNES C.W.	Tanner's Cottage	Private	Royal Sussex Regiment
FARNES W.	Shiremark	Gunner	Royal Field Artillery
FELTON W.A.W.	Friday St. & Garden Villa, Church St.	Able Seaman	Royal Navy
FLINT B.J.	Woodbarn Cottage, Denne	Stoker 1st Class	Royal Navy
FRANCIS F.	Daws Cottage	Private	Royal Sussex Regiment
FRANCIS F.H.	Warnham St. (Church St.)	Corporal	Royal Army Medical Corps
FRANCIS J.	Bell Cottages.	Private	Army Veterinary Corps
FUGGLES W.J.	Ends Place	Driver/ Mechanic	British Red Cross Society & Order of St John
GARMAN A.E.	Oak Cottage, Church St.	Private	Welsh Regiment
GARMAN H.	Corner House, Bell Rd.	Private	Coldstream Guards
GARMAN J.	Street Farm	Private	Labour Corps
GATES F.			Army
GLASS W.F.	Mayes Cottage		Army
GOACHER P.W.	Friday St. & Bell Rd.	Yeoman Signaller	Royal Navy
GRANT C.B.	The Firs, School Hill	Captain	Machine Gun Corps
GRANT I.	The Firs, School Hill	Captain	Khyber Rifles
GRANT R.W.	Stonyhurst	Captain	Royal West Kent Regiment
GREEN B.			Army
GREENFIELD A.	7 Station Cottages		Army
GREENFIELD R.A.	Station Cottages	Able Seaman	Royal Navy
GREENOP J.R.D.	Warnham Court Lodge	Lance Corporal	The Queen's
GREGSON H.G.	Ends Place	Lieutenant	Royal Wiltshire Yeomanry
HARDS A.E.	Goose Green	Private	Royal Sussex Regiment
HARVEY J.K.C.	The Chequers, Rowhook	Private	Army Service Corps
HASKINS J.	Warnham	Stoker 1st Class	Royal Navy
HAYLER F.C.	16 Church St.	Private	Army Service Corps
HAYLER G.B.	16 Church St.	Lance Corporal	Royal Welsh Fusiliers
HAYLER W.A.	Brickfield Cottages	Private	Royal Scots

HENDRIE C.	7 Friday St.	Private	Labour Corps
HIGGINS T.J.	Rowhook	Private	Royal Scots
HOARE C.G. MC	Warnham Court	Lieutenant	Guards Machine Gun Regiment
HOCKEN S.	Chickens Farm	Private	Devonshire Regiment
HOLT H.			
HUGGETT W.G. Croix de Guerre	Home Farm, Strood Park	Driver	British Red Cross Society
JACKSON G.T.	Westons	Private	Army Service Corps
JACKSON J.			Army
JOHNSTONE J.	Malt Mayes	Sergeant	Black Watch
JUPP H.A.	2 Friday St.	Private	Royal Sussex Regiment
JUPP W.	18 Station Cottages		Army
KEMP C.J.	Benland Cottage	Cadet	Royal Air Force
KEMP W.V.	Field Place	Private	Essex Regiment
KENNARD J.	Goose Green	Driver	Army Service Corps
KILLNER C.	21 Little London & Goose Green	Private	Royal Fusiliers
KILLNER E.	21 Little London	Private	Army Service Corps
KILLNER E.H.	21 Little London	Driver	Royal Engineers
KNIGHT F.	Friday St.	Private	Highland Light Infantry
KNIGHT W.A.G.	14 Station Cottages		Army
LAMBERT S.J.M.	Durfold	Major	Royal Horse Artillery
LAWRENCE H.J.	Rowhook	Private	Norfolk Regiment
LEADBETTER W.	Kingsfold	Sergeant	Royal Sussex Regiment
LEE J.	Goose Green		Territorial Force
LEE J.E.	Friday St.		Territorial Force
LEWIS L.G.	Golf Club Cottage	Lance Corporal	Labour Corps
LINDFIELD F.		Private	Royal Sussex Regiment
LINFIELD R.J.	Pear Tree Cottages, Warnham Lodge	Private	Sussex Yeomanry
LUCAS C.E.	Warnham Court	Captain	Royal Fusiliers
LUCAS G.M.E.	Warnham Court	Captain	Royal Inniskilling Fusiliers
LYON F.			Royal Navy
MADGWICK H.	Ends Place Lodge	Able Seaman	Royal Navy
MEREDITH J.H.	Warnham Court	Gunner	Royal Field Artillery

MERRITT H.G.	Dog and Duck Inn		Royal Navy
MERRITT H.W.	Dog and Duck Inn		Royal Navy
MERRITT J.L.C.	Dog and Duck Inn		Royal Navy
MERRITT R.A.	Dog and Duck Inn	Boy 2nd Class in 1911	Royal Navy
MILES F.A.	Church St.	Private	Royal West Kent Regiment
MILES G.			Army
MILES J.W.	Friday St.	Lance Corporal	Royal Sussex Regiment
MILES W.	Church St.		Territorial Force
MILLER G.H.	4 Sunnyside, Friday St.	Private	Royal Sussex Regiment
MILLS G.			Army
MITCHELL B.			Army/Territorial Force
MITCHELL C.R.	Station Cottages	Private	Army Service Corps
MITCHELL F.	Friday St.	Rifleman	Rifle Brigade
MORRIS W.C.F.	Warnham School	Gunner	Royal Garrison Artillery
MUGGERIDGE J.	Great Daux Cottage	Private	Army Veterinary Corps
MUGGERIDGE J.E.C.	Dervals	Private	South Staffordshire Regiment
MUNDAY C.	1 Byfleets Lane	Private	Royal Sussex Regiment
MYSON A.	Station Cottages		Army
NEWMAN W.	Mill Cottage	Private	Royal Engineers
NIGHTINGALE A.J.	Friday St.	Sapper	Royal Engineers
NIGHTINGALE C.	New Cottage, Friday St.	Private	The Buffs
NIGHTINGALE E.A.	5 Sunnyside, Friday St.	Private	Army Veterinary Corps
NIGHTINGALE G.W.	New Cottage, Friday St.	Private	Royal Sussex Regiment
NIGHTINGALE P.W.	3 Sunnyside, Friday St		Royal Sussex Regiment
NIGHTINGALE T.H.	New Cottage, Friday St.	Driver	Army Service Corps
OTTLEY C.C.	Goose Green	Private	Labour Corps
OTTLEY C.J.	Goose Green	Private	The Queen's
PACKHAM J.	Friday St.	Private	Royal Air Force
PAYNE W.G.H.	2 Lower Gables, Friday St.	Private	Labour Corps
PEARMAN J.B.	Northlands		

PETTIFER W.	7 Friday St.	Private	Labour Corps
PHILLIPS E.	Cider Mill Farm		Army
PICTON A.	Old Barn Cottage, Kingsfold		
PICTON F.	Old Barn Cottage, Kingsfold	Private	Manchester Regiment
POTTER R.	Church St.	Corporal	The Queen's
RAMSDALE G.			
READ G.H.	17 Station Rd.		Army/Territorial Force
READ H. MM	17 Station Rd.	Corporal	Middlesex Regiment
REDE R.L.M.	Brookhurst	Commander	Royal Navy
REDFORD G.A.	Robin Hood Lane	Private	Army Veterinary Corps
REDFORD H.A.E.	Church St. & Friday St.	Private	Machine Gun Corps
REDFORD R.	5 Friday St.	Gunner	Royal Garrison Artillery
REED T.P.	Serapis Cottage, Durfold Hill	Colour Sergeant	Royal Fusiliers
RENDALL F.F.	Bell-houses	Private	The Queen's
RENDALL J.	Bell-houses		
RICHARDS A.W.	Park View Cottage Bell Road & 3 School Hill	Able Seaman	Royal Navy
ROBERTSON F.M.B. DSO	Old Manor, Knob Hill	Lieutenant-Colonel	Black Watch
ROSE S.			Army
RUSH A.	Kingsfold	Trooper	4th Dragoon Guards
SADLER H.			Army/Territorial Force
SALMON D.L.	Keepers Cottage, Robin Hood Lane	VAD Nurse	Hants. 208 British Red Cross Society
SAYERS W.A.	Warnham Lodge stables	Private	Army Service Corps
SEAGRAVE F.A.	Goose Green	Driver	Royal Field Artillery
SECRETT A.A.R.	Gables, Friday St.	Lieutenant	Royal West Kent Regiment
SECRETT G.			
SELWOOD R.			Army
SHEPPARD G.W.H.	Fern Cottage, Rowhook	Private	Army Service Corps
SHORT M.	8 Friday St.	Private	Royal Defence Corps

SHORT M.H.J.	Friday St.	Gunner	Royal Horse Artillery
SIMMONDS F.		Private	Royal West Kent Regiment
SIMS W.			
SKEATES E.E.J.	Kingsfold	Acting Chief Stoker	Royal Navy
SMALLWOOD F.H.	Farthings Cottages	Private	Middlesex Regiment
SMART W.H.	Geerings Farm	Private	Labour Corps
SOAPER R.			Army
SPINK W.A.	Warnham Court	Private	Royal West Kent Regiment
STANFORD F.A.	Corner House	Gunner	Royal Garrison Artillery
STANFORD J.	6 Sunnyside, Friday St.	Private	Labour Corps
STARKES E.C.	Holbrook in 1911	Corporal	2nd Dragoon Guards
STEPHENS H.E.P.	Charmans Farm & Rowhook	Pioneer	Royal Engineers
STEPHENS M.H.		Captain	Royal Air Force
STEVENS E.A.	Serapis Cottage, Durfold Hill	Driver	Army Service Corps
STEVENSON G.	15 Station Cottages	Private	Royal Sussex Regiment
STONE C.R. DSO MC	Field Place	Major	Royal Fusiliers
STREET G.B.	The Gables, Friday St.		Army/Territorial Force
STUBBS K.S.		Captain	Rifle Brigade
TARRANT F.A.	The Laundry, Warnham Court	Lance Corporal	Royal Engineers
TAYLOR A.	School Hill	Private	Army Veterinary Corps
THORNS A.J.	Friday St.	Sergeant	The Queen's
TITTERINGTON A.L.	Home Farm, Warnham Lodge	Gunner	Royal Field Artillery
TULLETT F.			Army
TULLETT R.			Army
TYLDEN-WRIGHT J.T.M.	Westbrook	Flying Officer	Royal Air Force
VINCENT E.	The Mount, Durfold Hill	Private	Army Service Corps
WALFORD J.E.	Warnham Court Garden	Gunner	Royal Garrison Artillery
WALLIS D.B.	Graylands	Lieutenant	Connaught Rangers

WATTS A.F.	Park View Cottages 10 Friday St. & Bell Rd.	Private	Royal Sussex Regiment
WENHAM A.E.	Bell Cottages	Private	Army Service Corps
WHEELER C.E.	Park Villas, Bell Rd.	Lance Corporal	Military Foot Police
WHEELER F.J.	Park Villas, Bell Rd.	Private	Royal Sussex Regiment
WINCHESTER C.		Private	Royal Sussex Regiment
WOOD A.			Army
WOOD C.			Army
WOOD R.			Army
WOOD W.C.	Roberts Lane	Private	Royal West Kent Regiment
WOODMAN A.G.	Goose Green	Rifleman	King's Royal Rifle Corps
WOODMAN P.	Goose Green	Private	Royal Warwickshire Regiment
WOODS B.C.	Malt Mayes	Lance Corporal	Royal Sussex Regiment
WOODS L.C.	Malt Mayes	Sergeant	Northumberland Fusiliers
WOODS L.E.	Malt Mayes	Private	Essex Regiment
WORSFOLD A.	9 Brickyard Cottages	Driver	Army Service Corps
WORSFOLD G.	Kingsfold Place	Private	Royal Sussex Regiment
WORSFOLD G.	Church St.	Driver	Royal Fusiliers
WORSTER A.E.L.	The Greets, Friday St.		Royal Flying Corps
YATES A.			Army
YATES C.	16 Church St.	Sergeant	Royal Sussex Regiment
YATES J.	14 Church St.	Rifleman	King's Royal Rifle Corps
YATES P.	14 Church St.	Private	Royal Engineers
YATES T. DSM	School Hill	Leading Cook's Mate	Royal Navy
YEA C.V.	Village Hall	Air Mechanic 2nd Class	Royal Flying Corps
YEA H.A.	Village Hall	Sapper	Royal Engineers

Defence of the Realm Act

Sussex Emergency Scheme – Parish of Warnham

Chief Special Constable – Mr. C. J. Lucas
Head Special Constables –
Mr. P. L. Forwood.
Mr. G. N. Dicken.
Mr. Ernest Charman.
Mr. F. W. Freeman.
Mr. A. S. Hodgson.
Mr. ???

In the event of an invasion by a hostile force it has been decided to clear the County of everything that would be useful to the enemy and the plan to be adopted in Warnham is as follows:-

The whole Parish is under the control of the Chief Special Constable, Mr. C.J. Lucas. The Parish has been divided into five divisions each in charge of a Head Special Constable thus:-

No. 1. North East, or Kingsfold, Division – Mr. ???
No. 2. North Central Division – Mr. P. L. Forwood.
No. 3. North Western Division – Mr. G. N. Dicken
No. 4. Southern Division – Mr. A. S. Hodgson
No. 5. The Village, Mr. Ernest Charman
and
No. 6. Mr. F. W. Freeman takes control of the civil population and the removal of the women, children and the infirm.

Each of the above 5 divisions has been again sub-divided and each sub-division is in the charge of a special constable who is responsible to the Head Special Constable of his division as follows:-

No. 1. Division –
No. 2. Division –
No. 3. Division –
No. 4. Division – Mr. Albert Lovegrove, Mr. Frank Edwards, Mr.
No. 5. Division –
No. 6.

The principal objects to be accomplished are –

1. The removal of all transport and the destruction of any that cannot be removed.
2. The removal of all cattle, sheep and horses and the destruction of any that cannot be removed.
3. The removal of all food of all descriptions except Hay and the destruction of all that cannot be removed.
4. The destruction of Bridges etc.
5. The organisation of working parties.
6. The discipline and removal of the civil population.

A census of everything likely to be useful to the enemy has already been prepared throughout the Parish. Each Head Special Constable must have a copy of the list of everything in his division and each Special Constable must have a copy of the list of everything in his sub-division and they must superintend all the above duties in their divisions or subdivisions as the case may be.

In addition to his duties in connection with his own division each Head Special Constable is responsible for one of the above duties throughout the whole Parish as follows:-

1. Mr. A. S. Hodgson – Removal of transport etc.
2. Mr. P. L. Forwood – Removal of Cattle, Sheep, Horses etc.
3. Mr. G. N. Dicken – Removal or destruction of Food.
4. Mr. Ernest Charman – Organisation and Superintendance of Working Parties.
5. Mr. – Destruction of Bridges etc
6. Mr. Freeman – Discipline of and Removal of Civil Population.

Rendezvous or collecting places for transport and cattle have been decided upon and are known to the Chief and Head Special Constables and when the order to move is received all Transport, Cattle, etc are to be taken to their respective appointed collecting places where they will be received and organised by the Head Special Constable responsible for that particular duty throughout the Parish with the assistance of other Special Constables appointed for the purpose.

Each Head Special Constable is responsible, with the assistance of his own Special Constable, to see that all Transport, Cattle, Sheep, Horses etc, duly reach these appointed places and are there handed to the Head Special Constable in charge of each station.

When he has cleared his division and seen to the destruction of all food upon it etc, his duties there cease and he will give all his attention to the organisation in convoys etc. of the Transport, Cattle, Sheep, Horses etc as the case may be, directing them to the routes they will take, furnishing them with guides, and starting them safely on their journey.

In the case of the Transport Head Special Constable he must make proper provision and generally afford facilities for removing food, carrying fodder for cattle, and removing the women & children and the infirm, in co-operation with the Head Special Constables responsible for those respective duties.

Each Head Special Constable will forthwith notify every able-bodied man in his division of the arrangements that have been made and tell him that in the event of an emergency arising, Martial Law will at once be proclaimed and that he will be expected to perform any duties that may be required of him. He will further inform him of the nature of any special duties which he may probably be required to perform and appoint a rendezvous or meeting place for them to assemble. He will further instruct them that each man is to bring with him so far as he is able picks, spades, shovels and axes, three days food and blankets to sleep in.

Any men that are not required by a Head Special Constable for work in his own division are to be handed over by him to Head Special Constable Ernest Charman for organisation into working parties.

The Head Special Constable responsible for the organisation of working parties will organise three or four gangs of ten men each according to their trades with sufficient number of labourers in each gang to assist and with each gang under the control of a Special Constable and he will carry out whatever duties are assigned to him by the Military Authorities. He must be in possession of a list of tools available and see that they are produced when required and must appoint a rendezvous or meeting place where his men can meet him.

Head Special Constable Mr. G. N. Dicken will see to the removal of all Food in co-operation with the Transport Head Special Constable and when as much has been removed as possible he will see to the destruction of the remainder throughout the Parish.

Head Special Constable, Mr. F. W. Freeman will see to the discipline of the civil population and so far as possible will order them to remain in their houses and when so required by the Military Authorities he will, in conjunction with the Transport Head Special Constable, arrange for their removal, sending as many as possible on foot, and taking the infirm and the younger children and some of the women in wagons.

He will further endeavour to arrange that each family provides itself with food and some money for three days and plenty of blankets to sleep in and that the younger irresponsible children shall be labelled with their names and addresses.

The Head Special Constables responsible for the removal of the Transport and Cattle etc. will get into touch with the Head Special Constable in adjoining Parishes and arrange the routes to be followed and get them approved by the Military Authorities.

BY THE KING.

A PROCLAMATION.

GEORGE R.I.

We, being persuaded that the abstention from all unnecessary consumption of grain will furnish the surest and most effectual means of defeating the devices of Our enemies and thereby of bringing the war to a speedy and successful termination, and out of Our resolve to leave nothing undone which can contribute to these ends or to the welfare of Our people in these times of grave stress and anxiety, have thought fit, by and with the advice of Our Privy Council, to issue this Our Royal Proclamation, most earnestly exhorting and charging all those of Our loving subjects the men and women of Our realm who have the means of procuring articles of food other than wheaten corn, as they tender their own immediate interests, and feel for the wants of others, especially to practise the greatest economy and frugality in the use of every species of grain: And We do for this purpose more particularly exhort and charge all heads of households to reduce the consumption of bread in their respective families by at least one-fourth of the quantity consumed in ordinary times; to abstain from the use of flour in pastry, and, moreover, carefully to restrict or wherever possible to abandon the use thereof in all other articles than bread: And We do also, in like manner, exhort and charge all persons who keep horses to abandon the practice of feeding the same on oats or other grain, unless they shall have received from Our Food Controller a licence to feed horses on oats or other grain to be given only in cases where it is necessary to do so with a view to maintain the breed of horses in the national interest: And We do hereby further charge and enjoin all Ministers of Religion in their respective churches and chapels within Our United Kingdom of Great Britain and Ireland to read, or cause to be read, this Our Proclamation on the Lord's Day, for four successive weeks after the issue thereof.

Given at Our Court at Buckingham Palace, this Second day of May, in the year of our Lord one thousand nine hundred and seventeen, and in the Seventh year of Our Reign.

GOD SAVE THE KING.

Printed by Eyre and Spottiswoode, Ltd.,
Printers to the King's most Excellent Majesty. 1917.
For His Majesty's Stationery Office.

• (38) 2951b 20,000 5/17

Glossary of terms and abbreviations

Military terms

Other ranks	All ranks below 2nd Lieutenant
Pte	Private soldier also known as Driver, Sapper (Royal Engineers), Gunner (Royal Artillery), Trooper (Cavalry), Rifleman (some infantry units)
NCO	Non-commissioned officer
Sgt	Sergeant
C/Sgt	Colour Sergeant – a senior Sergeant in a Company
CSM	Company Sergeant Major
RSM	Regimental Sergeant Major
Lt & 2nd Lt	Lieutenant and 2nd Lieutenant
CO	Commanding Officer
MO	Medical Officer
Capt	Captain
Subaltern	A junior officer below the rank of captain
ADC	Aide-de-camp (Military officer acting as personal assistant to a senior officer)
AB	Able Seaman
Coy	Company
Bn	Battalion
Bde	Brigade
Div	Division
Unit	A general term for a formation of fighting soldiers, could be a battalion, brigade or division together with associated personnel, eg medical, catering, engineers etc which make up a specific group to which individual soldiers show allegiance.

VAD	Voluntary Aid Detachment
WAAC	Women's Army Auxiliary Corps
RE	Royal Engineers
ASC	Army Service Corps
TF	Territorial Force
RDC	Royal Defence Corps
RFC	Royal Flying Corps
ANZAC	Australian and New Zealand Army Corps
BEF	British Expeditionary Force
MEF	Mediterranean Expeditionary Force
EEF	Egyptian Expeditionary Force
AEF	American Expeditionary Force
HMS	His Majesty's Ship
HMT	His Majesty's Troopship
SS	Steamship
HQ	Headquarters
GHQ	General Headquarters
CCS	Casualty Clearing Station
Redoubt	Additional fortification providing a refuge in a trench system
CB	Confined to Barracks
First 100,000	Volunteers answering Kitchener's Call to Arms in August 1914
The Old Contemptibles	Soldiers of the Regular Army serving in France and Belgium in August 1914

Campaign Medals

1914 Star	For service in France or Belgium between 5 August and 22 November 1914.
1914-15 Star	For service in any theatre of war between 5 August 1914 and 31 December 1915.
British War Medal	For service in a theatre of war between 5 August 1914 and 11 November 1918.
Victory Medal	To commemorate Victory and awarded to all who received the 1914 or 1914-15 star.
The Silver War Badge	Issued in the United Kingdom to service personnel who had been honourably discharged due to wounds or sickness.

All recipients of the 1914 or 1914-15 Stars automatically received the War Medal and Victory Medal. Those joining from 1916 onwards were not eligible for the Stars. A Star plus the two medals were known colloquially as 'Pip, Squeak and Wilfred'

Other abbreviations used in this book

MCC	Marylebone Cricket Club
CWGC	Commonwealth War Graves Commission
CLB	Church Lads' Brigade
YMCA	Young Men's Christian Association
WSCT	West Sussex County Times
WSRO	West Sussex Record Office

Bravery Awards (mentioned in this book)

DSO	Distinguished Service Order awarded to those with the rank of Major and above and very occasionally to a more junior officer, for distinguished or meritorious service usually in the presence of the enemy and under fire.
MC	The Military Cross was a decoration for gallantry during active operations in the presence of the enemy awarded to commissioned officers with the rank of Captain or below.
DSM	Distinguished Service Medal was an award for bravery whilst on active service and was for other ranks of the Royal Navy.
MM	The Military Medal was awarded to warrant officers, non-commissioned officers and other ranks for gallantry in action against the enemy.

Mentioned in Despatches was not an award of a medal, but a commendation of an act of gallantry. To be 'Mentioned in Despatches' was when an individual was mentioned by name and commended for having carried out a noteworthy act of gallantry or service. A Despatch is an official report written by the senior commander of an army in the field. It would give details of the conduct of the military operations being carried out. An individual could be mentioned in despatches more than once. This commendation and the Victoria Cross were the only two awards for an act of gallantry which could be made posthumously.

Conversion of money

1d (one penny) = ½p (approximately);

6d = 2½ p;

1/- (one shilling) = 5p;

10/- = 50p

In 1918 £1 was worth approximately £50 by today's standards. This was half the value it had in 1914. There was massive inflation during the Great War

Sources

Bibliography

Boraston, J H *Sir Douglas Haig's War Despatches 1914-19 and maps* J M Kent 1919

Brown, Malcolm *1918 – Year of Victory* Sidgwick & Jackson with IWM 1998

Brown, Malcolm *Imperial War Museum Book of the Western Front* Sidgwick & Jackson with IWM 1993

Coombs, Rose *Before Endeavours Fade, a guide to the battlefields of the First World War,* Battle of Britain Prints International Limited, first published 1976

Cooper, G T *Horsham's Heroes of the Great War* Friends of the Horsham Museum Society 2009

Cooper, Jilly *Animals in War* Imperial War Museum 1983

Coppard, George *With A Machine Gun to Cambrai* Papermac 1986

Falls, Captain Cyril *Official History Egypt and Palestine (Vol II)* HMSO 1930

Gliddon, Gerald *VCs of the First World War: Cambrai 1917* The History Press 2012

Hastings, Max *Catastrophe – Europe goes to War 1914* William Collins 2013

Holmes, Richard *The Western Front* BBC 2008

James, E A *British Regiments 1914-1918* Naval and Military Press 1993

Macdonald, Lyn *1914* Penguin Books 1989

Muggeridge, Ron *Warnham, A History* The Field Place Press 1985

O'Neill, H C *The Royal Fusiliers in the Great War* Heinemann 1922

Overton, Richard *A Wartime Engagement* Private publication

Powell-Edwards, Lt Col H I, DSO *The Sussex Yeomanry and 16th Battalion Royal Sussex Regt 1914-19* Andrew Melrose Ltd 1921

Richards, Goodson and Morris *Sketch Map History of the Great Wars and After 1914-1964* Harrap 1966

Sheffield, G D *The Pictorial History of World War 1* Bison Books 1988

Stone, Christopher *A History of the 22nd (Service) Battalion Royal Fusiliers (Kensington)* Naval & Military Press 1923

Talbot-Booth, E C *The British Army, Its History, Customs, Traditions and Uniforms* Samson Low, Marston & Co Ltd 1941

Taylor, A J P *History of WWI* reprinted Macdonald & Co Ltd 1988

Westlake, Ray *Tracing British Battalions on the Somme* Pen & Sword Books Ltd 2009

Wojtczak, Helena *Jack the Ripper At Last?* Hastings Press 2014

History of the 20th Century 1900-1965 Purnell for BBC Publishing Ltd, London 1968

Official Histories of the War Reprinted by the Imperial War Museum

Parish Magazines for the Deanery of Storrington (including Warnham), 1914-1920

Warnham Parish Registers

West Sussex County Times 1914-1920

West Sussex Gazette 1914-1920

Warnham School Log Books and Minutes of Meetings of School Managers

Organisations

Charterhouse School

Christ's Hospital

Loxwood Historical Society

National Archives, Kew

Queen's Own Royal West Kent Regiment Museum, Maidstone

Southwater Local History Group

Surrey History Centre, Woking

West Sussex Records Office, Chichester

Individuals

Barry Fleming, Historian of the Royal Fusiliers

Bridget Meads, Spink family tree

Duncan Voice, Yates family tree

Gary Cooper, author of *Horsham's Heroes of the Great War*

Helena Wojtczak, author of *Jack the Ripper At Last?*

Matthew Ralph, Dinnage family tree

Internet

Ancestry www.ancestry.co.uk

Find my Past www.findmypast.co.uk

- Census returns 1841-1911
- Service records
- Service pension records
- Medal cards
- Army wills
- Du Ruvigny's Roll of Honour
- UK Soldiers died in the Great War, His Majesty's Stationery Office 1921
- Naval casualties
- Naval medal and award rolls
- London Poor Law records
- Probate index
- Birth, marriage and death records and indexes

BBC History www.bbc.co.uk/ww1

Commonwealth War Graves Commission www.cwgc.org

Forces War Records www.forces-war-records.co.uk

Gallipoli www.ataturktoday.com

Godalming Museum www.godalmingmuseum.org.uk

History Learning Site www.historylearningsite.co.uk/world_war_one.htm

London Gazette www.london-gazette.co.uk

Machine Gun Tactics on the Western Front www.essentialsomme.com/articles/british_machine_gun_tactics.htm

National Army Museum wwwnam.ac.uk

Old Bailey online www.oldbaileyonline.org

Royal Horticultural Society www.rhs.org.uk

Royal West Surrey Regiment War Diaries http://www.queensroyalsurreys.org.uk/war_diaries/war_diaries_home_new.shtml

The Long, Long Trail www.1914-1918.net

The Times online www.thetimes.co.uk/tto/archive

Wikipedia en.wikipedia.org

Various UK Regimental sites

Regimental sites of Canada and Australia

www.webmatters.net

www.whallen.org

Acknowledgements

The publishers would like to acknowledge the sources of the visual and certain other material and thank copyright holders for permission to reproduce material, both visual and written where copyright applies. Although every effort has been made to contact copyright holders, we apologise to anyone whose rights have been inadvertently overlooked and will be happy to rectify errors and omissions. In particular the publishers would like to thank the following for permission to reproduce photographs, illustrations and other material in this book.

Inside front cover:
John Cannon: School Hill, Warnham.

Page 2:
John Cannon: Church Street.

Page 8:
John Cannon: The Forge.

Life in Warnham:
John Cannon: Rev Richard Bowcott, Military camp at Warnham, St Margaret's, Warnham Stores, Warnham Post Office.

Susan Overton: Captain Corbett, Warnham war memorial, Invitation to memorial dedication.

Imperial War Museum: Belgian Refugees, German Soldiers at Christmas Truce, Women felling trees.

Horsham Museum (William Albury Collection): Posters.

G T Cooper (Friends of Horsham Museum): Volunteers at 8 Causeway, Members of the WAAC, Queuing for margarine.

Olive Thornton: Latter-day remembrance parade.

Warnham and the 1911 Census:
Rodney Dales, Steve Lancaster and K Wiles.

Warnham School:
John Cannon: Warnham School, Mr Stroud & pupils, Schoolroom 1920s.

Map of the Western Front:
Steve Lancaster & Susan Overton.

Page 51:
G T Cooper (Friends of Horsham Museum): 1/4th Battalion Royal Sussex in Park Street.

Biographies:
Regimental badges:
http://www.freewebs.com/irishregimentsofthebritisharmy
www.heartsanddaggers.co.uk
www.militarybadgecollection.com
www.northeastmedals.co.uk
www.britishempire.co.uk

Wikipedia: Regimental badges, Trinity College Toronto, River Scarpe machine gun post, Battle of Loos, Tyne Cot Memorial, HMS Prince of Wales, La Ferte-sous-Jouarre Memorial, Christopher Stone, Royal Crest.

CWGC: Menin Gate panels, Ploegsteert memorial, Cologne Southern Cemetery, Thiepval memorial to the Missing, Chocques Cemetery.

ww1photos.com: Bates, Chinnery.

NYTimes: Germans in sheepskin coats, Troops going over the top on the Somme.

Susan Overton: Bowles grave, Balcombe War Memorial, Coole's gravestone, Station Road cottages, CH War Memorial, Hayler's gravestone, Sunnyside, Horsham War Memorial, Salmon Family grave, Passchendaele today, Wooden gravestone of Wood, Roberts Cottages, Broken gravestone of Woodman, Broadbridge Heath War Memorial.

Edward Arnold: British soldiers playing cricket.

Illustrated War News: German observation post destroyed by shellfire in Mametz Wood, Destroyed German trenches at Passchendaele.

Barry Fleming: Panels on Menin Gate, Somerville Wood, Vadencourt British Cemetery.

Warnham Historical Society: Friday Street.

Alfieri Picture Service: Beach at Anzac Cove.

Duncan Voice: Warnham Contingent, Alfred Comper.

Alan Ramsay: Tom Yates outside his cottage.

Myra Hayden: Tom Yates & Amelia, Marble Clock.

Charterhouse School: House photo.

Matthew Ralph: Ernest and Frances Dinnage.

Imperial War Museum: German Storm Troopers, Surrender of Jerusalem, Passchendaele.

John Cannon: Warnham String Band, Warnham old school, Warnham Stores & Staff.

Christ's Hospital: House photo.

G T Cooper (Friends of Horsham Museum): Digging in at Delville Wood, A Casualty Clearing Station, Evacuating from Suvla Bay, 1/4th on the march in Palestine, 4th Bn at Bedford, Roffey Camp, Exhausted troops at Passchendaele, British tanks in a ruined village.

Central Council of Church Bell Ringers: Memorial Book, St Pauls Cathedral.

Steve Lancaster: Stonyhurst, Chapel Cottage.

Rachel Hamer: Fakenham War Memorial.

Mary McConville: Capt F W Paddon.

www.royalpioneercorps.co.uk: Pioneers Sweeping the road.

Illustrated London News: British Troops moving a gun.

Southwater Local History Group: Emily Barker.

Horsham Society (Brian Slyfield): Graylands and the Boyd Wallis Boys.

Inside back cover:

West Sussex Record Office ref WSRO Par 203/7/60: Roll of Honour.

Back cover:

John Cannon: Greetings postcard Christmas 1915.